There's a Cow in My Garden

All good wishes
Diana Lancaster
Thank you for calling
at 309 Honey.
Have fun!

1993

DIANA LANCASTER

THERE'S A COW IN MY GARDEN

A guide to producing home-grown food

ANGUS & ROBERTSON PUBLISHERS

To Kaara, a friend with a contageous sense of adventure
who gave timely encouragement.

AN ANGUS & ROBERTSON BOOK

First published in Australia in 1990 by
Collins/Angus & Robertson Publishers Australia
First published in New Zealand in 1990
by Collins/Angus & Robertson Publishers
New Zealand

Collins/Angus & Robertson Publishers Australia
Unit 4, Eden Park, 31 Waterloo Road, North Ryde,
NSW 2113, Australia

Collins/Angus & Robertson Publishers New Zealand
31 View Road, Glenfield, Auckland 10, New Zealand

Angus & Robertson (UK)
16 Golden Square, London W1R 4BN, United Kingdom

National Library of Australia
Cataloguing-in-Publication data:

Lancaster, Diana.
    There's a cow in my garden.

    Bibliography.
    Includes index.
    ISBN 0 207 16153 4.

    1. Self-sufficiency. 2. Home economics. 3. Gardening. 4.
    Animal culture. 5. Cookery. I. Title.

640

Typeset in 12/13 pt Baskerville
Printed in Australia by Griffin Press

C o n t e n t s

Contents

Introduction

Come, buy wine and milk
without money and without price.
Why do you spend your money for
that which is not bread,
and your labour for that which
does not satisfy?

Isaiah 55: 1-2

We're very lucky. From a suburban upbringing to a city education and finally a country lifestyle, I feel among the most privileged. We have green hills and animals around us. All we lack is money. My first title for this book was *Free Food*. In our first year, although I worked full time in town, we ate, drank and partied on $15 each a week when the average food bill for a family of four was $160. So the motivating force was economic. We milked a cow, made butter and cheese, grew vegetables, kept chickens and rabbits, made wine and farmed bees because we couldn't afford to do otherwise.

Then I found that the occasional restaurant meal or "takeaways", instead of being a treat, was a let down. The food didn't taste as good as ours. Flavour continued to motivate us. (One needs "motivation" because there is lots of work and little "free time".)

Then we heard about the hole in the sky and dumping of nuclear waste and acid rain. I was ashamed for my part in the greed and casual waste that is destroying our lovely planet. We continue to try to find small ways of cutting down unnecessary consumption.

Our ambition is a "minimum impact" lifestyle. We plant trees, encourage the bees, tend the animals on a small scale and limit travel and extravagance. This book is the saga of our learning experiences: not an encyclopaedia; not how things should be done; just how it is working for us.

I have 112 cookery books (and I dare to preach about unnecessary consumption!). I didn't believe it when George grumbled quietly that I had "at least 80" one day when I brought home another. I believed it even less when he told me that I didn't use them anyway! Of course I did! I read them like novels. I have at least eight open if I want to make anything . . . I had this idea of myself that I couldn't make anything without a book—but at last I have been brought to realise that with eight books telling me what to do I felt safe to ignore the lot and try it my way.

That is what I hope readers will do with recipes in this book. They were chosen because ingredients are mostly home produced and the method quick and easy (time, to me, is the most expensive ingredient). But ignore them by all means. I am still enjoying the new sense of freedom I have knowing that I don't *have* to follow a recipe. Just pick out the ideas.

I'm no cook. My "menu planning" is done in the first commercial break of the television evening news and my cooking in the second. If it takes longer, the meal has to last three days. Thank goodness for freezers and microwave ovens!

That's what we mean by "minimum impact". We're grateful for the gifts of time that our technology gives us. We're grateful for birdsong, clean rivers and fertile soil. We just don't want to waste any of it. Trying to use and recycle as much as we can has led to our adventures in good eating and fairly basic, fun living. In town or the suburbs we would do the same. Being in the country is just a glorious bonus because here we can live with Phoo and Ben and Spike (dogs), Nicodemus and Alfonse (donkeys), Bonnie, Basil and Willie (rabbits), Rosie and Honey (cows), Bagpuss (cat), Suzie (pig), the sheep, the bees, and the chooks that take up where Spiderman, Doodledoo, Black Mama and Hoppity left off.

This kind of life needs to be shared. George gets mentioned in dispatches throughout the book. That's his special and very precious gift to me because he is a private person and would so much like to remain anonymous. I'll thank him privately.

But I would like to place on record my gratitude to the writers and publishers of the cookbooks and "how to" books that I have enjoyed reading and have listed in the bibliography. It feels comfortable to receive encouragement from those who have "been there, done that".

I have a list of quotes pinned above my desk from that book of good sense, the Bible (Revised Standard Version). When I'm tempted to nip into town for greasies or a TV dinner, I read: "He shall eat curds and honey when he knows how to refuse the evil and choose the good" (Isaiah 7:15). On the other hand, if there's a party going . . .

"Bread is made for laughter and wine gladdens life" (Ecclesiastes 10:19).

Have fun!

Milk

PREAMBLE

Susie was my gesture of rebellion. We had heavy mortgages. Neither of us had the kind of job that would bring in the money to repay them, so I decided to teach the whole bullying money world a lesson and refuse to pay for milk.

Well, it looks *peaceful enough! — now read on.*

First I thought of a goat. We lived on a small house plot and I fancied the image of my self (wearing ample petticoats and an apron, presumably in blue gingham) leading the willing animal daily to its new pasture. The image blurred suitably on the bundles I would have to carry: a stool, a bucket, a hat, an umbrella, hot water, towel . . . It faded altogether when somebody else's goat got at our fruit trees.

We moved to more space. We both still worked five, and often seven, days a week. Money was even tighter. I worked out that if a cow gave me two pints of milk a day she would pay for herself in two years and we would still have the cow. And there would be a calf, which after all was another cow . . . Surely it was simple economic good sense?

George, who fortunately knew about cows, was tactful enough not to mention accounting items like housing, feed, water supply, but instead took a cow in exchange for a week's farm labouring.

Susie was not beautiful. She was black and white, squat, scrawny and lonely. Rosie, who has succeeded Susie, is not beautiful either. When I first saw her long, long ginger-striped nose, barrel of a body and dainty ankles I rudely collapsed in giggles. She has never quite forgiven me and I don't blame her.

Both cows had been chosen for the same quality: they were gentle beasts who stood quietly for milking.

My initial calculations were out on one important point: Susie didn't deliver two pints of milk a day. She gave eight pints. And I was lucky: with a "better" cow, it could have been 32 pints a day. Which gave me a problem! Being born in the war, I am stamped through like seaside rock with the slogan "Waste Not, Want Not". To preserve cream one made butter, didn't one? To preserve milk one made cheese, didn't one? So one began.

Or tried to. We were now living in a rural area to make room for George's bees. I asked local farmers' wives, "How do you make butter? Cheese?" Drew a blank. I went to the museum, a converted dairy factory, and saw vast implements of torture for dissecting milk and walloping cream. I found a book that was three-quarters taken up with methods of scrubbing and scalding antique equipment and a quarter telling me why my cream might not "clabber". The most likely cause was witchcraft.

Finally I found a farmer's wife who said: "Stick it in the mixer and press the button." That was the sort of advice I needed. Two hours later I rang back and said, "Nothing's happened." It took a few adjustments, but I had found what I was looking for: a modern way of taking a basic skill out of the "quaint" category and making it accessible to people like me.

CHAPTER 1   COW, COMPANION AND CONSTANT HOT WATER

It is not necessary to keep a cow to make butter and all the cheeses. And it is certainly not necessary to clutter the kitchen with churns and separators and butter-washing boards. Fortunately, it is not critical these days for the dairywoman's hands to be "smooth as butter, white as milk, and cool as spring water" (Dorothy Hartley *Food in England*, Macdonald, 1954).

Amazing factories cows: feed in grass and out pops butter, milk and cheese.

Scrubbing and scalding all equipment, benches, floor and walls used to be the main chore of dairying. Every book I have come across dealing with milk, labours the need for perfect hygiene. And quite properly. Bugs love milk. But I am assuming that these days we understand about dirt and bacteria and the need for clean kitchens, clean tools and clean hands. With our fabulous plastics, wallboards and stainless steel in the kitchen, it seems pointless to go into wearisome detail about scouring pine draining-boards.

Constant hot water is the darling of this particular dairymaid. This year we splurged on a wood-burning stove with a wetback. What a happy winter we had! Really hot (free) water to clean the milking bucket, the dog's milk jug, the ice-cream container for the cream, the margarine carton for the butter and to rinse the milk bottles: dairying is a breeze! Go easy on soap or detergent on surfaces that come into contact with milk. Always rinse with hot water and, if possible, turn containers upside down on a rack to dry rather than use a cloth.

The best thing and the worst thing about having your own cow is that circumstances force you to process milk daily. When you run out of containers and can cram nothing more in the fridge, you have to do something. That's what propelled me into action initially. Now that I have the taste for our cheeses and butter and milky puds, I would very quickly find a source of fresh, cheap milk if Rosie dried up.

Butter can be made from bought cream and cheese from milk in bottles or cartons, but you don't save money that way. (A goat is good for milk and cheese. Butter from goat's milk is possible but not worth the trouble.

Milk

I have heard goat milk criticised as "too bitter" and "too sweet". Taste depends on the animal's diet.) Access to a cow is a project worth giving a bit of energy to.

SHARE A COW
A group of friends with enough grass and water between them could rotate a cow, sharing expenses and taking milk one or two days a week each.

LEASE A COW
If you live not too far from the countryside, find a friendly dairy farmer who would enter into a plan to rent a cow. Perhaps once a week you could provide a carrier service for him—oddments he needed from town— and he could exchange as much milk as you were able to carry back.

CHOOSE A COW
Another possibility is to buy a cow and arrange with a dairy farmer for him to run her with his herd. The arrangement could be that he keeps the calf, or half her value when she goes to the works, or takes some milk when you don't need it. Some permutation should appeal and your family has the fun of visiting and watching over its cow.

GET A COW
Best of all if you have the space and can accept the tie of regular milking (train friends to help as soon as possible) is to get your own cow. Rosie pays for herself easily at least twice a year.

Looks in cows don't matter. (Susie soon fattened up, became sleek, matronly and very handsome. Her milk yield was low but she put on a lot of meat and rewarded us well when she had to go to the works. She was a herd reject because she didn't get in calf. We couldn't get her in calf either.) Rosie still makes me laugh if I'm not careful, her legs so elegantly slender and her bulk with its chopped off tail so ungainly. She stays half-starved looking but gives masses of milk and has brought up a fat naughty calf.

Even the quantity of milk produced is relatively unimportant unless one cow has to feed several families. Oversupply rather than undersupply is more likely to lead to problems. Lots of cream is a bonus. Enough for regular butter making, plus cream for some cheeses, plus cream for dessert and cooking treats—that's real luxury!

Check on a cow's health. It is reassuring if she comes from a herd that is regularly tuberculosis tested and has a clear record. In spacious comfortable surroundings, away from the rest of the herd and being regularly hand-milked, your cow should stay healthy. If you talk to your cow when you see her and milk her every day, you will soon notice if

4

there is any difference in her condition. Some cows get irritable when they are "bulling"—every three weeks when they come into season—and their bellies feel warmer.

When you have your cow, unless you have been very cunning and made arrangements with a dairy farmer, you have to milk her. This is where I am glad there are two of us to share the chores. Although I find them all pleasurable, they do take time. If one person can look after the milking shed and the other the dairying, then everything can be fitted comfortably into half an hour. There is still time to rescue the fire, feed the chooks, walk the dogs, check the vegie garden and put on make-up before taking off for work.

George and Susie taught me to milk.

If you've never milked a cow before, be patient with yourself. George and Susie were very patient with me. And I spent hours feeling so stupid. Milking is like any other motor skill: your muscles as well as your brain need time to register the new sequences of movements.

To begin with, get the co-operation of your cow. Learn where and how she likes to be caressed. Rosie doesn't like her head interfered with but she will accept a pat and a rub bum-end if she's in the mood. Honey, a hand-reared very friendly Jersey with long horns, likes hard scratching on the neck. Susie was placid and enjoyed a back rub. Once she was in the milking bail (which George fixed up in a broken-down shed), she appreciated a friendly chat about the weather and a pat on the rump before getting down to the business of sliding a hand across to her udder to give it a wash in warm water and then a towelling.

Usually the udders are pretty clean, though not when the cow is bulling. Then she does everything to annoy for a couple of days, including lying in a pudding of nice fresh dung. When it has been raining heavily, mud washes off quite easily, but unless you dry her flank, rainwater mixed with mud dribbles steadily into the milking area. Obviously, it is important to keep the milk clean.

The worst that can happen is that the cow puts her foot in the milk bucket. A tender teat, flies and sandflies, boredom, bulling or a sudden fright when a cat jumps in the door can all make this happen. Neither Susie nor Rosie would be stroppy for the sake of it, though some cows can be.

There are two possible precautions: keep a leg rope anchored to the wall and tie it loosely but firmly to the back leg nearest you when milking so that she can't step it forward into the bucket or kick. The other precaution gives early warning of movement: when milking, push your head against the cow's flank above the udder. This both steadies her and gives you muscle-to-muscle warning of what is about to happen—enough time usually to grab the bucket out of the way and hold the leg back.

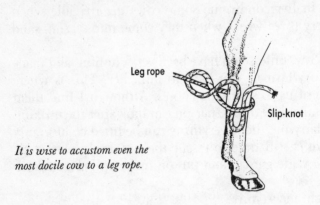

Leg rope

Slip-knot

It is wise to accustom even the most docile cow to a leg rope.

Milking Technique

We were lucky. When we lived on our small section by the beach, all sorts of things arrived on the tide. One of those was a three-legged milking stool, firm and the right height. An upended nail box would do. After greeting and soothing the cow (that's assuming you are still on speaking terms after she has made you run round in circles to get her to the milking shed), distract her attention with something tasty to eat in a box in front of her (there are various preparations available, some doused liberally with molasses), and some hay where she can reach it. Persuade her to move the back leg furthest from you forward so that the nearest back leg leaves a gap for you to get at the udder.

Both Rosie and George enjoy the quiet rhythms of milking time to plan their days.

Those teats are actually tougher than they look. Watch how a calf belts and bullies its mother for milk. Don't be afraid of using a strong grip, but the action is neither like pulling down on a bell rope nor one of sliding the hand down. That makes both you and the cow sore.

Press your hand as close to the udder as you can, close your fist around the teat and squeeze downwards with thumb and index finger, middle finger, ring finger and little finger in sequence. It's no good just squeezing: the milk needs to be squirted downwards with pressure. And you have to aim straight! The object is to hit the inside of the bucket. Your fingers will ache and your wrists feel like dropping off until the muscles are used to their new job.

Persevere. The exercise is frustrating for you to begin with and boring for the cow. You might of course be a "natural" and take to it straight away. It took me weeks. I would struggle, squirt milk everywhere except in the bucket, carry on doggedly to extract every drop, then George would take over to "finish off"—and get going those lovely long sizzling squirts that filled the bucket with warm froth in no time.

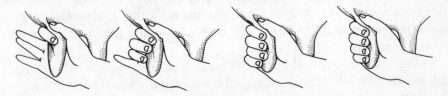

Milking: Not only should a dairymaid have hands "smooth as butter, white as milk and cool as spring water" but they also need to be strong.

Unless there is a calf to share the job of milking, it is important to strip the cow of all her milk. The less you take, the less she will make. If small amounts of milk are left in the udders, there is more danger of the cow developing mastitis.

Hand milked cows have a good chance of escaping mastitis, but some cows are more prone than others and a bad bump or missed milkings can bring it on. (Udders are divided into four "quarters", each with its own milk and one teat. The milk in these four quarters does not mix.) Basically, mastitis is a clogging of the nipple openings. The milk goes stringy and hardens. If it is not bad, an experienced milker can clear the quarter. If mastitis is allowed to get bad, it becomes painful for the cow and wasteful. It can be treated with penicillin but the treatment can cost the equivalent of a month's milk production, not counting what you lose while you wait for the penicillin to clear from the cow's system. Don't drink the milk, although it is perfectly all right for the dogs, chooks or pigs.

The other worry about cows and milk is tuberculosis. It was a real problem in the old days, but now it is not common. Most dairy herds are regularly tested and infected cows culled out. Even cows with a positive reaction to TB testing do not necessarily have TB, and even if a cow does have TB it is not transmitted to humans through the milk itself but by flakes of dry skin from the udder falling into the milk. Some home milkers put muslin over the bucket to make extra sure this doesn't happen. A cow bought with a clean bill of health, loved and living in airy, pleasant conditions without undue stress should be well out of danger. If it makes you feel safer, get the vet to give her an annual check-up.

CHAPTER 2   CREAM AND BUTTER

Now that you have your pail of frothy, warm milk, strain it (unless it has come from the clean, chilled vats of your friendly dairy farmer). The sooner the milk gets chilled after leaving the cow, the more efficiently the cream rises to the surface. We strain our milk through two fine-nylon sieves into one or two plastic five litre pails with lids, and fit it into the fridge to stay until next morning.

Soured milk, cream and butter is attractive to some people. Many books still instruct the use of wide-mouthed open containers to be left overnight, skimmed in the morning and then the cream left to "ripen" for another 24 hours before making butter. We prefer our drinking milk, cream and butter to be as "sweet" (fresh) as is practicable.

Where to work?   The kitchen will do. Of course, if you have a large, airy, stainless-steel lined, empty room with spare cooker, fridge and bench space . . . use that! (I have a luxury in my kitchen, apart from the wood burning stove. Inside the larder, I have put a workshelf and two power points. That means that mixer, food processor, toaster, coffee machine and rechargeable torch can all be left instantly operational, out of the way and behind a closed door. I love my shelf.)

What to work with?   An electric mixer, a fridge, freezer, plastic containers (begin to save all kinds of containers from now on!), hot water, plastic measuring cups and clean hands. And a timer clock with a bell.

Taking off the cream.   When George goes down to milk Rosie, I take the plastic pails of milk (donated the day before) from the fridge and, using a light plastic half-cup measure with a handle, scoop the yellow cream off the blue milk. The cream is fat and globby and slithers over the edge into the measure, then I empty it into a two litre ice-cream container, gouging it out of the measuring cup and off the outside with a clean finger. There are a few strands of yellow cream still evading capture by the time I have finished, but I like just a little cream in our drinking milk.

The milk I pour into milk bottles because they store conveniently in the refrigerator. The cream also goes into the fridge and waits there for more cream over the next couple of days until I have nearly the full two litres for buttermaking. Two litres makes about 500 grams of butter— a little more or less depending on the thickness of the cream and my success in skimming it without too much milk.

Proper cream separators are much more efficient if you want to take more cream from the milk or separate large quantities. With one family and one cow, I am content with our system. A plastic half-cup measure takes a shorter time to wash than a cream separator.

Pasteurising   To do or not to do? We don't. Rosie is healthy. We are healthy. We found no difficulty in becoming accustomed to raw instead of cooked milk. If you choose to destroy all the bacteria and yeasts in milk (the good and the bad), heat the milk and cream to 72°C for sixteen seconds then cool it quickly. Or, keep the milk slightly cooler, between 65°C and 70°C, for thirty seconds. Bought milk is already pasteurised.

Devonshire cream   To make clotted cream that is rich and thick, choose a time when you have a glut of milk and cream. Let your whole (unskimmed) milk set in the fridge overnight and, to make it worth the effort, add any extra cream you can afford. Heat the milk to between 90 and 95°C and hold it at that heat for several hours. It begins to look like the skin on old paint but wrinkled, with butter puddles. Let it cool then refrigerate again and skim the next day. Now I know why genuine Devonshire cream fudge and toffees are so expensive to buy!

The following are milk and cream recipes for times of plenty. If you have ample milk available and a dollop of cream, soups using practically any vegetables are quick to make, nutritious and filling for cool or warm weather.

Winter Green Vegetable Soup

1½ cups cooked greens (choose from peas; spinach; silver beet; a mixture of mustard greens, beetroot tops and comfrey—tasty and terribly good for you; frozen green beans; Brussels sprouts; celery; cabbage)

1 onion, coarsely chopped

fresh herbs to taste

3 tablespoons butter

3 tablespoons flour

black pepper to taste

2 cups milk

1 teaspoon salt

1 cup stock or water

¼ cup cream

Optional: honey, chilli sauce, bacon, lemon zest

In a blender, purée the cooked greens with the softened onion (fried, boiled or microwaved), along with a selection of fresh, green herbs.

Melt the butter in a saucepan, then take the pan away from the heat source. Mix in the flour and black pepper to taste. Slowly stir in milk and salt. Bring to the boil and keep it plopping gently while you stir it for 3 minutes. Add the blended vegetables and stock or water. Reheat and add the cream before serving.

Optional additions are a flavouring of fried bacon pieces and/or a mixture that I find cheers up vegetable soups and gives them a "sweet and sour" interest—either a dash of chilli sauce or a fresh chilli (chopped), with 1 tablespoon honey and the grated rind of half an orange or lemon. Using rind zest instead of juice avoids the problem of the milk curdling.

The same basic recipe is suitable for tomatoes and sweetcorn. If it is one of those glorious years when mushrooms suddenly whiten the nearby pastures, fry about 250 g with the onion in about 6 tablespoons butter, then add 4 tablespoons flour, make a paste and stir in 6 cups of milk. Season with salt and pepper and add cream before serving.

Our winter standby is pumpkin soup, made with kumikumi or whatever mixture of pumpkin is available—and I make plenty, freezing some for emergencies.

Pumpkin Soup

Kumikumi have very hard shells in winter. To avoid cutting my hands, I attack the shells with a cleaver on a block of wood on the lawn. When I have gathered up the pieces and washed off the grass, I scoop out the seeds (give them to chooks or donkeys) and fit the bits, shell outwards, in a microwave proof bowl with ½ inch water, cover them and microwave on "high" for 20 minutes. When they have cooled, the flesh spoons off easily and leaves the brittle shells for the donkeys.

"Pure" pumpkin soup from my *Maori Cookbook* is just pumpkin, butter and 600 ml of milk with seasoning. The editors, Glenfield College Home and School Association Auckland, suggest simmering slices of bread in the soup for five minutes before serving. Our family prefers the soup made with fried-up onions, bacon and chopped green ginger, with parsley stirred in.

Chilled Pink Mint Soup

A refreshing milky summer soup using home-made yoghurt and tomato juice.

Blend 300 ml plain yoghurt with 300 ml tomato juice, then add the juice of an orange and leaves from two sprigs of mint. Blend again and season to taste.

Depending on the sweetness of the orange, it might need a little sugar or a teaspoon of lemon juice—or both. Serve with a finely chopped mint topping. For a more subtle version in a lighter drink, instead of using yoghurt, try fresh buttermilk from your buttermaking.

Quiche

This is no longer a luxury dish when you have your own milk source, especially if you keep chooks too. The basic custard is made with milk, cream and eggs.

Use enough pastry to line two shallow quiche dishes—make your favourite pastry or use the recipe for Rabbit Custard Tarts described in the Buns section. Spread grated cheese (home-made of course) over the bottom. Settle on whatever mixture of fried onions, bacon and ham, peppers or prawns your family prefers and pour on the custard.

For this, combine 4 eggs, 1 cup cream, ½ cup milk, salt and pepper. Decorate with paprika and sliced gherkins, or with slices of tomato and parsley. Cook in the oven at 180⁰C for 40 minutes (or longer at lower temperature in a wood-fired stove) until set and allow to stand a few minutes before cutting.

— ◈ —

MILKY PUDS

Only imagination limits what can be done for puds if milk and cream are "free". Personally I have never been able to face the thought of tapioca, semolina and sago since lumpy school meals in post-war England, but rice pud has taken on a new life since we have made our own. Dried fruit, depending on our whim (dates, apricots, figs, crystallised ginger or prunes) with sliced almonds or crumbled walnuts, make it quite a different experience from the tasteless globs used as "fillers" at school. And made with honey and cream there is no comparison. Rice, sago, tapioca and semolina are all used in about the same proportions with the milk: about 30 g or 2 good tablespoons (it doesn't have to be too accurate) to 600 ml of milk with 25 g sugar. The secret of a creamy milk pud is to cook it slowly in a cool oven.

Our Rice Pud

Wash 2 tablespoons long-grain white rice and mix it with the milk in an ovenproof dish. (Some recipes tell you to butter the bowl but I haven't found it makes a lot of difference to the dish washing, and I hate buttering dishes!) We add a tablespoon of honey, some chopped almonds and sultanas and often a luxury sprinkling of chopped crystallised ginger. For a more austere and traditional pud, just sprinkle with nutmeg. If I have used a skim milk, I mix in ¼ cup cream or float knobs of butter on top. (Semolina and tapioca can be brought to the boil with the milk on top of the stove before putting in the oven.)

I usually put the pud in the oven after lunch and remember it again about afternoon tea—generally about 2 hours at 120 to 150ºC. It benefits from a stir within the first hour. The family prefers it cold.

Custards of various kinds are a wonderful standby. They can be made well ahead of a meal and they slide down easily after a rich or heavy first course. With fruit they are a meal in themselves.

The standard instructions for the kinds of custards that don't come in packets is: 1 egg to 300 ml milk and 2 tablespoons honey or 25 g sugar. The more egg, the firmer the custard.

A simple and delicious custard is a New Zealand Milk Promotion Council recipe that I have served hot or cold with innumerable variations since I found it on one of their calendars five years ago.

Crème Brûlée

1½ cups topmilk or cream
3 eggs
2 tablespoons sugar or honey

¼ teaspoon vanilla
brown sugar for topping

Warm the milk and cream until the first small bubble appears.
In a large bowl, mix the eggs just enough to combine whites and yolks, and add the sugar or melted honey. Stir in the warm milk and the vanilla.
Pour the mixture into a heatproof baking dish or individual moulds and stand them in a baking pan of hot water. Bake in a moderate oven (180ºC) until firm— 30 to 45 minutes.
Sprinkle with brown or raw sugar and melt under the grill for a few minutes. This makes a luxurious caramel crust.
When I make double the recipe, I use 2 cups of milk to 1 of cream, and then double the remaining ingredients.

A "custard" that is really a junket goes down very well in the summer and is even easier to make. Simply warm milk and cream to blood heat and mix in any goodies you like—chopped nuts, chopped dried fruit, ground spices—and add sugar or warmed honey to taste. Take the mixture from the heat source and stir in thoroughly a teaspoon of rennet. Leave the bowl covered in a warm place until it sets (10 minutes), then put it in the fridge. If any is left after the first meal, the curds and whey will separate, but both are delicious.

Carrot Halva

I cannot desert the milk section without including our "buck-me-up" winter treat. When all the glorious fruits are finally finished and the vegie garden is growing

"green manure", we combat winter blues with the only thing left in the garden: carrots. Carrots, milk and sugar (or honey) make an incredibly delicious sweet, cheap on money but very expensive on time.
I usually double the quantities because the time is more valuable to me than the ingredients—and because we're greedy with the stuff!

500 g carrots	*a few strands of saffron (soaked in 2*
1800 ml milk	*teaspoons warm water) if you have them,*
375 g sugar/honey	*or a little turmeric*
30 g raisins	*crushed seeds of 2 green cardamoms*
60 g butter	*(optional)*
	almonds, blanched and sliced finely

Grate the carrots as finely as possible. (Even better, boil carrots, make carrot wine with the juice, and puree the carrots.) Bring the milk to the boil and add the carrots. Simmer and stir when necessary until thick and creamy. Then add sugar and raisins until you get to the "very thick" stage. (It *is* hard to decide the difference between thick, very thick, and ready!) Then add the butter and saffron until rich and golden and it is done. There seems to be no way to avoid the stickiness—so sprinkle it with almonds and enjoy it in fudge-sized squares. (Hide what you can rescue in the fridge. It would freeze, given the chance.)

— ◁▷ —

BUTTER
I have read books that say home-made butter should have a grainy texture or be soft or sour, but my aim is always to make it just like bought butter. The difference is that it tastes better, you can vary the salt content to suit the family and you know it is fresh. It takes about 35 minutes to make including cleaning up, but those 35 minutes don't have to be in a single hit.

If I have a two litre ice-cream container full of cream in the fridge, I empty it into the electric mixer when George goes to milk Rosie and set the timer for ten minutes. I use the wire whisk attachment (not the batter beater—that takes for ever) and set the machine at medium speed. To avoid splattering everything else on the shelf, I cover the bowl and attachment head with a tea-towel. I can forget about it for the first ten minutes until the bell goes, and get on with skimming cream and organising the dogs' milk and washing the eggs.

Washing milk containers is something I like to do as I go along, not leave till the general dish-washing. I transfer milk frequently so that I know nothing in the fridge for drinking is more than two or three days old. I rinse with cold water, then wash with detergent, rinse with very hot water and leave to drain. Or if I know everything is fresh, I just use the very hot water.

Milk

After ten minutes' whipping, the cream has changed from a flat yellow, filling half the mixing bowl, to a whipped white up to the top of the bowl and trying to get out. I set the clock for another ten minutes and carry on with the chores. At the end of that ten minutes George has usually arrived back with a pail of milk to be strained. The butter has usually begun to creep down the sides of the bowl again but is still foamy, so I clean the sides with a spatula, turn off the machine and go out to do chooks and dogs—take apples or carrots to the donkeys if we're not late—and enjoy the morning.

If it is a work day, the mixture in the bowl waits for me until I get home. I have even left it until next day, but that butter turned out very soft. Cream has a way of getting back at you if you abuse it too badly.

When I am ready to finish off the butter, I put on a plastic apron and have a plastic strainer ready sitting on the ice-cream carton that the cream came out of. If I had kept the machine running in the morning while the cream was still cool from the fridge, the whipping would have taken another ten minutes. When the mixture has all day to warm up, it makes butter almost instantly (it "clabbers"). Turn on the machine at medium, but be ready to turn it down and off so that the buttermilk that has separated from the fat does not slosh all over the kitchen.

Now for my big secret! Temperature is important in buttermaking. One book told me that it was all right not to have a separate dairy, so long as I kept my kitchen at 10⁰C. I would freeze! And anyway, the stove is in the kitchen and alight all the time. My solution is simple and it works. I fill an ice-cream container with water and freeze it. When I put the cream in the mixer, I take out my ice block and put it in a small bowl of water. By the time the butter is ready, the water is cold even in summer at midday.

In the mixing bowl, you will have yellow globs of fat and blueish liquid buttermilk. Pour the buttermilk through the strainer, back into the original ice-cream container. Keep the buttermilk. It is pleasant for a cool drink once you have got used to it not being milk; it has all the vitamins and goodies of milk without the fat; it is useful for cooking, and dogs and chickens love it. But beware—"buttermilk" in some recipes refers to a cultured product, made like yoghurt.

Pour chilled water over the butterfat while you clean up the mixer and organise salt and a container for about 500 grams of butter. I use a margarine container, but something oblong to fit into the butter conditioner in the fridge would be better. Then comes the fun part: cool your hands (which of course are scrupulously clean) in the cold water. At this stage I usually glance at the clock and comfort myself that within five minutes I will have butter the way I want it, whatever tricks the fat still has up its sleeve.

14

A local woodcarver has made me a pair of butter "hands" to finish off square or rolled butter pats. Made in 250 gram pats, wrapped in freezer paper, the packet is convenient and a useful gift.

The idea is to gather up the globs of yellow fat from the water and squeeze out the white liquid, the buttermilk. If it is behaving properly, the fat will not be as sticky as you expect it to be. If it is being really difficult, it will be horribly sticky, but that, fortunately, is unusual. Pick up the globules in the reasonably small lumps that you have shaken or scraped off the mixer attachment and join them together, squashing out the buttermilk like you would squeeze water from nylon tights in the days before washing machines.

Squash them all together and begin to press the butter into a single pat between the heels of your hands. The plastic apron is to stop squirts of buttermilk getting on your clothes. To start with it is hard to get the butter "working". That is because there is still a lot of buttermilk between the fat globules. After a while you will find your hands take on a rhythm of pressing and turning the butter so that your fingers stay out of the way. I find I tire less if I stand up straight, lift my hands to my chest as if in angelic prayer and look out of the window while my hands do the work. It is a good time to practise regular deep breathing, and I am sure the exercise keeps the hands supple, strengthens the upper arms and develops the chest! All that and a pound of butter!

Rinse the butter in more cold water and squash it until it is the texture of bought butter. We find that half a teaspoon of salt is enough. Distribute the salt with more squashing, then make a ball of butter and plop it in the container. I smooth it off with a knife, just for looks. If you prefer to finish off with butter "hands", soak the two wooden paddles in the iced water while you work the butter. Making different shapes is fun and takes some skill.

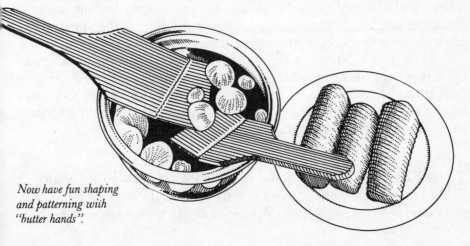

Now have fun shaping and patterning with "butter hands".

The butter keeps well in the fridge or freezer, but I think it is most delicious of all if it can be eaten up fairly quickly at the temperature it was made, without more cooling.

I have tried other ways of storing partially made butter, by cooling and freezing at various stages. Some efforts have demanded more subsequent labour in getting the butter to "work" again, others have given me a hard time with sticky fingers, but eventually each has given us a satisfactory pat of butter. This method always works for these quantities. When I have tried to be greedy, the mixer bowl has overflowed and my wrists have ached with the kneading.

The only time my butter has refused to "clabber" has been when condensation has watered the cream or when I have included too much milk in the cream or on the odd occasion that I have begun to make the butter and then left it to go really soft before getting back to it the next day. The answer is the same in each case. Hook a fine sieve over an ice-cream container (you'll probably need two) and tip into it the contents of your mixing bowl. The excess whey will drain through. Tip the thickening cream back into the mixer and try again. It is in the nature of thick cream without whey to become butter: it *has* to "clabber". Unless, of course, witchcraft in your area is more potent than in ours!

Making fancy butters is very easy. Just add the extras at the same time as you add the salt. Sometimes the operation needs a bit of planning ahead. It is annoying to have to stop and peel and crush garlic in the middle of buttermaking—especially if you have decided to make only half the butter garlic and the rest, say, cinnamon and orange. There is an awful lot of hand scrubbing to do.

I regularly add caraway seeds to some of my buter—just half a teaspoon with the salt and then keep on working the butter until I see it is evenly distributed. I use the same method for crushed garlic with ground black pepper and chopped green herbs, but the butter does become sticky. I don't use the butter hands in case the wood takes up the smell of the garlic. If I am thinking of making pancakes, I add fine sugar, cinnamon and the zest of a lemon to the butter. The variations are infinite and the fun of experimenting makes the job of buttermaking more interesting once it has become a regular ritual. It is also quite impressive to visitors when you unwrap a perfect pat of already flavoured butter. (Buttermakers have earned the right to show off a little!)

GHEE

If you like to cook Indian food, it is a treat to use clarified butter. It is not hard to make and is a good way to make the most of butter that stays obstinately sticky or soft. Beware of books that tell you to boil the butter for two hours! I tried that. The solids fall to the bottom of the saucepan while a froth rises to the top. Skim the top and pour off the fat *before* the solids on the bottom turn brown and then black. I still have a bottle of black butter! I thought ghee would stay liquid, but it goes solid. It keeps in a jar unrefrigerated for many months without going rancid.

CHAPTER 3   CHEESE

Just to write the heading "Cheese" sends a flutter to my anticipatory area, somewhere near the solar plexus—whatever that is.

I know I am being daring to the point of foolhardy to put my findings in print at this stage. Cheesemaking is a lifetime's adventure and, as with winemaking, an expert should be elderly, established and have done the same thing repeatedly a hundred thousand times. So far, I have discovered one cheese that I can rely on to turn out well every time (I made it by experimenting before I found any recipes) and perhaps another ten or so "interesting" cheeses where I have approximated other people's recipes. With those miserable credentials I will still share what I have learned, because both making and tasting are fun and enormously satisfying. And save money.

A ghoulish row of cheeses: a lapse in hygiene and they could smell as bad as they look.

My approach to cheesemaking was the same as to buttermaking: millions of people have made it over thousands of years, so it can't be so difficult! And it is not. In general outline, cheesemaking is simple. Make the milk separate into curds and whey. Drain off the whey, squash the curds together and wait a bit. That's all there is to it. But temperature, timing and manipulation of the curd make the difference between cheeses, and these have to be precise.

On the other hand, if you throw caution to the winds and begin boldly taking ignorance as your baseline, you can evolve cheeses that have never

Milk

before been tasted. Or you can have a hanging row of hideously orange and stinking bags like grisly skulls perfuming your house for three obstinate months. Both have happened to us.

The first step along our cheese trail was a request from a visitor for junket—just like he had eaten when he was a kid. I bought a bottle of rennet, put a teaspoon in finger-warm milk just like it said on the bottle, waited ten minutes, put it in the fridge and—what an excellent cook I was!—there was junket.

Then came a bleak patch. I made enquiries among our rural neighbours about cheesemaking. The steadiest reply was that it was a waste of time with less than ten gallons of milk from a single milking. Poor Susie: she was doing her best.

The same friend who gave me the clue about butter told me she had tried cheese once upon a time. She had filled bags with junket, let them drip, then hung them on a line across her studio. It sounded simple enough. She couldn't tell me what the cheese tasted like because a rat had eaten it.

I spent a lot of milk and a lot of energy repeating her experiment. I wrote down every variation—temperature, cream ratio, date—and mixed some with herbs, some with garlic. I pressed the bags under wood and rocks, re-tied them, rescued them when the rocks slipped . . . and put up with the smell. I thought all dairies must smell that way.

I had gleaned many snippets of "knowledge" on my enquiries. One was: "It has to be left at least three months to mature". I left those stinking bags, eight of them, each with its numbered tag, as they turned yellow, turned orange and moulds disfigured them.

At last three months was up and I took down the first one.

Lucky Kaara. She didn't know what a good turn that rat had done for her!

I attacked it with a cleaver. It was harder than a pumpkin. In the very middle were a few millimetres of cheese that hadn't completely dried out. With great ceremony, I tasted a sliver.

It was the ultimate. Vile. It tasted worse than it smelt. It took me a month to feed it all to our three long-suffering dogs and I couldn't look them in the eye until it was gone. Yuk!

I've made some bad cheeses since then, but not that bad.

It took a while to rekindle my courage—I clung to the "ten gallon" excuse. But what to do with the skimmed milk? Susie kept on sending me a daily bucket of milk with her love.

To give myself time to think and to reduce the milk's bulk, I turned it into junket. While the butter machine whirred, I heated up the skimmed milk, put in rennet, stirred it and left it. At that stage we only had the

18

electric oven. I heated that for a few minutes, then turned it off and put the junket inside to set. I left it there all day while I went to work and in the evening, cut it through with a long knife to release the clear whey from the curd.

Sometimes the curd was thick and heavy and there was a lot of whey, and sometimes it was fluffy and there was little whey. The temperature of the milk and of the oven made the difference. The hotter the temperature the more solid the curd. Before I went to bed, I drained the curds and whey through a double cotton cloth. The cloth came from a huge roll of stretchy stockinette used in the meat industry to cover mutton carcasses. I boiled up generous squares of it and used it for everything.

After pouring off as much whey as I could, I heaped the cloth on top of the curd and let it drip out until the morning. (The whey went into a bucket for chooks and a neighbour's pig. It can be used in cooking but the volume is overwhelming.) By the morning, there was a flat solid disc of white curd. Taking a tip from a friend who had worked in a dairy factory, I broke it in pieces and washed it.

Not knowing what to do next, I filled up plastic boxes and hid it in the freezer. When I had run out of plastic boxes and freezer space and had a weekend to play, I got them all out and let them warm up and mixed in salt.

Cheese, I had heard, had to be pressed. We had a cider press so I lined the barrel with a large square of stockinette and ladled in the curd. There must have been ten kilos of curd. We crammed it all in, folded the cloth over the top and put on the pressure. Whey came oozing out most satisfactorily.

Next problem was where to keep it. With lingering memories of cheese smells, we decided on the garage under the house where it was cool. The rats soon found it there. So it went into the honey house and dribbled for a weak under increasing pressure. I left it another week until there was a spare afternoon to rescue it. We hoicked it back onto the balcony and faced the problem of how to get the cheese out of the press.

The cloth around the curd had wedged itself between the slats of the cider barrel and had hardened. The only thing to do was to use brute force: wind down the press. The bag burst. Ten kilos of crumbled curd burst onto the balcony.

Terribly disappointed, I tasted a lump. It was delicious! Mild, but definitely cheese. Triumphant, we scooped it all up, put half back in the freezer and half in the fridge to use for cooking. I used it in soups, quiches, macaronis, and pizzas for the next six months.

At last I had proved that we could make something that tasted cheesy. Now we had to make it look like a cheese. We tried lining the cider barrel

Milk

with pieces of perforated tin, but they wouldn't slide out when they were under pressure from the cheese. We cut the bottom from a cake tin and put holes in the sides for the whey and made wooden discs with holes for top and bottom. That was nearly right, except the holes were too big and the cloth popped through and went hard and we couldn't push the cheese through.

We sorted that one out. Freezer Cheese is still our most reliable standby. I have since learned the rules of cheese making and Freezer Cheese breaks most of them, but it has a fresh Stilton flavour, is pleasantly moist and is firm enough to slice but crumbles if you want it to, like fetta. The best thing about it is that it is quick and easy to make, a genuine "no fuss" cheese and quick to mature.

309 Freezer Cheese

An uncooked cheese. I claim the right to name the "309"—the number of our street—because it breaks the rules of traditional cheese and so is "new".

The size of pans and bowls and the amount of milk available are the only limit on quantity. Skim milk is fine to use, but for a creamier cheese add half the cream you skimmed off the whole milk. Heat the cream first to about blood heat and tip it in to the cold milk. That stops the cream rising to the surface of the curd.

I heat eight litres of unpasteurised cheesemilk to a temperature comfortable for my finger, 32°C. (Slightly cooler and the cheese will turn out softer and moister, hotter and it will have a tougher, rubbery texture. For Freezer Cheese it doesn't much matter, but try to keep your system the same for each block of curds you intend to use in the same cheese, otherwise with a soft and tough mixture the texture will be uneven and crumble too easily.)

Stir the cheesemilk to distribute heat. Take it off the heat and add a teaspoon of rennet. (Before I read cheesemaking books, I added rennet direct to the cheesemilk. Now I mix it with a few tablespoons of cold water. I haven't noticed any difference.) Stir for twenty seconds. Leave the pan, covered with a tea-towel against dust, in a warm place. (A "warm place" used to be my electric oven, warmed for a few minutes then turned of, with the door slightly open, and is now the plate rack over the woodburning stove. A towel snuggled around the pan would keep in enough heat for the rennet to work.)

The rennet takes about half an hour to turn the liquid into junket. Transparent yellowish whey begins to separate around the edge of the white bulk which is the curd. Nothing bad has happened to me when I have left it all day. At a time convenient to you, slice through the curd to let out the whey.

For formal cheeses that have proper names and exact recipes, the size and regularity of the cut curd matters. My system with Freezer Cheese used to be to use a long bladed carving knife and cut down through the curd one way and then the other in rather crooked lines, leaving about 1.5 cm between each cut. I left the curd again until I was ready to scoop it into a cloth for draining. Then I used a plastic measuring cup with a handle (big sister to the half-cup size used for skimming cream) and cut across the curd in layers. That way I ended up with cubes about the same size. Now George has devised a wire gadget for horizontal cuts.

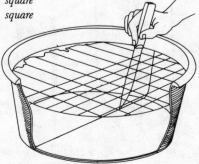

The only problem with a square cutter is that you need a square saucepan.

The cubes won't be perfect but make them as regular as possible.

Plastic and nylon sieves and colanders of suitable size take the hassle out of cheesemaking. It is worth collecting them. A two-part lettuce shaker, half solid and half perforated, has been my most useful whey drainer. The perforated half rests over the solid half. With a cloth lining the top, curds and whey can drain without the need to tie and hang them. A colander that fits over a plastic bucket works as well.

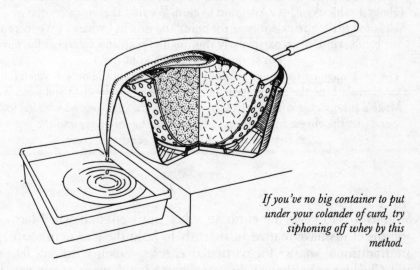

If you've no big container to put under your colander of curd, try siphoning off whey by this method.

It really is important to boil up the cheese cloth for at least five minutes, whatever you use. "Dirty" cloth contributed to my first cheese disaster: I didn't boil the cloth because it was new and, I assumed, clean. The dressing in the material reacted badly with the acid in the whey and triggered that awful smell and the hectic orange colour.

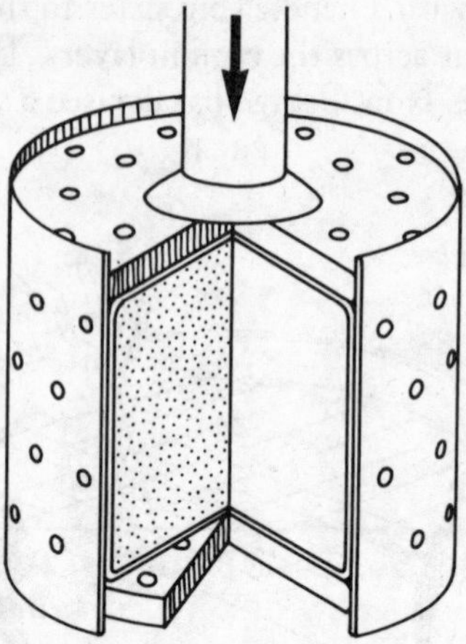

If a cheese is pressed into a snug, tidy shape, there will be fewer bumps and crevices for moulds to grow during ripening.

Having ladled the curds into a cloth over a colander and poured off as much whey as you can (to prevent it spilling over in the night) go to bed. Next morning the curds will have settled into a matted disc. It is a simple matter to wash the disc in cold water, break it gently to fit into a freezer box, put it away and rinse the cloth.

When you have collected enough curd and have the time, let the curd thaw. Combine as much as you can handle with the moulds you have ready, and warm it through gently—in the sun under a dark cloth or above the stove but not on direct heat.

You need salt, but how much depends on your family's tastes. A guide is 20 grams (about 1 tablespoon) per kilogram of curd. We find that quantity too much but half is too little. Sprinkle it over the curds and mix in by hand. (When you wash your hands, rinse them particularly thoroughly: soap and detergent flavours come out strongly in cheese and butter.)

The next stage needs some explaining. Stand your mould on a wooden follower (see above). Line the mould with a clean cloth. Ladle the curd and push it down. Make a tidy packet with the ends of the cloth. Fit on a second wooden follower and put the cheese in the press. The mould, the followers and the press are necessary for all hard and many semi-soft cheeses.

Mould

Moulds are to keep the curds together until enough whey has escaped and the curds have matted sufficiently to hold the cheese in shape. There are traditional shapes for particular cheeses. Edam is round, feta square and Cheddar cake-shaped. Freezer Cheese is whatever shape you like to make it, but I have found cake shape to be the simplest.

To achieve this, we use a 23 cm length of 150 mm diameter plastic water pipe with small holes drilled round the sides. We have also made moulds out of plastic piping of a smaller diameter: with Freezer Cheese, smaller cheeses are ready for eating more quickly so a selection of sizes is useful. We have two 120 mm diameter moulds made from the cut-out middles of two-litre plastic containers and two from 90 mm pipes. The moulds need to be at least twice as tall as your final cheese will be deep as curds sink down when the whey is expelled. (I have read recently that plastic piping is unsuitable for cheesemaking because it is of a material that cannot be properly sterilised. We have had no problems: the material is hard and shiny and there are two layers of cloth between it and the cheese.)

FOLLOWERS

Followers are perforated discs (or squares) to fit each end of the mould. Ours are made from plywood with drilled holes. A firm plastic would do. They must take pressure and distribute it over the cheese. They need to fit snugly into the mould otherwise cheese oozes up around the edges.

Once you begin cheesemaking, you will notice flower pots, baskets, tins, tubes and containers of all sorts that can be converted into moulds.

PRESS

For a long-lasting, big, hard cheese, a press is absolutely necessary. For most home-sized cheeses, an improvisation is good enough. I took the idea of a press too seriously and used a powerful cast iron press made for pressing beeswax. I pressed the poor cheese to death. The only way we could tell it from chalk was the cardamom seeds inside.

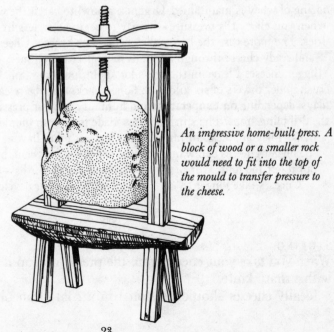

An impressive home-built press. A block of wood or a smaller rock would need to fit into the top of the mould to transfer pressure to the cheese.

Our wine press is good because I can see the cheese and the amount of whey that is coming out, but there is no gauge to indicate pressure. Cheeses need a gentle touch to begin with: just enough pressure to encourage whey to ooze out steadily but not spurt out. That means that if your press is a wind-down one, it needs adjusting hourly to begin with until the flow slows.

Probably a weight pressing the cheese is kinder. Propping everything in place takes ingenuity. You need something the right size to fit in the mould on top of the follower, then a platform to take the weight. Rocks, or a bucket filled with increasing amounts of water, are suitable weights. Or if it is a big cheese and you need more pressure, something cunning can be done with a car jack and the underneath of a firm shelf.

Don't make your press too complicated. The cheese needs to be turned regularly so that it drains evenly and keeps its shape. And most of the parts of the press will have to be cleaned between cheeses.

Back to 309 Freezer Cheese

. . . the curds are tidily packed into a cloth inside the mould. The ends of the cloth are a nuisance because you have to start with a big cloth to hold all the curds. Just pack them in. You can change the cloth after two hours when the cheese holds its shape. Use a smaller cloth then and put it back in the press under increased pressure to get rid of the dents. The more regular the shape of the end product, the easier it is to dry and control moulds (the blue, green and orange varieties).

Begin with light pressure on the cheese and increase gradually so that a regular oozing of whey is maintained. Organise a bowl to catch the whey. Turn the cheese when you check the pressure—hourly to begin with, less frequently as the cheese dries. The more care the better the cheese, but Freezer Cheese survives as a rough and ready cheese through all kinds of neglect (cleanliness is the only 'must').

Bigger cheeses I leave in the press for about four days. Smaller cheeses (which I crush under towers of six kilogram honey packs) can be released after two or three days, depending on temperature and humidity in your pressing room—whenever the dribbling stops. The small cheeses made in 90 mm moulds can be eaten within a week. They are pleasant immediately but get more flavour if left the extra days. The bigger cheeses can wait until you are ready for them, but they begin to dry out if left too long. Our maximum so far is four months—a very tasty cheese. Cheeses take longer to cure in winter and flavour develops more slowly.

STORING

When you take your cheese from the press, unwrap it and trim off ridges with a sharp knife.

Ideally cheeses should be stored in a cool clean place with a flow of fresh air for about 24 hours for the outer skin to form. If the temperature is too hot, the cheese cracks and moulds creep inside. If it is too humid, drying is slow and moulds get established. I have found care of the young cheese to be the most tricky and frustrating part of cheesemaking. Cool dark cellars were the answer in the old days, and caves, but not many people have these, and if they do, rats and flies probably have access.

With varying success I have tried all the following recommended methods.

Wax dipping A coat of paraffin wax keeps moulds away from the cheese, but it is an expensive and messy procedure. Unless you make candles or take up beekeeping you are unlikely to have a large saucepan used specially for wax—and wax is difficult to clean up. If you do choose to use wax, be careful of wax's low flash point. Heat slowly over water and never leave the room while it is heating. Dip the cheese a portion at a time, allowing each portion to harden so that you can hold it. I have tried brushing on beeswax but moulds grow underneath.

Smear the dry cheese with butter or lard. This works well for a while but has to be renewed frequently. If you make your own butter, it doesn't seem so extravagant. Cooking oil is an alternative.

Let the cheese dry naturally without any covering. This is sometimes recommended for brined cheeses—those that have been salted by leaving them in saline solution for 24 hours. I have found that because the cheeses dry slowly (salt attracts dampness), moulds still make their home on the skin. At certain times of the year when drying conditions are perfect, a good rind can form naturally but it is a matter of luck. I have also tried dry salting and wiping with alcohol.

Flour and water paste. I keep coming back to this method and I use it immediately the cheese is unwrapped, without waiting for the rind to harden. Make a paste from about two teaspoons of white flour and enough water to make it the consistency of prepared mustard. Spread it on the cheese with a pastry brush as soon as it comes out of the press, then stretch a single layer of boiled cheesecloth, muslin or stockinette over it and bandage it securely.

Label the cheese with its type and date, and a number to correspond with a record of how you made the cheese. Let it stand on a rack or undyed rush mat so that air can circulate (a mat on egg cartons is ideal). Turn it daily for a week and then less frequently until it is ready to eat. (Finding suitable mats was a problem until I hit on the idea of cutting off the bottoms of our bamboo matchstick blinds. They work perfectly.)

Moulds take up residence anyway, but I have decided not to object to them. When the cheese is unwrapped, they can be scrubbed off the skin with cold water, leaving the cheese respectable for the table. Cut off the

Milk

rind: it is a perk for dogs, birds, chooks and cat.

Let your imagination run riot with flavouring. When you sprinkle salt on the curds, try adding pressed garlic, crushed cardamon seeds or chopped walnuts and orange. Herbs are a possibility, but experiment with smaller cheeses: I have been disappointed with patchy discolouration of the white cheese.

When you need help deciding which you like best, have a party!

PASTEURISING MILK FOR CHEESE

There are different opinions about the need to pasteurise milk, most of them held strongly and expressed forcibly. It is the law in New Zealand and Australia that cheese made from unpasteurised milk cannot be sold. Small-scale cheesemakers maintain that cheese from unpasteurised milk is safe and better tasting. They have been fighting battles with the authorities for years. Larger dairy companies all pasteurise and standardise milk.

The New Zealand Dairy Research Institute which services the larger commercial enterprises wrote to me: "It is a dangerous practice to advocate the use of unpasteurised milk in cheesemaking and we would certainly not recommend it." In the same letter, I was referred to Chr. Hansen's Laboratories, a Danish company established in 1874 which makes the results of advanced cheesemaking technology available to small producers. They can supply rennet, a wealth of "starter" cultures, cheese moulds and cheese colourings in reasonable quantities. Their representatives told me: "Forty years ago in New Zealand milk had to be pasteurised. These days it is probably a waste of time." The major advantage of continuing the practice was "repeatability" in cheeses.

There is always some danger associated with home-produced foods, though statistically insignificant against the dangers of travelling in a car. We remain vividly aware that milk is a perfect breeding ground for bad bugs as well as good ones. Whatever kind of mess my house is in, the dairying equipment is always given immediate "hospital" treatment and milk spends as little time as possible between the cow and the fridge. The faintest suspicion of staleness or a less than fresh smell and the milk, cream, yoghurt or cheese goes straight to the animals.

The most impressive and comprehensive book I have read on cheesemaking is by Professor Frank Kosikowski. In *Cheese and Fermented Milk Foods* (published by the author, 2nd ed. 1977) he writes:

Most cheeses are safe and in recent years little has been heard of disease epidemics resulting from cheese. But it is well to remember that home cheeses have a greater potential for causing food poisoning than commercial cheese, if not properly made and protected.

ADDING LACTIC STARTER

I had never needed to use a lactic "starter" while Susie and then Rosie gave me plenty of milk. But just as Rosie was drying up to have her calf, I was asked by our local Polytechnic to offer a course in cheesemaking. I wanted to demonstrate four cheeses, and to have some stages prepared in advance. That meant even if I starved the pigs and dogs I wouldn't have enough milk. And of course it was the dry time for local dairy farmers' herds. I had to buy shop milk which was pasteurised, and pasteurised milk won't make cheese.

Fortunately for me, Hansen's had just opened a branch in New Zealand at Hamilton. Their kind and patient manager, Owen Scott, expressed surprise that I had achieved any success with my hit and miss methods. His life's experience of cheesemaking was with factories and carefully controlled environments. He sent me a 100 gram foil packet of freeze-dried cultures suitable for turning up to 5000 litres of milk into Goudas, Edams, Danbos, mould-ripened cheeses, semi-hard cheese with holes, and other soft cheeses.

Mr Scott started to ask on the phone how I made my "mother culture" but gave up and began talking about fishing when it became obvious that "mother culture" to me meant something to do with teenage daughters. He promised to send me technical information. According to that technical information:

> Treatment of cheesemilk prior to curdmaking normally comprises clarification and possibly thermization, fat standardization, pasteur-ization and/or bactofuge treatment, ripening and final adjustments with various additives such as calcium chloride and colouring or discolouring agents.

I'm glad I didn't read that before I began making delicious cheeses by mistake!

I'm finding again and again, with wine, bread and cheese, that the raw materials just *want* to become food. However badly my ignorance treats them, and so long as the priority is spotless hygiene, they turn out okay.

There were no specific instructions with the freeze-dried granules of cultures about how to make three litres of milk into a Gouda cheese. I bought skim milk and received my packet of cultures the evening before fifteen students arrived for the demonstration. The only instructions were to ripen the milk for "a few hours" before use. I guessed five hours was a "few", rose early, heated the milk to blood heat and added the "starter"— about a quarter of a teaspoon (another guess). Later in the morning I read that the ideal heat for propagating should have been between 19°C and 23°C. Scared that I had killed off the culture by overheating, I slipped back into the demonstration room during morning coffee time and tipped in a few more granules before warming the milk again ready for rennet. I was nervous.

The milk coagulated beautifully and produced a "Gouda" type of cheese with quite a different flavour from the various other cheeses that I had produced with Rosie's unpasteurised milk. In fact, that had been a problem: I could get a good range of textures with different curd treatments, but all my cheeses had begun to taste the same (although a different flavour in the winter from the summer). Using starter gave me a new world of flavours to explore.

The "mother culture" is the original ripened milk. Instead of using all my three litres of milk to make the Gouda, I could have kept some in the fridge and used just a portion of it to "ripen" the next batch of milk. (The same principle applies with yoghurt and cultured buttermilk. A small amount of yoghurt added to milk at blood temperature—and left a while in the warm—will turn all the milk into yoghurt. Small amounts of cultured buttermilk will turn more warm milk into buttermilk.)

With freeze-dried cultures from Hansen's, the granules can be added direct to the cheese milk or they can be used to make a mother culture. If you really need to know, the cultures contain *Streptococcus lactis*, *Streptococcus cremoris*, *Streptococcus diacetylactis* (for aroma) and *Leuconostoc cemoris*. The "O cultures" for cheeses that don't need carbon dioxide to make holes contain no *Streptococcus diacetylactis* or *Leuconostoc cremoris*. Most of the different kinds of starters are currently stored at Chr. Hansen's Laboratory (Australia) Pty Ltd in Victoria, Australia but can be obtained through Mr Scott in Hamilton.

If you choose to do without commercial starters, try the advice of Polly Pinder in her book *Soft Cheeses* (Search Press, 1978). Her cheeses are all made from skim milk (bottled or in a carton). Her starter is simple: into half a teacup of milk heated to 35°C crumble 14 grams of bought hard cheese. Cover with a clean cloth and leave it in a warm room temperature for 24 hours. That is a "mother culture", enough to start four litres of cheese milk: choose the cheese flavour you like best to influence your own cheese. Fresh commercial buttermilk also has suitable bacteria for cheese.

HEATING CUT CURDS
The other step not practised with old fashioned cheeses but recommended in modern books is cooking (scalding) the curds after they have been cut. This is not a difficult operation but it takes time because the curds have to be heated slowly and the heat to which they are brought is critical.

The advantage of heating the curd is that whey runs out more quickly. The heated curds compress more efficiently so that pressing and curing time are shortened and the cheese, being drier, takes on longer-lasting qualities. I am not convinced that flavour is improved, but cooking at different temperatures gives scope for experimenting with cheeses that have a variety of textures and uses. Some grate more smoothly and others melt sensuously on toast.

With cooked curd cheeses, the whole skill of the cheesemaker rests on that moment when the decision is made: the curds are done!

With a shift in emphasis away from producing cheeses and towards marketing them, when cheese became "business", expectations about cheeses and even definitions of how cheeses should look and taste changed. Cottage cheese is a good example. It began as the most simple cheese a cottage housewife could make: she left milk to sour (probably skimmed milk because she had taken the cream for butter) and when it was solid she hung it in a cloth for a few hours for the whey to drip out. It was then cottage cheese. But since cottage cheese has been sold in plastic cartons and recommended for the diet conscious, everybody has learnt that cottage cheese comes in little round globules bound lightly together with a pale cream.

Getting these little globules to maintain exactly the right shape and softness has become a talent more easily exercised by the big factories where standardisation is the secret of mass production. In the kitchen it is a lot harder. But if you would like to experiment with cooked cheeses, cottage cheese is a good one to start with, simply because you can sample the results instantly instead of having to wait weeks or months for a mature cheese.

Cottage Cheese

Use any quantity of skimmed milk. Cottage cheese keeps at the most for a week under refrigeration so there is no point in making too much.
There are several possible starting points:

(a) Let raw milk sour naturally, keeping it lightly covered to keep it clean, at a comfortably warm room temperature (about four days in winter, less in summer).
(b) Use raw milk but add buttermilk or yoghurt to make it sour more quickly with a flavour you like.
(c) Use raw milk, bring it to blood heat or slightly less, add ½ teaspoon of rennet mixed in two teaspoons cold water for four litres of milk, take it off the heat and allow to set (30 minutes to an hour depending on temperature).

Milk

(d) Use pasteurised skim milk, warm it slowly to 24°C then stir in fresh commercial buttermilk or a lactic acid starter culture and take it off the heat. Let it rest a few hours then continue as for (c).

Whichever method you start with, all should reach a stage of set curd. Cut the curd in cubes about the same size, about 2 cm. Put the curd back on a slow, very controllable heat source (this is where it is easier to have a computerised factory than a common kitchen).

Professor Frank K. Kosikowski, who has researched small factory cheese production at Cornell University, in a chapter of his book *Cheese and Fermented Milk Foods* writes that curds (made without rennet) from ten gallons of skim milk should be brought up to approximately 50°C and over a period of 90 minutes, letting the temperature rise uniformly five degrees in every ten minutes. I like this test for the proper degree of cooking: ". . . the curds should . . . hold together, rather than spatter, when dropped from waist level to a dish on the floor."
Other authorities recommend heating curds to 43°C, or 35-38°C, washing the curds with water at a temperature of 80°C, or leaving the curds at 32°C "until they hold their shape".
You choose! I tried heating curds to 43°C and swishing them around by hand until they were properly resilient (that is, they jump back into shape when squashed between the fingers) but the result was tough little balls that squeaked when we chewed them. (Mind you I did leave the curds on the stove when George called me to help separate the calf from Rosie, which I shouldn't have done.)
Lower heating suits our tastes better. Our best results have been obtained by warming the curds with the addition of hot water over a 2 hour period, to a temperature of about 43°C.
To finish off: drain the whey off the curds and wash them. Tip them into a colander lined with muslin and leave them for about half an hour, then salt lightly and mix them with cream. They are really good with home-made lemon curd in pancakes.

If you understand what different speeds of heating and degrees of heat can do to your cottage-cheese curds, then you have acquired a basic competence to tackle any cheese. Scale of operation becomes the limiting factor. Some flavours, of a perfectly matured Stilton or Cheddar for instance, can never be reproduced in small scale cheesemaking because they do have to come from big cheeses. Small cheeses dry out before they can mature to the necessary degree. The special gifts of small cheeses are delectable, fresh and different flavours.

CHAPTER 4   COOKED CHEESE AND SOFT CHEESE

In her book *Food in England*, Dorothy Hartley has a recipe for Cheddar cheese from around 1700 AD. Of course, the cheese has to be made in Cheddar in Somerset, England. Made elsewhere or at a time of year other than that specified, the cows could be on different pasture and the flavour would change. Every notable dairying district in England had its cheese: Cheddar, Caerphilly, Gloucester, Wensleydale, Stilton, Cheshire. Essex wasn't too great. Dorothy Hartley quotes a poem about Essex cheese:

> *Those that made me were uncivil*
> *They made me harder than the devil*
> *Knives won't cut me, fire won't light me*
> *Dogs bark at me but they can't bite me.*

(Just like my Cardamom Chalk cheese.)

All our Cheddars these days are an approximation, and methods of making them vary in almost every detail according to the authority consulted.

309 Freezer Cheese, although it is made with modern gadgets and to suit my lifestyle, is an old-fashioned cheese. It is made according to the rhythm of cheese making reported from the eighteenth and nineteenth centuries but omits three procedures recommended in most more recent cheesemaking books. They are: pasteurising the milk, adding a "starter", and re-heating cut curds.

309 Freezer Cheese is an uncooked semi-soft cheese. Gouda is another semi-soft, but cooked. Cheddar is classed as a hard cheese (though not as hard as Parmesan, Emmental or Gruyere) because when properly ripened, it has less moisture remaining. Cheddar is also a "cooked" cheese and cooked to a higher temperature than Gouda. An approximation of both cheeses can be made successfully at home on a small scale.

Cooked Cheeses

Gouda

Any quantity of milk can be used—it depends on how big you want the cheese and what is available. Three litres makes a rather small cheese (about 5 cm high in a 12 cm mould) so 5 litres makes the effort more worthwhile.

Warm 1 litre of cream to blood heat. Pour it into 5 litres of skim milk and warm to 32°C. (I am assuming the milk is either unpasteurised or ripened—see page 9). Add 1 teaspoon rennet and stir thoroughly for about 20 seconds. Leave covered and in a warm place for about an hour.

Cut the curd into 1.5 cm cubes as evenly as possible. Slowly re-warm curd to 34°C, stirring gently so that curds hold their shape, but keeping heat evenly distributed. Hold the heat at 34°C and stir the curd for about half an hour or until individual curds loose their "squashiness" and return to shape when gently pressed with the fingers. (The more moisture left in the curd, the softer the cheese. Experiment. The preferred result is simply a matter of individual taste.)

Capture the curds in a clean muslin cloth, reserving the warm whey. Do this operation under the whey if possible. (There is a logistical problem with Gouda: in factories, the curds are gathered and squeezed while still in whey and no air is allowed to find its way between the pieces of curd. I have found that I get a good result from lifting the curds out of the whey, salting them, then returning them to the warm whey and squeezing out the air while they are immersed.)

Add salt—about 25 g to 1 kg of curd, or to taste. Mix it in by hand and bundle up the curds in the muslin. Return the bundle of curds to the whey and press out air gently and press out as much whey as possible.

Remembering that more whey will drain from the cheese, set up a mould and follower on a mat or draining board and pack the bundle of muslin-wrapped curds into the mould. Make the excess cloth as tidy as possible on top of the cheese and put a wooden follower on top of that.

Press lightly to begin with. Put a hunk of lead (weights from a diving belt or weights from old kitchen scales will do) on the top follower for the first half hour, pressing occasionally with your own weight to keep the whey flowing out of holes in the mould.

Turn and press from the other end, putting the cheese under increasing pressure over 24 hours (see pages 23–24). Press cheese (changing cloth for a smaller one if you wish) for about four days, depending on climate—if cold and damp, four or five days; if hot and dry, three or four.

Take out of press and unwrap cheese. Commercial dairies have a PVA glue that is painted onto the outer skin of the cheese and which hardens and goes transparent. I treat Gouda the same as the other cheeses and use a flour paste and cloth bandaging (see page 25). Label and encode to tally with your notes.

Ripen in cool, vermin-free place for about six weeks, or longer if the weather is cold or the cheese is large. As the cheese matures, the crust gives a more "hollow" sound when you flick it.

It takes about half a day to make Gouda to the stage of getting it in the press. Of course, it can be speeded up or slowed down but I have found that there is a danger both ways. If the operation is speeded up so that the curds have less time in the whey, there is a flavour loss. When I have left the curds warming for too long, they have become too acid: the texture becomes spongy and it is impossible to make cheese. It doesn't smell good either.

Cheddar

Cheddar takes longer, needs, if possible, more milk and is more labour intensive. The extra trouble gives you a cheese that can be ripened for longer because it is dryer, and the flavour has more chance to develop and mature.

Warm 2 or 3 litres of cream to blood heat (37°C or just under), pour it into 10 litres of skim milk and warm to 33°. (For pasteurised milk, see steps for adding lactic starter and ripening milk on page 27.) Add 1½ teaspoons rennet and stir thoroughly.
Leave covered in a warm place for about an hour.
Cut curd into small even cubes, about 1 cm. Slowly, over a period of about 1½ hours (you *can* cheat a bit) re-warm curd. The maximum temperature is warmer than for Gouda but cooler than for Cottage Cheese. Aim for about 38°C. Stir with the hand to distribute temperature evenly. In factories, the temperature is brought up using a water-jacket casing around the vat. I find that heating a little whey and tipping it back into the curd works well, or even tipping in hot water if the whey is not to be used for something else.
Hold the temperature steady for a further half hour or until the curds hold their shape when pressed with the fingers (very hard to judge until you have got the "feel" of differently heated curds. You want them independent but not squeaky to chew, soft but not squashy).
Away from a heat source but still in a warm environment, let the curd settle under the whey. (It "mats".)
Pour off the whey and cut the matted curd into slabs. Using 12 litres of milk and cream, six slabs is a convenient number.
Layer the slabs in pairs on a sloping smooth surface so that more whey can drain off under pressure of the curd's own weight. Use a tilted meat roasting pan. Keep warm under a damp cloth. Repile the slabs over a few hours. This process is called cheddaring. Towards the end, put a light weight on the slabs.
When the curd is relatively dry, mill it. Commercially, curd is milled to the rough size of potato chips. At home I crumble the curd much more finely. I have tried breaking it in a food processor because for a large quantity the process is hard on the fingers. The cheese didn't suffer but I felt that the treatment was a bit drastic and have since plodded away and done it by hand. I try to keep the curd pleasantly warm through this stage. The curd can be washed or not—washing gives a milder cheddar, but be careful not to wash away too much whey because the cheese needs some acid to mature properly.
Put a mould on a follower, line it with a clean, warm, damp cloth (rinsed in whey) and ladle in the milled curd (clothes pegs on top of the mould help keep the muslin cloth in place). Press it down, fold the cloth in neatly and cap with the other follower.
Press. Cheddar definitely needs a press. Begin with light pressure, turning hourly until the whey flow decreases. Turn daily for a week, gradually increasing pressure as cheese shrinks. Don't press too hard too fast or cheese texture will be lost. Keep

Milk

the whey trickling, but don't make the curds ooze through the mould holes. Take out of the press—sometimes a bit tricky if you have forgotten to turn the cheese regularly. Take off the cloth and trim rough edges of the cheese. Paste, bandage, label.

Ripen in cool airy place. Leave up to 12 weeks.

To serve: in *private* rip off the now blue bandages and scrub rind in cold water with a vegetable brush. If it passes the "sniff test" and sounds pleasantly hollow when you flick it, you can probably take the risk of cutting it in front of guests. I like to have a taste first, just to make sure! Have your notes handy because there will be those who want to know how you did it.

Soft Cheeses

Soft cheeses are the easiest to make, but unfortunately I find them the least satisfactory. They are not cooked or pressed and most should be refrigerated until they are used. To me, the flavour is "delicate" to the point of insipid, but of course the are plenty of herbs, fruits, and spices that can liven it up.

My favourite soft cheeses of all are the French Camembert and Brie which can, apparently, be made at home but they need a special mould which is introduced to the cheesemilk at the same time as the lactic starter. That is an adventure for the future, but the results could certainly turn my assessment of home-made soft cheeses upside down.

Since soft cheeses have to be eaten soon after they are made, it makes sense to use smaller quantities of milk. And if you are using less milk, then it seems a good time to experiment!

There are a number of curdling agents for milk apart from rennet. All of them can be used for different soft cheeses. Rennet is the most "neutral" in flavour and the most reliable in its effect on the milk, that is why it is usually chosen for the more elaborate efforts that go into a semi-soft or hard cheese.

I remember my mother's wartime cheeses as being a delightful treat. She simply hung up sour milk in a cloth and waited until it became cheese. With a little salt, the flavour was unbeatable. I have had less success using the "natural" method. By the time I have had milk hanging around for four days waiting for it to go "bad", I have usually got bored with it and given it to the pig. I think I miss out through being over particular.

Lemon juice gives curds an interesting flavour, or orange juice (any acid will make milk curdle). The point at which the milk curdles is rather dramatic. I warmed some milk, stirred in the lemon juice and immediately long strings of curdled milk wrapped themselves round the spoon—quite

34

a different reaction from the gentler rennet. Vinegar has the same reaction and makes a dryer curd. There is no strong flavour if you use white vinegar but the smell seems to stay with the curd.

Curd made with any of the curdling agents is an excellent base for dips and spreads. Skim milk is alright to use, but a creamier spread holds its flavour better. An orange and lemon curd is an unusual base for sweet or savoury spreads.

Orange and Lemon Spread

2 l milk

250 ml cream (or more)

(juice and some pulp) of 3 oranges

juice of 3 lemons

honey to taste

pinch of salt

chopped dried apricots, cinnamon, chopped blanched almonds (optional)

Warm milk beyond blood heat to about 50°C and stir in the citrus juice. Take off the heat source and leave to settle for about 15 minutes.

Line a colander with boiled muslin and pour in the curds and whey so that the whey drains through. Tie up the corners of the cloth to make a bag and hang it on a hook or a pole to drain for about an hour. (The citrus flavoured whey is pleasant to use as the basis for drinks with the addition of honey, or for sauces or in cooking. It keeps well in the fridge or it can be frozen.)

Warm the honey until it is liquid, then mix it with the curds, and add salt, apricots, spices and nuts. It's lovely.

Cream Cheese

I was determined to make cream cheese with cream. But it didn't work. I tried souring cream naturally and hanging it to mature. I hung it for ten weeks and it still tasted to me just like butter. Only the flecks of milk left in the cream had anything like a cheesy taste. I tried adding rennet and treating it like milk, but the "cheese" still tasted like butter, not cheese. It was useful for mixing with my normal curd for dips and spreads. Then I looked in the books and discovered that cream cheese is made with milk as well. Use about the same proportion of cream and milk, then use the normal curd-making method.

Warm cream first and pour into milk. Warm milk to blood temperature, put in a teaspoon of rennet and stir. Take off the heat but leave in a warm place for an hour. Cut the curd. Drain the whey. Salt. Either mix in flavouring or keep refrigerated until use.

For a good spread using cream cheese, add chopped crystallised ginger, dates, honey and a teaspoon of lemon pulp.

Garlic and Ginger Spread

This spread is our family favourite for "happy hour" biscuits, and moreish with French bread or baked potato.
For a strong flavoured spicy cheese, white vinegar is suitable as a curdling agent.

2 l skim milk
1 l cream (or less)
3 tablespoons wine vinegar or cider vinegar
salt
honey
lemon pulp
1 clove garlic crushed

1 teaspoon crushed root ginger (or use celery seed if preferred)
1 fresh chilli, cut very small and without seeds, or chilli sauce
olive oil (just sufficient to soften, depending on the dryness of the curd)
black and yellow mustard seeds soaked in wine vinegar to soften

Warm milk to about 50°C. Stir in vinegar and leave for half an hour. Pour through muslin to drain whey. Hang until curd is the desired consistency.
Break the curd into a food processor and mix in salt, then honey (amount depends on type of honey used—taste it) balanced with lemon pulp (the part that is left in the squeezer when you have juiced the lemon—the soft bits), then the garlic, ginger and chilli. The olive oil is to adjust the spreading texture and the mustard is for decoration and an unexpected texture treat.
This spread might be a bit sophisticated for youngsters but I am often surprised by the people who do enjoy it.

Chutney Spread

The quickest and easiest spread, and usually one of the most popular, is made when I pinch a bit of the 309 Freezer Cheese curd and mix it with homemade chutney (apple or whatever).

2 l milk
½ l cream
1 teaspoon rennet

salt to taste
sunflower seeds
chutney

Warm the milk to blood heat or just under (about 35°C) and stir in rennet. Leave in a warm place for about an hour then cut curd. Tip into a colander lined with muslin and let drain overnight. Break curd into food processor. Add salt and sunflower seeds and chutney and process to desired consistency, or just stir it all together.

For elegance at a dinner party or a bit of family fun, there are moulded soft cheeses with proper names that can be made at home. Coulommier and Colwick are made with the same basic recipe, but the treatment of the curds gives them different shapes. In fact, the only variations between soft cheeses are in the shape, the colouring or in the non-cheese additions, such as dried grape pips squashed into the "rind" or a coating of toast crumbs or biscuit crumbs.

The soft cheeses ripened with special moulds are a different matter: they have built-in flavour. (It's tricky that both kinds of "moulds" are used in cheesemaking. In this context I mean the living mould not the rigid kind.)

Coulommier Cheese

1 l (or less) cream
3 l skim milk

1 teaspoon rennet
salt

The equipment that you need is what makes Coulommier different. Two moulds cut from the same 120 mm pipe so that they fit exactly on top of each other will do. Apparently there are special moulds available in shops that sell supplies to cheesemakers, but I haven't come across them. I find it better if the moulds have small draining holes in the sides. Without the holes, the whey takes forever to drain.

Warm cream to blood temperature and tip into milk. Warm milk and cream mixture to 32°C and stir in rennet. Leave, warm and covered, for an hour. Arrange the bottom part of the mould (the bottom part should be two-thirds and the top part one-third of the total length—whatever is convenient for your mouldmaker is okay, but I suggest 140 mm and 70 mm) on a plain straw mat over a basin or draining board. Carefully take off small slices of curd and layer it into the mould. At about four stages during the ladling add salt (probably about 1 tablespoon in total will be sufficient) between the layers. Hold or tape on the top part of the mould and continue until full. That's all. Then let it drain.

The curd could take 24 hours to drain in winter, to the point where it has sunk below the top mould. A soon as it is safe to take off the top mould, put a second straw mat over the cheese and turn the cheese to drain the other way. Depending on the weather, keep turning and draining the cheese for a few days.

When you tip it out, it should hold its shape. You can choose what you do with it next. Either eat fresh or refrigerate for a few days to let the cheese mature. I have also read that the cheese can be left at room temperature to mature for a few weeks, but when I have tried that, the cheese has gradually collapsed. There is too much whey left in the cheese. It might work in other dryer, warmer conditions.

Colwick Cheese

Make the basic curd from the same recipe as Coulommier. Line a mould with a boiled muslin cloth. Ladel the curds into the cloth. As the curd sinks, pull up the sides of the cloth and tie them above the cheese so that the edges curl inwards and there is a crater in the middle. Pull up the cloth several times over the hours while the cheese drains.

The secret of Colwick's deliciousness is in the serving. Many recipes suggest filling the hollow with strawberries and cream. (But eat immediately. The acid in strawberries can react badly with acid in cheese). Melon balls and liqueur are an attractive alternative. For a popular family dessert, I have had no complaints about a layer of raspberry jam, a dollop of ice cream and nuts or grated chocolate sprinkled on the top. Honey crystallised ginger and a little brandy can substitute for the jam. Individual portions are more fun if you have enough moulds. The advantage of small cheeses is that they drain more quickly.

Records

It really is worth keeping records. Temperatures and timing are critical in cheesemaking and they are easy to forget. It is very frustrating to taste a really successful cheese ten weeks after you have made it—and know that there is only luck to help you recreate it. Scribble down *somewhere* the recipe of your experiments and cross reference with a number attached to the ripening cheese. On the cheese label write the general type of cheese, the date it was made and the date you think it should be ready. Ten greeny-blue cheeses in a row look very similar.

PART TWO

Bees

PREAMBLE

Bees were a joke when we had our citrus orchard. In the cool of the summer dawn George would set off on the tractor to mow around the trees. Perhaps I had got as far as hanging out the washing and I would see this distant figure making a rapid and ragged approach from a long avenue of mandarins, wildly slapping at head, air and breast, yelling and leaping. That was George when the tractor bumped into a hanging swarm of bees. He didn't like them. They were brown wild ones and they nested in the kitchen and bedroom walls and droned all night. I was very calm about them and never made a fuss, but I got stung and he didn't, and when I got stung I swelled up like a balloon. I have photos taken by unkind friends when the poison was new and I had a round face and slit eyes like a teenage Eskimo (no wrinkles!) and then again when the poison had dropped and I had jowls like Queen Victoria.

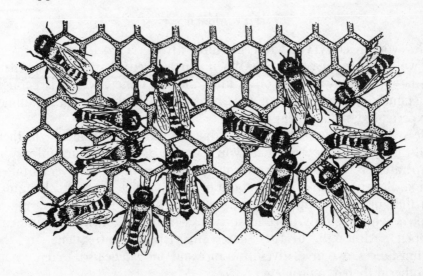

Bees

It came as a surprise when we sold our fish shop and George said: "I think I would like to keep bees." Naturally, I laughed. We had a small section by the beach, absolutely no experience with bees and no tools for making hives. But he won me over when he said: "They're interesting."

They are. Cows and sheep can be managed because we can out-think them, but each beehive has up to 90,000 bees and they have a new trick in store for every problem solved. Every hive is different, conditions change all the time, no year is like the last. Bees would have to be a good investment for an alert old age. Our pattern had been to enjoy getting new projects into smooth running order but then to lose interest in "just maintenance". Bees would never be "just maintenance".

As is our style, we flung ourselves into bees, all available resources and more. On reflection, that is not a way we would recommend.

You can nurture, cajole, feed, talk to, mulch and water one tree or even four thousand citrus trees. You stand a good chance, if you read the right management books, of coming out on top. But suppose you applied for the job of controlling the flora and fauna of the Himalayan range of mountains. There would be a change of scale. To be an intelligent manager you would need to study the threads of interdependence already established in the highlands, scrublands and rhododendron forests of the foothills. Then you would attempt to exploit trends and patterns to suit your overall management plan. That is how you have to work with bees. The variables are devastatingly complex, but the basics of beekeeping are simple: encourage your bees to help themselves and they will provide for you of their excess supplies.

And they *are* fun, believe it or not!

How Many?

Unless you are crazy, you will begin modestly.

Two hives are safer than one. When a hive is settled and thriving, there can be an annual surplus of 30 kilograms of honey, which is enough for a family. But hives, like animals, can suffer setbacks, particularly under inexperienced management.

Bees have to cope with a climate that isn't always considerate to their needs, and with flowers that won't give up their nectar unless the temperature is right and then only at certain times of the day over a limited period. Bees need the correct amount of space (which is always changing) and they need a young strong queen to keep replenishing the army of workers who live only three to six weeks in the summer. Anything can happen. Although disasters are surprisingly infrequent in the circumstances, two hives gives insurance and one can be used to rejuvenate the other if there is a problem.

40

However many hives you have, they must be registered. You will be allotted a number and that must appear on your hives. When you are deciding where to put your hives and how many, take notice of any other hives in the area and the feed sources. The official limit is one kilometre between apiaries. (An apiary is usually defined as having ten hives or more.) If there are other hives near to you, get in touch with the other beekeepers and negotiate. There is usually room for a couple more so long as there is enough feed to go around. It's not much good having bees if there are not enough nectar sources to provide the raw material for honey. And your hives, being young and new to the area, will be the ones to suffer.

Towns are a good place to keep hives. Commercial beekeepers usually find sites in the country where they will be out of the way and have access to flowering trees and clover. Town bees can take the pickings from gardens and parks that are carefully planned to have flowers all year 'round. Neighbours and by-laws could possibly create a problem, but with careful siting of your hives you should avoid complaints.

If the hives are up high (as they would be in trees), then the bees have no need to bother people walking on the ground who inadvertently get in the path of their flight to or from the hive. Sitings on top of flat roofs are excellent. We had a particularly successful hive on the top of a 1000 gallon wine vat that we used as a woodshed. It looked a bit silly when it towered seven boxes high but it faced a main road and picnic area, and no-one was ever stung.

The other good thing about having two hives is that they can share your attention, and halve it. A hive takes about a week to settle back to its work if it has been opened and interrupted but to learn about bees, one has to see inside the hives. That gives you a good excuse to keep taking the top off and having a look. If there is only one hive to take the pressure of your curiosity you could easily reach mid-summer with no honey and very frustrated bees.

The best thing you could do is offer your services on an irregular basis to another local beekeeper. There is a lot of heavy work in beekeeping and there are times of the year when having two people makes the job a whole lot easier and pleasanter. The beekeeper will be delighted with your help and you get the opportunity to look into his hives, pick his brains and learn skills with no expense to your own bees.

Which Ones?

Attending a hive that is cooperative is pleasant work. Get a stroppy one and you wonder why you bother with the little brutes. Ill-bred bees attack without provocation, run away from inspection, pester you making an irritating high pitched whine and keep it up until you give in and go home—and then they chase you. To begin with, invest in well bred, big furry yellow Italian bees with a young queen.

Once again your friendly local beekeeper will be the one to help. If you organise the woodwork for a hive, he or she will probably enjoy getting you started with the right stock. It is in his interest anyway: the better the class of bee in his area, the better chance his new queens have of finding suitable partners on their mating flights, but that's another ball game.

On the other hand, it's a shame to turn down a swarm of bees that is easy to catch. The best managed hives lose a swarm sometimes and you could be picking up good stock. Even brown wild bees can be gentle and industrious. It is the crossbreeds that make the beekeeper's life unpleasurable, but there is a way to teach them good manners: change the queen bee.

Every bee in a hive is the daughter or son of the queen. Minute by minute in the running of a hive, messages come through from mother. If she is calm and busy, her offspring go about their work without fuss. If she is fidgety and flighty, the hive crouches on the edge of panic.

The queen is almost twice as long as her daughters, the worker bees. Her body is shiny and her wings are short. Her walk is what gives her away when you are looking for her among hundreds and thousands of bees on a frame: she has a dignified regal sway rather than a run. To begin with, before queen-spotting becomes second nature, you might confuse her with her bulky sons, the drones, but they are fluffy with square rumps.

The queen is big because she is full of eggs. A few days after she hatches, while she is still a virgin, she tests the air with a few exploratory flights and then takes off on the adventure of her life to the high flight lanes where normally only the men venture.

The men, the drones, do not concern themselves with hive work. On a wet day or early in the morning, they congregate in the men's clubs at each end of the hive as far as possible from the work area where the young are being reared. At about ten o'clock when the sun is pleasantly warm and they are bored with the smell of hivehold chores, they fly to their other club grounds, higher than their worker sisters dare venture. When the young queen arrives (from another hive), up to eight or nine drones will sacrifice themselves for the joy of fathering a new generation. They mate and die, and she flies back to the hive, avoiding predatory birds, and her body grows and she begins to lay eggs.

The workers prepare cells in the wax comb to be cradles for the new babies (the brood). If the cell is a perfect shape, the queen pops in a fertile egg which will hatch as a female bee who will begin her career as a nurse, graduate to a guard and mature to a nectar and pollen gatherer. If the cell is irregularly shaped or large, the queen will lay an unfertilised egg and a drone will hatch.

The young fluffy drone is spoiled and pampered by the nurses and workers, even fed by them although he can feed himself, and allowed free access into neighbouring hives without the mandatory offerings of pollen or nectar (which he cannot gather). He doesn't even have to fight to protect the hive against robber bees, wasps and mice: he is equipped with no sting. His life is enviable until the season ends and the nectar flow dwindles; then his sisters take him bodily and push him outside the hive. If he can't find a welcome anywhere else and he pushes back in, they bite off his wings and leave him to perish.

CHAPTER 1   HOUSING

A hole in a tree or a wall cavity is the sort of home bees choose for themselves. We often find that bees do best in crumbling boxes that we hope other beekeepers won't notice—the kind that three seasons ago we said: "Well, perhaps just one more season." But when it comes to housing, it is the convenience of the beekeeper rather than the preference of the bees that matters. When the bees had their choice, the only way to separate them from their honey was to kill them. When a reverend gentleman named Langstroth last century though of a way to organise hives so that waxed frames could be slotted in and out of the bee boxes, he saved an awful lot of furry lives.

A hive is built like a house, except that it comes to pieces and can grow taller or shorter according to the number of bees it has to accommodate. Usually, it sits on two solid treated timber runners. They are the only part of the hive that can be made from arsenic-treated wood.

On to those runners is nailed the bottom board, the floor of the hive. That has to be the same dimensions as the boxes that will rest on it, except that it is longer at one end to provide a landing platform for the bees. Around three sides, where the boxes will rest, it has nailed, stapled or glued strips of timber about one centimetre high. The long end with the landing platform is left open for the bees' entrance.

Not all parts are used at once but all are necessary.

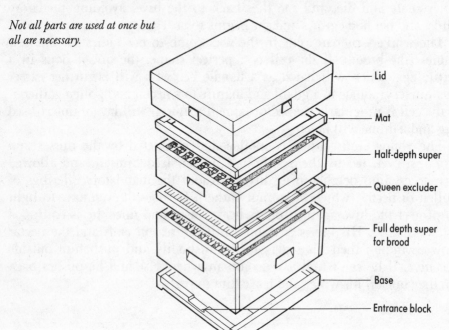

- Lid
- Mat
- Half-depth super
- Queen excluder
- Full depth super for brood
- Base
- Entrance block

The "rooms", called boxes or supers, are a standard oblong but vary in depth. The deepest box (boxes don't have tops and bottoms—they're square tubes) called a "full-depth super", is put on the base board. In a mature hive, there are two full depth boxes where the queen lays her eggs and where the colony of bees spends the winter. When spring comes, the queen begins to lay eggs very fast (up to 1200 a day) and the hive expands rapidly as food becomes available. That is when the beekeeper piles on more boxes.

If the beekeeper has any regard for his human frailty, he will choose to load on three-quarter-depth boxes to be filled with honey. They can be heavy enough to lift when they are full of honey, but full-depth boxes are back breakers—50 kilogram boxes, stuck together, hard to grip, well defended and at an awkward angle. Half-depth boxes are easier to handle, but more expense and more work is involved for less honey. Half-depths are often used to collect comb honey: the sort that is cut into squares and solid in plastic boxes.

On top of the boxes goes a ceiling mat, and then the lid. The perfect hive has not yet been devised, all have to be a compromise and every beekeeper has his pet methods and ideas for improvements. For instance: bees need a warm, draught-proof home where they can keep the temperature of the brood at 35°C, but ventilation is very important. They need fresh air, but the entrance must be narrow enough for the bees to guard it against wasps and mice. The beekeeper has to be able to take the hive to pieces, and yet it must be sturdy enough to stand up against strong winds and curious cattle who see it as a rubbing post.

The secret of the Reverend Langstroth's revolutionary beehive rested on a measurement (6.4 mm) called the bee space. If there is a smaller gap in the hive, the bees will glue it up with a sticky substance called propolis. If there is a bigger space, they will fill it with wax comb, sculptured according to their creative urge. If the space is just right for the bees to use as a corridor, that is a bee space. Unless there is a carpenter in the family, it is wise for the beginner beekeeper to buy ready-made hive parts with accurate bee spaces.

The furniture of the hives is the removable frames. These slot into a recess cut around the top of each box and they hang eight, nine or ten to a box. When the colony is very young—just a queen, a frame of ready-to-hatch brood (capped) with its nurse bees, two frames of pollen and honey and some worker bees hijacked from another hive—it is called a nucleus. Sometimes special half-size boxes are used for the nucleus and sometimes it is put in a full-depth super with empty frames, ready for expansion.

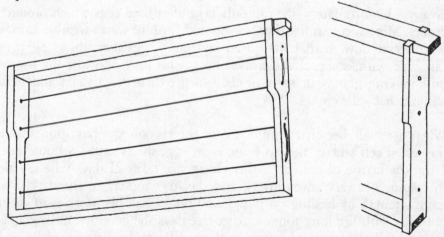

Full-depth frames have either three or four wires melted into the foundation wax to keep it secure.

The young colony has to be treated like a young animal and given special attention until the queen and her team have raised enough mature bees to bring in supplies to keep the family going. They might not be able to afford many teenagers to guard their entrance, so they need a cut-down entrance hole, and they will probably use up more honey and pollen than they can bring in, particularly if the weather is windy, wet or cold.

The frames are wooden and one of the most fiddly jobs for the beekeeper each year (until he or she has built up a good supply of used frames) is to thread them with thin wire and secure it on small nails at each end so that three or four strands stretch across full-depth frames, two strands across three-quarter frames and one strand across half-depth frames. A sheet of wax indented with the shapes of cells is called "foundation". This foundation is attached to the wires with heat. For a small number of hives, it is simplest to buy frames that already have wires and wax.

Bees have a few tidy traits that can be relied upon. One is to finish any job they come across in their hive that has been started. During their growing up they all learn to do everything (the women, that is; the drones only do One Thing). That means that bees will take up any task at any stage so long as they have suitable glands. Since the foundation sheets have the base shapes for cells indented onto them, the bees build up the sides of the cells with their own wax ready for the queen to lay her eggs in or ready for storing pollen and nectar.

There are regular stages in the life of a female bee, but if there is a crisis in the hive, those stages can be reversed and juggled on instruction from the queen or in response to external factors. A dramatic example of adaptability is shown if the queen dies and there are no young eggs laid. Any ordinary, sterile worker bee can take on the role of queen and lay eggs. Unfortunately, she can only lay unfertilised eggs which produce drones. More successfully, if an unseasonal flush of warm weather brings on a nectar flow so that the queen lays more eggs than the nurse bees can cope with, some of the worker bees, who long ago lost the use of milk-making glands in their heads, can get them reactivated and help with the babycare chores.

When a female bee first climbs out of the cocoon she has spun inside the sealed cell where she was born as an egg, she is called a house bee. From the laying of the egg to her emergence takes 21 days. She is pale in colour, not very adventurous, and she likes to stay in the dark. She gains strength by feeding on pollen and honey and her work is to clean out cells with her long tongue. After five days she develops milk glands in her head and can feed larvae in their cells (grubs, between three and eight days since laying). The milk fed to larvae that will become ordinary worker bees like herself is the same as that fed to the potential queen and called royal jelly. Regular bees simply don't get as much of it as royalty.

It is the quantity of bee milk fed to a grub that decides whether or not it will hatch as a queen. In the ordinary course of hive life, a special elongated cell is built by the bees for an egg to be given royal treatment. That happens when conditions are becoming overcrowded or their queen is ageing and they think it might be time to swarm away from the home hive with a new queen. If an accident befalls the queen (for example, the beekeeper squashes her) then the bees can select any of her freshly laid eggs, feed it with extra rations of bee milk, stretch out the cell to accommodate the bigger larva and rear a virgin queen.

At about ten days from hatching, the young bee gives up nursing and becomes a builder. Her wax glands in the abdomen become active and the milk glands dry up. She builds cells and puts wax caps over cells that are filled with mature honey or carry larvae eight days old who like privacy while they spin their cocoons.

Not all bees go through the next stage and some stay there the rest of their lives. Their venom glands become active (nurse bees don't sting) and they go on guard at the entrance to the hive. Some stay only a few days on active service, others enjoy the work and take it up as a permanent career.

After guard duties, at about three weeks old, the bees become factory hands on their most popular production line: honeymaking. The glands on their heads that secreted milk for the grubs go into action again but produce the enzymes that convert nectar into honey. The factory hands, still called "house bees" because they prefer the darkness and warmth near the broodnest, "chew" nectar that they take from the foraging bees. They actually stretch it out for minutes at a time, exposing it to warm air so that excess moisture evaporates, then mix it with saliva that contains enzymes. The rest of the moisture content is reduced while the honey is in the cells.

Honey drying is a task for the whole hive. When the workers arrive home at dusk after a busy day of foraging, the fanning begins. All the bees turn in the same direction and vibrate their wings to bring warm dry air from the entrance and send it out again the other side. You can hear the hum of wings and feel the draught. If you hold a blade of grass at one side of the entrance it will be sucked in, and at the other side it will bend with the force of air blowing out. Bees can make honey from nectar in three to five days if ventilation in the hive is good, but it can take three weeks in a damp, clammy hive.

At last, three weeks to a month after hatching, the bee feels her wing muscles begin to develop and she becomes curious about the light. After a few orientation flights, she becomes the bee that is most familiar: the forager. She collects pollen to rear the young bees, nectar for honey and water for cooling. There is yet another career open to her: she could devote herself to the repairs and maintenance trade. Bees that collect sticky plant materials and mix them with wax and other bee goodies to make propolis, tend to specialise. They develop the expertise to use the propolis in the hive to plaster up holes and stick boxes together. (I have also read that a liberal coating of propolis inside the hive keeps the bees healthy. I hope it has that use because it is a big nuisance to the beekeeper.)

Bee books abound and most of them give charts, lists and diagrams to explain about the stages in a bee's life. I found particular delight in Eva Crane's *A Book of Honey* (Oxford University Press, 1980) which as well as a very solid foundation of facts gives a feeling for the depth of fascination admirers have felt through the ages for bees and their products.

Siting

When bees swarm, they can take weeks in the open trying to decide on the best position for their new home. They have to take into consideration many factors and we have learnt the hard way that finding a site where the bees feel happy is the key to good honey production.

There are obvious pointers, but beekeeping keeps you humble: bees don't operate on human logic. You can think you have given them the perfect spot—and they hate it. For some reason the hive doesn't thrive. Another hive you can put in a crazy place and suddenly it is bursting at the seams. A change of entrance angle or a move of a few centimetres could make the difference, but beware of moving a hive a short distance from its original position. It has to be a move of less than a metre or more than three kilometres.

Bees are creatures of habit and they learn the route to and from their hive by certain visual markers. If they suddenly find themselves in a completely new place, they will go on orientation flights and pick out new markers, but if they are near the old site, they are still guided by the old markers and when they land "home" and there is no hive, they get confused. They stay there and die.

There has to be enough food for the bees. This is not usually a problem with two hives. Bees can fly up to five or even ten kilometres to find pollen, nectar and water, but it stands to reason that the shorter distance they need to go for supplies, the more time and energy they will have left over for honey production.

They need protection from wind and rain, and maximum sun (or midday shade in very hot places). Slope the hive entrance downwards so that rainwater cannot collect on the baseboard. In the southern hemisphere, it is best for the entrance to face north-east (in the northern hemisphere, south-east) so that the bees can begin work with the first rays of the morning sun. Actually the bees can sense more of the sun's rays than we can: ultraviolet is for them a colour, so they can see as sunshine what looks to us like shade. They dip out at the infra-red end of the spectrum. (Our white they apparently see as a blue-green, but oranges, greens and yellows look the same to them. There is more lovely stuff about bee senses in Colin G. Butler's *The World of the Honey Bee*, Collins, 1974.)

We are learning to "feel" a good bee place. It has a stillness, the bird calls are clear and the sound of a river makes it perfect. A sheltered dip in the ground or against a sunny wall are good starting places. The bottom of a hill is preferred so long as it is not a wind tunnel: the bees can climb up the hill while fresh and without a load, then fly down tired and laden. It is not a good idea to face a hive into a footpath. Bees are attracted by movement and the last thing you want is people stung—besides, you lose good worker bees that way. Airborne noise doesn't worry them. Very serious people told us early on that we must pass on family news to the bees, but the calming effect must be on the teller not the told because bees have no receptors for air vibrations. They don't like sudden movements or bangs on their hive.

The other hazard is washing lines. Bees like to keep their hive clean (they drag dead spiders, wasps, bees and cockroaches out of their entrance—though I have yet to see them tackle a dead mouse) and they go on communal "cleansing flights". They save up waste, sometimes for weeks, then set off in a group to find a suitable target. I don't know why they prefer freshly laundered white sheets hanging on a washing line, or a newly painted white wall, but they do. We had a white house once. I've painted this one green, *and* I've dyed our white clothes khaki.

For the sake of good neighbourly relations, try to divert the attention of your bees away from the next door patch. We have found the best way to do this is to face the bees fairly close to a bush or hedge so that they have to fly upwards from the hive, out of people and washing-line zones. And don't site hives too near to family pets: bees react badly to animal smells. Our dogs have learnt to keep well away from the hives.

Bigger animals with thicker hides, or woolly sheep, take longer to learn. Hives exposed to these hazards might need a fence. An electric fence is all right, but beware of high tension power wires overhead: the bees sense an electrical field and become aggressive.

It takes a while to begin to think like a bee, especially to think like 20,000 to 90,000 bees all at different stages of development and with different jobs to do . . . And that is only one hive.

CHAPTER 2   HANDLING

When we went to the bee supplies shop to buy George his overalls I was very firm: "Bees are *your* choice. I don't need overalls. I don't need a hat and veil. Or gloves." But I had to agree that there would be the odd occasion when he needed help: how can one person alone lift a heavy wobbly hive about half a metre square (or nearly square)? We came away both fully equipped, including a hive tool each—just in case I needed to open up a hive for any reason and take out frames.

Beekeeping is like that: it is easy to get involved. Sometimes I have had occasion to wish I hadn't. Because we had to try to make a living out of beekeeping, we had to increase our hive numbers fast from the very beginning. And increase our sites. I often had this wish about not getting involved in the middle of a moonless, drizzly night somewhere on a totally strange farm with George saying: "I think there is a steep bank here. Can you see a gate? Mind the blackberries. The farmer said he would be taking his bulls out of this paddock . . ."

Beehives have to be moved at night. The bees don't fly in the dark but they certainly crawl. On these midnight expeditions we were usually carting with us twelve or so newly acquired hives, often in disrepair, bumping them on the trailer behind a tractor over slippery unknown territory. Poor things. They came out of every crevice like a black wave, up our arms and legs when we tried to carry them and into any lights we dared shine.

I was glad we had good gear. My strong advice to any beginner would be: wear complete protection. There are enough things to remember and learn about beekeeping without the worry of sudden attack.

Many people have told us (people who have never kept bees) that bees won't sting if you are well disposed towards them. I agree that bees are not vicious like wasps, and I will happily pick flowers among working bees or spend time unprotected beside a hive just watching bees. But in working with a hive, accidents happen. If a bee's hive mate gets crushed under a frame, she is not likely to hang around to work out that you didn't mean to do it. She will respond to the distress signal or the smell of venom and attack. If she and the avenging band she rallies only punish your heavy leather gloves or bombard your protective veil, you will probably be willing to continue learning the skills of beekeeping. If you get a great number of stings at one time, the volume of poison in your blood can be dangerous—apart from being very uncomfortable.

An essential item is a veil held out by a hat with a brim, or a hood like fencers wear with protective gauze over the face that zips onto a top. Gloves are the most expensive item. Bees can sting through light gloves.

A puff of smoke buys time while the worker bees return home for a quick snack of honey.

Even with good thick soft leather, the points of the stings can get through and scratch the skin. Gloves need gauntlets to cover your cuffs so that there is no gap for bees to crawl up your arms. The same at the ankles: tie your trouser legs or tuck them firmly into boots. Once you have felt bees crawling up your legs you will never need to be told that one again. Sew up any unnecessary openings in your overalls: bees find the tiniest hole and tell their friends about it.

Avoid bright colours, especially blues, that will attract the bees. Avoid animal smells (don't cuddle the dog wearing your bee overalls). And don't wear pure wool socks or pure wool anything. The bees dive into woolly hats and socks in desperate kamikaze.

If a bee does get to you, scrape off the sting with a fingernail. Don't squeeze it. The back end of a sting is still attached to the venom sack and muscles that pump the venom into the victim. The longer the sting stays in your skin the more venom can be pumped in, even though the bee has fallen off. Then leave it. The first ten minutes are the worst. *Don't scratch it*! That spreads the poison. If it is any consolation, after your first few stings, the swelling that accompanies them will become less noticeable, and if you can keep up an average of four or five quickly-scraped-away stings in not-too-sensitive places per year, you can begin to take stings quite casually! (They still hurt, though.)

51

If a bee gets lost in your hair, smack it and squash it quickly before it has time to burrow in.

Bee venom is like snake venom, complex and nasty in big doses. If you take a lot of stings, the body can go into shock: get yourself to the doctor or hospital for a shot of adrenalin. George has taken about 40 stings round his ankles (woolly socks—he won't do that again) and has been unaffected, but in more sensitive places they would have to be taken seriously.

You could get kicked in the head by a horse, tossed by a cow with a calf, or run over by a car. With proper precautions bees are no more risky.

So, dressed up like a spaceman, you approach your hive with a piece of hooked flat iron called a hive tool. You could use a nail on a bit of wood to help hook out the frames, but a hive tool designed for beekeepers and refined by them has so many uses it is worth the investment. It can lever off boxes, unstick propolis, scrape off burr comb and, in emergencies, pull out nails.

Smoker: a beekeeper's best friend.

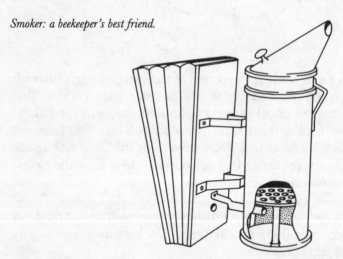

Your other friend is a smoker. Smoke has been used to divert bees for at least 4000 years, according to cave drawings. It has the effect of sending bees scurrying back into their hives to feed from the stored honey. The theory is that when they are fat and full they are not so aggressive and that they cannot curl round so easily to sting. It works anyway.

The smoke puffing machine is a tin can with a spout attached to bellows. A lot of fires have been started with smokers so they deserve to be respected. They take a bit of getting used to. George has a method of lighting a piece of newspaper inside the protecting wall of a super, then lighting a rolled up strip of sacking from the flames. That is stuffed into the smoker and fanned with the bellows to keep it going. Once the smoker is properly alight it needs only occasional pumping to keep the right volume of smoke available. My job is usually pumping it alight and holding things while George sorts out the rest of the equipment.

Carrying bits of beekeeping equipment can become complicated and it is a good idea to organise a box with a handle like a carpenter's tool box, then you can have spare sacking, pieces of wood for hive blocks, sheets of newspaper in case hives need joining, and somewhere to keep your hive tool. That is probably not necessary for only two hives, but one thing can lead to another, and bees *are* fascinating . . .

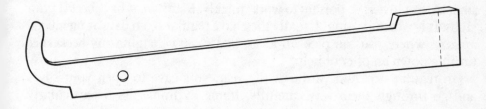

A good quality hive tool will save you stings and frustration and save bees' lives.

Smoke takes about a minute to work and the effects last ten minutes. When the smoker is going, puff about three puffs in the entrance of each hive, wait a minute, take the lid off the hive gently, without bumping, loosen the hive mat and squirt another puff underneath, working with the wind. Experiment with your fuel: some fuel has really horrid fumes. Aim for cool white smoke. Old sacks are best; corrugated paper, grass clippings and pine needles are okay.

These instructions are for ideal conditions. If your bees are anything like our bees, they will gum up their lids and mats so efficiently with propolis that bumping and banging is unavoidable. But try to calm your movements. Jumpiness and fast hand movements irritate the bees. Even if they sting you, you are allowed to speak harshly because the bees can't hear, but curb your instinct to take a swipe at them. Try smoking your arms to take away the "human" smell.

When you take off the lid and mat, the fascinating part begins. If it is midsummer and the "flow" is on, your hive mat might be stuck to the frames with burr comb. As you lift it off and the burr comb breaks, oodles of glorious liquid honey spills out. The temptation is to rip off your gloves and plunge in a finger. That would be silly of course.

If you have chosen a fine sunny day after the dew has melted, most of the worker bees are out gathering and the house bees are too busy to bother with you. Somewhere down below, the queen is laying like crazy and her recently hatched babies are cleaning out cells for her as fast as their tongues can twitch. Don't at any time leave the hive uncovered for long because if you don't steal the honey, other bees will. They are terrible robbers. If they can save themselves the trouble of gathering and processing their own honey, they will. Once they get in a robbing frenzy, the only thing to do is close down the hive, restrict the entrance and go home.

Each time the hive is opened and smoke used, the routine is disrupted and production lost. On the other hand, a beekeeper has to practise handling bees in order to streamline his movements. It is important to keep operations smooth, but just as important to work quickly. Many areas have beekeeping clubs. It is worth joining. Usually they have regular open days at members' apiaries where you can pick up ideas, and I can't imagine any beekeeper turning down an offer of help.

On regular occasions through the year, you have to open your hives and go through them very carefully, frame by frame. Two particularly important inspections are for disease (regulations in many places require a beekeeper to make a check and report problems) and, in spring, to look for and destroy queen cells that the bees are making in anticipation of swarming.

The beekeeper's year should really begin in midwinter. Every year we get caught out by the spring and promise ourselves that next year we will begin preparations earlier and be ready.

Winter is when all the surplus gear is stored away in the shed. It is a good time for repairs and maintenance, cleaning frames, experimenting with wasp-discouraging devices and making up nuclear boxes. The bees are having to cluster around their queen and brood nest to keep warm, so they are wintered down in one or two full-depth supers. They have blocks across their entrances so a hole only big enough for one or two bees is left. Some method has been devised for maximum ventilation without letting in too much cold air. (That's a hard one.)

Our most valuable asset stored in the shed is the drawn comb from the season before. The bees use more time and energy to build wax comb on foundation than to make honey. That is why it is reckoned that it takes a hive about three years to come into full production. We had a disastrous winter our first year without realising until it was too late.

There is a small blue-grey moth called wax moth who insinuates herself through invisible cracks in woodwork and lays her eggs in comb. Within a very short time there is a revolting tangle of joined up cobweb, chewed wax and huge, white, greedy grubs where the nice clean wax had been. The wax moths took our whole first-year crop of drawn comb and our bees had to begin again. There is a chemical stocked by beekeepers' suppliers that discourages the moths. Keep the crystals on tin lids in the stack of supers and frames, but renew them when they evaporate. The smell is not as pleasant as wax and honey, but the alternative is to seal the boxes in gas filled chambers.

If each hive has been left with one box of brood and one box of honey at the end of the season, the bees should have enough supplies to last through winter, but don't abandon them. If the weather is particularly trying, with long periods of rain when the bees haven't been able to get out at all, they could have gone through all their stores. More dangerous are the false starts to spring. If winter seems short and the warm days come then change their minds and go back into a cold snap, the bees might have been fooled into anticipating a nectar flow. If the queen has laid a lot of eggs, the house bees could have used up all honey and pollen supplies to rear the brood.

If you have no honey to use in an emergency, the bees can be fed sugar. There are several methods of feeding. A simple way is to drill a hole in the hive mat and sprinkle raw sugar on the mat under the hive lid. A sugar and water solution makes sugar more immediately available to the bees and is used if the bees need a boost to get them up to strength ready for the honey flow. Feeders made of plastic are available, or you can glue and tack hardboard on a frame leaving a hole at the top. If you push in small twigs the bees can sit on those to drink the sugar solution.

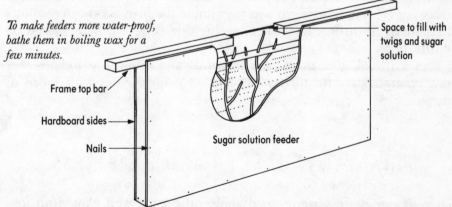

To make feeders more water-proof, bathe them in boiling wax for a few minutes.

Space to fill with twigs and sugar solution

Frame top bar

Hardboard sides

Nails

Sugar solution feeder

Queen bees can live up to six years but they become less productive as they get older. Their egg laying gets patchy and more of their offspring are drones. The ideal is to have a new young queen every year. George finds it hard to kill queens who seem to be doing a good job and some of ours survive two seasons.

Queens can be bought and arrive in the mail in little plastic boxes with five or six attendants. They need warmth and water as soon as they arrive. We rear our own queens. It is an exacting and fraught time: so many things can go wrong that George is in a state of anxiety for a month, but when he sees his big fat yellow queens happily hatched and laying he is so pleased. For two hives I would recommend buying in queens, but rearing queens is a most intriguing sideline if bees get you hooked.

The most likely time to get swarming is during the spring build-up. It is the natural way for bee colonies to reproduce themselves but represents a huge loss to the beekeeper. Just when you need the colony at its strongest to bring in the nectar for honey, the queen takes off leaving ready-to-hatch queens in capped cells, and with her go most of the mature workers and half the drones. Only the nurse bees are left with stores and a stack of brood to busy them. Honeymaking will have to wait at least three weeks until there are new nurse bees to release the originals for foraging.

There is no foolproof way to prevent swarming, but there are precautions. Usually the bees prepare to go when space is short, when the queen is old, or when everything is fairly comfortable and routine in the hive: they get bored. So we give them more space, a box to fill with honey, or some foundation to draw out as comb. (That is the term. Actually they build on, not draw out.) Another trick is to join a weaker hive with a stronger and they all become so busy sorting out relationships that they ditch the plan to swarm.

Whatever diversionary tactics you choose, it is wise to keep a watch for the swollen warts that appear on comb and are queen cells. Smash them. And if one swarm gets away, examine the hive. Swarming follows the pattern of earthquakes: after the big one there can be a succession of little ones.

Bees will look after themselves in spring and summer as long as they have enough space for their stores and no major hassles with wasps or disease.

CHAPTER 3 HEALTH AND HAPPINESS

There is one bee disease dreaded above all others. AFB (American foul brood) is the big bogey.

Most other problems can be cleared up by renewing the queen or by giving the hive a warmer site and better ventilation. A faulty queen can begin to lay eggs that are susceptible to a creeping mummification as they develop into grubs. This is called chalk brood, and re-queening is the answer.

A pile of dead bees outside a hive is a bad sign and it could mean that the hive is under attack from the equivalent of our bad colds, flu and pneumonia. It is obviously weakened and a target for robber bees and wasps, so it needs special care. If there are no more ominous signs after an inspection of the brood, close the entrance to one bee width. Check that rain hasn't accumulated inside, that the bottom board is clean, that there is no dead mouse inside and that there are plenty of stores. Just keep a watch: the hive will probably right itself. If it doesn't, ask someone who knows to take a look.

AFB is a different story. It is a serious enough disease to keep the beekeeper constantly alert to the point of neurotic. We have never had it in our hives, but every time George opens a hive he is suspicious and stays that way until he is satisfied. The law in New Zealand demands that once a year every hive be thoroughly inspected and the beekeeper sign a declaration to the effect that there has been no trace of AFB in hives under his care. If you know of any slack beekeepers around who might have unregistered or uninspected hives, AFB is a strong argument for putting their weights up.

The name tells us what to look for: the brood turns foul. Normally, capped brood looks fresh and the grub has a pearly glow. Capped brood is crusty, golden and domed. When something is wrong, the wax caps sink and go greasy and dull; some are perforated. There is a nasty smell and the larvae turn into gluey brown blobs. Pull out the mess on a stick and it stretches in a string.

AFB is highly infectious. It is carried on spores in the air, in honey and in wax: if buried, it can survive at least 50 years. For these reasons, never leave honey from other apiaries open near your own hives. If you do find signs of AFB, close the hive right down after the bees have come home in the evening and do not wear any of the same protective gear or use the same hive tool when you are attending another hive. Report the hive immediately. The danger is that it has become weakened and that neighbouring bees have been robbing the honey and infecting themselves.

Intense heat is the only means of destroying the AFB spores. If you do not burn your own hive, the Ministry of Agriculture and Fisheries in New Zealand will arrange to burn it. There is good reason for panic until all potential sources of infection are destroyed. One infected hive can wipe out apiaries for miles around, and very quickly.

Less dramatic, but a persistent source of irritation, are wasps. Wasps are bigger and stronger than bees and they like honey. One wasp can kill a lot of bees. It takes several bees to kill one wasp. If a hive is strong, the bees will keep up a courageous defence but it takes the time and energy that they should be using to raise brood and make honey. After constant pestering over a long period, even a strong hive can give up the struggle and let wasps rob freely. It soon becomes a weak, then a dead, hive. A pile of chewed wax on the landing platform is a give-away that a hive is under strong attack.

It helps the bees to have a smaller entrance to defend, so an entrance block is the first emergency procedure. Although wasps are larger than bees, they seem able to enter a hive through a smaller hole, so seal up all back doors too. It is easy to distinguish between wasps and bees around a hive. Returning bees head confidently for the entrance and land on the platform or fly in, but wasps hover and watch and nag. When they see their chance, they swoop and dive in. They are very quick.

One way of reducing the entrance without cutting down ventilation is to tack perforated tin over the entrance just leaving eight millimetres for a bee.

Another way to discourage the wasps, used with success by some beekeepers, is to attach a sheet of tin or aluminium above the entrance so that the wasps have to travel through a long dark tunnel before they reach the comparative safety of brood nest and nurse bees. It slows the wasps down but they are fearless animals and confident of their own strength. They keep on attacking.

There are various poisons available for wasps but some of the things that attract wasps also attract bees. We tried mixing poison with stewed apple but that killed as many bees as wasps. Wasps will take prepared meat but it becomes expensive. The ideal is to find and kill the wasp nests.

Finding a wasp nest is not as difficult as it sounds. Wasps are heavy creatures and don't fly nearly as far as bees. Usually the nest is within half a kilometre and the wasps fly in a straight line from their nest to the hive they are attacking. They can nest in trees or walls but the most usual is a hole in the ground. They will choose a place on a steep riverbank or slope if they can. Their only enemies apart from man are intense cold and rain. They are smart enough to live where it is going to take a lot of rain to flood them out, and they will site themselves towards the sun.

Be wary when tracking wasps. The line of working wasps will lead you to their hole, but you don't want to stumble over it before you are ready. Wait until evening once the hole is pinpointed, then put on full, protective bee-gear. As petrol fumes are the traditional weapon against nests, take a bottle of petrol and a spade. The idea is to invert the bottle of petrol and let it leak out gradually so that the fumes kill the wasps and their brood. That is not always so easy because holes are often sideways into a bank and not straight down. And if it is a big nest there is more than one hole. The spade is to alter the shape of the hole, fill in with dirt around the bottle and fill in alternative entrances.

Probably, in the dark on a steep bank with wasps still more active than they are meant to be, you won't want to spend too long in their area doing your gardening. What we have found very effective is the use of petroleum-based fly killers on sale in garages. They come in waxy slabs to hang up in houses. We cut those into three and nail each piece on a stick. They need to be treated with care because they are extremely toxic to bees as well as wasps. They have to be well wrapped and stored away from bees and never handled with beekeeping gloves. A strip pushed well down a hole on its stick and left a week to spread its fumes has so far done the job effectively.

If possible, be ruthless with those wasp nests and put them at the top of your priority list. They survive mild winters and can grow huge. We hear horror stories of nests dug out and needing three trucks to cart away the brood. Killing wasps is not the pleasantest chore, but if you can get the cooperation of neighbours in spotting nests you will be helping everyone in a wide area by getting rid of them, and especially the bees.

Cattle can be more of a problem than they might at first seem. I have had a very depressed George come home just at the beginning of the honey flow. He's worked like a maniac rearing queens, readying the hives, building them up and they start bringing in beautiful honey—then he goes to an apiary on a farm and finds fifteen tall hives spread across the paddock smashed and open, the honey robbed and queens dead. He's lost a year's production and three months of hard work. It's been a continuing story. The theory goes that beekeepers are gentle people. On that kind of occasion I wouldn't be surprised to hear the farmer had come back to find a paddock of dead bulls, each savagely mutilated with a hive tool.

Which brings me to the ultimate enemy of the bees: man. Once a colony of bees has been displaced from its natural habitat high in trees where it is safe from predators except birds and bears, it becomes vulnerable. It is not only the beekeeper who steals honey. Non-authorised personnel also take it. And they take hives, parts of hives and loose bees, especially now that hives of bees for pollinating fruit vines and trees have become big business.

If your hives are in your own garden, they should be safe. If that is not practical, don't leave them in a public place. Most people with orchard or pasture should welcome them for the increased crops and fertility they give in exchange for their keep, plus the traditional gift of honey from the beekeeper for access to that land. The important part is the beekeeper's relationship with the farmers, orchardists and neighbours whose land he is using. Keep in touch. Deliver their honey regularly. Be extra careful to leave gates as you found them and crops untrampled. Make sure he has your telephone number to let you know if lids are blown off or hives down. And try to pick an intelligent farmer who will remember to turn on your electric fence before he lets his bulls into the paddock.

CHAPTER 4   HARVEST

We have to remind ourselves fairly frequently that our object is honey production, not beekeeping. Cultivating that attitude does make a difference to hive management. I still hear George muttering things like: "Get your bum into gear, girlie" when an obstinate bee sits on the edge of the hive mat waiting to be crushed when the lid goes on. He hates to hurt a bee, and of course we tread very carefully in the paddocks, but the human honey producer has to take his cue from the bees: it is the hive that has to survive and individual bees are a means to that end.

Even with two hives in the garden, if the main flowering in your area—from gum trees, clover, tea tree or whatever—is only a few weeks away and one of your hives is still sluggish, sacrifice it. Join the weak hive to the strong one and kill the weak queen. One strong hive will bring in much more honey than two weak ones. It is easy to join them. Take the lid and mat off the strong hive, cover it with a sheet of newspaper then add the brood chambers of the weak hive. By the time the bees have chewed through the newspaper, the smells of the two hives will have intermingled and there will be very little fighting. The bees in the top boxes have to use the entrance at the bottom of the hive. Their journeys through the hive acquaint them with the peccadilloes of their new queen.

A perk of beekeeping is that flowers are so important. We have become aware of tiny, delicate, pale flowers that the bees love but that were insignificant to us before. We can enjoy the rhythm of flowering through the year, welcoming especially the trees and weeds that give pollen and some nectar when the bees would otherwise have a lean time. There is usually only one main nectar flow in the year, during the late spring and early summer. Most flowers need warmth to produce nectar. In our area, the tea tree (Manuka) flow begins the first week in November and finishes the first week in December. We move our hives in December and catch a clover crop in January.

Honey flow chores are pleasant ones: keeping ahead of the bees, preparing boxes of waxed frames for them (drawn if possible, or foundation for the strongest hives to draw) and giving them space for honey. The bees get very frustrated if rain or cold winds stop the nectar flow. It is best to attend to them only on warm sunny days.

When enough moisture has been evaporated from a cell full of honey, the bees cover it with a wax cap. It can stay safely packed away for literally thousands of years. Four-thousand-year-old honey from the Egyptian pyramids is reported to be good but, as with all foods, I prefer the new stuff. (Even Hundred-Year-Old Eggs I find overrated, though they are quite good with a slice of pink ginger and a glass of whisky. I had a boyfriend once who snacked that way in the bath every evening after work . . .)

You are unlikely to want to leave your honey that long, but it can be left until the end of the season or taken as soon as the frames are full. The less disruption to the bees the better. It is most comfortable to harvest before the flow has stopped because the bees are busy and happy and less likely to rob or pester. The bees need a box of honey per hive to take them through the winter anyway so if you take what you want early, it gives them a chance to build up their own stores again.

You can blow, brush or trick the bees away from the frame of honey. We blow. We use a backpack machine with a plastic nozzle designed to clear leaves and litter from football stands. It is a quick way because we can clear a whole box at a time. Brushing with a light brush is fairly efficient if you are organised with a box ready to receive clean frames and somebody standing by to operate the lid for it. Some bees get rolled in honey and the brush gets sticky, but for a couple of hives the method is good enough. Or you can buy a bee escape. Bee escapes are cunning contraptions like turnstiles: bees can go out but not come back. The escapes need to be put on the hive the evening before honey harvest day.

When the honey is off, prepare to extract it as quickly as possible. Two reasons for this: honey is easier to extract when it is warm from the hive where the bees keep it at about 34°F, and the longer a box of honey is stored, the more likely the bees are to find it and rob it. We lost 20 full-depth supers full of honey in about four days before we completed the bee-proof room in our shed. That was about 600 kilograms of honey.

It is not worth getting an extractor and pumps and filters and tanks for a few hives. Many bee clubs have small hand operated extractors that members can borrow, or if you time it right, a commercial beekeeper would put your frames through his machine for you. He would make a small charge per frame or take capping wax in part payment.

Honey doesn't have to be extracted at all. If you have been successful in smuggling your frame of honey back to the kitchen without leading a procession of vengeful bees, that first plunge of eager fingers into the crisp white cappings of a new comb takes some beating. The most elegantly prepared meal would never measure up to the pleasure of scooping white wax and golden honey, warm from the hive, and dribbling it straight into waiting pink mouths. People have done that since we all lived in caves and it still tastes as good.

When the feeding frenzy has died down, the rest of the honey and wax can be scraped off the foundation into a colander or sieve and left to drain. The wax that is left can either be given straight back to the bees for them to clean out or be washed in a little cold water to take out the honey. The syrup is a good start to meadmaking. The wax can go for candlemaking or furniture polish or as a base to some cosmetics. You see how one thing leads to another?

The major snag with scraping the foundation is that you lose a supply of drawn comb for the next season. And the family could start complaining about chewing mouthfuls of wax. If you can borrow the bee club's extractor, plan to extract after dark when the bees are not flying and get a slave or two to run behind you with a cloth when you are ferrying frames of honey to your house or shed: it is unwise to leave a trail of dribbled honey.

Honey cleans off easily with cold or warm water. Wax is the difficult one. If it falls on the floor, it pays to clean it up before it can get trodden in. Wax clogs up brushes and filter nets and sticks inside plastic pails. Scrape and wash where possible, use kerosene on difficult spots. Although the temptation is to use hot water with honey, there are far fewer problems with cold because the wax particles don't melt and stick.

The honey extractor is a drum. It has wire baskets inside to hold the frames of honey and a handle or motor to spin the baskets. The honey is thrown to the sides of the drum by centrifugal force. It slides down the sides and pours from a gate at the bottom into your container. Big extractors for 8, 16, 32 or more frames are set up with pumps and vats to filter wax and surplus bits of bee from the honey and maintain the right temperature. For home extraction, it is probably enough to filter the honey through a nylon sieve. When the honey settles in the container, wax and debris float to the top and can be skimmed off.

Before the frames of honey go into the extractor, the cells holding the honey have to be uncapped. It is worth rigging up a jig to balance your frames while you cut them. Drive a long nail through a slim wood batten that spans your cappings container, then rest a corner of the heavy frame on the nail over the container. A long-bladed kitchen knife will slice off the cappings, but will do it more efficiently if it is hot, so keep a container of hot water beside your cutting area. Two long-bladed knives would be even better so that one can warm up while you use the other. Electrically heated and steam-filled knives are available from beekeeper suppliers.

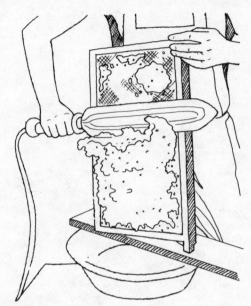

You work for this moment all year.
Soon the honey will be yours.

The idea is to balance the frame on the nail and skim the knife just under the crust of cappings so that as little honey as possible is lost from the cells. The bees do not always cooperate. If the frames have been too far apart in the box, say eight to the box and not evenly spaced, then some will be big, fat frames with odd shaped burr comb interfering with your neat, slim crust. Other frames will have bumps and hollows unsuited to your straight, long blade. It is slow work to begin with, but it is surprising how slick you can get. Some honey is easier to deal with than other: tea tree is very sticky and heavy on the wrist but the knife slides easily through clover honey. When you have uncapped one side of the frame, swivel it on the nail and do the other.

Beeswax from cappings is valuable. Give the cappings back to the bees to rob the honey or wash the cappings. Be careful to clean up honey thoroughly or the bees will very quickly be in to help you.

Now that you have rows of containers with sparkling clear honey, turn to Part 3 for the moods of honey, how to store it and how to enjoy it. Bon appetit.

Honey

PREAMBLE

Honey is more than something to spread on bread—although 100,000 tonnes goes that way every year. From anointing infants to embalming the dead, honey has played an intimate part in human affairs for at least 10,000 years and was available and waiting for us long before we were invented.

For a long time nobody knew where honey came from. They were painfully aware that bees collected and guarded it, but the nectar, they thought, was exuded from heaven like dew. It was the regular food of the gods, to be shared with them on special ritual occasions.

Honey keeps its mystery, even though 800,000 tonnes is now produced annually, and its analysis is unromantic. According to Janet Pleshette in *Health on Your Plate* (Hamlyn Paperbacks, 1983), a 100 gram "average" sample of honey contains:

Calories	288	Copper	0.07 mg
Protein	0.25-2.75 g	Iron	0.4 mg
Fat	trace	Manganese	0.2 mg
Fructose	27.25-44.26 g	Phosphorus	17 mg
Glucose	22-40.75 g	Vitamin A	trace
Sucrose	0.25-7 g	Vitamin B_1	2-12 mcg
Maltose	2.7-16 g	Vitamin B_2	7-145 mcg
Higher sugars	0.13-13.2 g	Vitamin B_6	1-480 mcg
Water	14.4-22.9 g	Pantothenic acid	0-360 mcg
Potassium	51 mg	Nicotinic acid	4-590 mcg
Sodium	11 mg	Vitamin C	0.5-6.5 mcg
Magnesium	6 mg	Biotin	3 mcg
Calcium	5.3 mg	Folic acid	trace

An analysis of a human body reads in the same sort of way, but nobody

has yet been able to concoct a human body from its chemical analysis, neither have we been able to manufacture a synthetic honey. A list of parts cannot tell the whole story. We might not even have the whole list. Other authorities (Eva Crane) state that up to 181 different constituents have been identified in honey, some not found in any other substance. And if we don't know what other things we are looking for it is hard to find them.

Honey is a health giving and delicious food, taken straight from the hive or used in cooking. It is an excellent medicine used internally or externally: there are even claims that it prolongs life. Used on its own or with other ingredients it gives beauty to the skin and hair. It used to bring good luck, fertility and protection from devils. It has been used to pay the rent and to encourage rain to fall. Once upon a time the penalty for stealing honey was death. And a dip in honey is even good for rooting plant cuttings.

In our modern wisdom, we know that honey comes from the nectar of flowers. We also know that the nectar of every flower has minute quantities of different ingredients and these all go into honey. No two spoonfuls of honey are quite the same—unless it has been treated and heated and blended for efficient marketing from supermarket shelves.

The perfume of the flowers is the perfume of fresh honey. Some of the delicate oils are lost from the nectar when the bees store it away in wax pockets, fan it to evaporate excess water and chew it to mix it with the enzymes that turn nectar into honey. Some are lost when the beekeeper uncaps the wax pockets of the comb and spins out the honey. The stronger flower perfume dominates the lighter ones. If more than 45 per cent of the honey has come from nectar of a particular flower, say clover, then the honey is called Clover Honey. We can never be quite sure which other flowers have contributed. There are techniques for counting and identifying microscopic pollen grains but the results are of only academic interest.

The moods of honey are worth understanding. Honey can be a clear liquid, cloudy and runny, just right for spreading like margarine, hard and granular, or divided so that it seems to be part syrup and part hard white rock sugar. All that can happen in the same pot of honey, and it will taste the same and have the same miraculous properties whichever mood it is in.

Time, temperature and moisture affect honey. Good honey, though perhaps with fewer subtle flower flavours than when it was first harvested, has been found in Egyptian tombs and calculated to be 2400 years old. It was probably crystallised, but the cool, dry, constant temperature of the desert tomb would have kept it in perfect condition.

Moisture is the main enemy of honey. Once the bees have reduced the water content to between 17 and 20 per cent they seal their honey with wax and keep the hive temperature at about 30°C. If dampness gets into honey, yeasts begin to work and the honey ferments. Mixed with warm water in the right conditions and if the yeasts are well bred, after a little while the mixture turns into mead, the Elixir of Life, Ambrosia of the Gods. Without good yeasts and a winemaker's care, it can turn into a bitter disappointment.

At 30°C, when the honey leaves the comb, it is a clear liquid. Honey from some flowers flows more easily than from others. Clover honey flows easily, heather and manuka produce a honey that flows more slowly and has to be bullied out of the comb with vibrating needles. In the old days, people ate honey with the wax incorporated, plus pollen, young bee grubs, bits of dead bees and whatever other protein was preserved in the wholesome and sterile environment of the honey. These days for a fussier market, it is filtered. Possibly we leave some of honey's fabled curative powers behind in the nylon mesh.

The honey molecules are sociable. They seek to cluster together. They can use a particle of pollen, a dust speck or an air bubble as a life-raft from which to start growing a star shaped crystal. Depending on the temperature, they will arrange themselves quickly into small crystals (if it is cold, between 16 and 18°C) or slowly grow into large crystals (if the temperature is warm, between 19 and 25°C). The smaller the crystal, the easier honey is to spread, and spreadable honey is preferred in most families.

The more viscous honeys, the slow flowing heather and manuka types, keep their molecules in suspension longer. They rearrange into clusters more slowly so that granulation makes the honey coarse and hard. Where less resistance is offered to the moving molecules, in quick flowing honeys like clover and pohutukawa, the crystals are small. With a combination of low temperature and a light, less viscous honey, the ideal fine crystal emerges. Other honeys can be tricked into reacting the same way.

There is a technique used by beekeepers, large and small scale, to encourage honey to take exactly the right consistency. Fortunately crystals imitate each other. Like sheep, they follow a leader down an exact track. If a small quantity of fine crystal is introduced carefully after the honey is extracted, all the newly forming crystals will take the same shape. If the honey is then cooled and kept cool (but not refrigerated) the results should be a perfect, spreadable, creamy honey, whatever its floral source. Of course, it doesn't always work out that easily because honey, coming straight from the bees, is, happily, as unpredictable as all natural products.

Honey is equally accommodating in the kitchen. To make it liquid, heat the jar very gently and keep it in a warm place. Honey does not conduct heat as quickly as water and is inclined to burn on the outside while staying cool on the inside. Either warm the honey in a pan of hot water keeping an inch of water between the honey and the heat source, or, if the container can stand it, put it in the microwave on defrost for a short while. If you keep bees and have a 20 litre pail of hard honey, put it in a box or cupboard with a light bulb warming it for a day or two, but not to a temperature of more than 40°C.

To harden honey, put it in the salad or butter compartment of the fridge. Some honey on supermarket shelves is presented and labelled as clear honey. (Its shelf life as "clear" honey is about three months.) "Clear honey" has been flash heated: heated to a high temperature for a short time and heated again after cooling, a method of killing the yeasts in honey and of delaying its tendency to crystallise. This pasteurising also cooks out many of the more delicate flower oils and helpful enzymes so that clear honey becomes virtually a sugar syrup. Any heating beyond the temperature of the hive (maximum 40°C, ideal 35°C) damages the balance of sugars, minerals, acids, vitamins, proteins and enzymes that gives honey its unique properties.

CHAPTER 1   BEES AND THEIR HONEY: WHY BOTHER WITH BEES?

Wasps give bees a bad name, and yet they are mortal enemies. Wasps are vicious and greedy and they pester and sting without provocation. Because we keep bees, people complain to us: "I was chased by this bee and it wouldn't leave me alone." If asked were they sure it couldn't have been a wasp, the inevitable reply is that it could have been. Be assured— it was.

Unless their hive is threatened or an individual bee is about to be crushed, bees don't sting. They have to give up their lives to sting and they are usually much too busy surviving and helping the hive to survive to waste lives casually. But when an animal or a human wants to rob their hive, take away supplies collected to save them from winter starvation, then they sting. And it hurts. However "immune" to stings a beekeeper becomes, the stings, in most cases, still hurt like blazes.

So why bother with bees? The short answer is that it is worth it. Honey was first produced up to 20 million years ago. We don't know if dinosaurs and pterodactyls robbed the bees but they probably did. When bears, monkeys and birds were invented, *they* did. And as soon as man arrived a million or two years ago, he joined the honey thieves. It was to remain the only sweet food apart from fruit for the next million or so years, until in the 1600s commercial sugar plantations in the West Indies began to develop the world's sweet tooth. From the odd lucky find of a bee swarm and a feast of honey perhaps twice a year, per capita sugar consumption has gone up world wide to 20 kg each with a great deal more than that being gorged in the rich countries.

In every ancient civilisation that we know anything about, honey was collected and bees encouraged. There are some delightful cave and rock drawings showing the hazards of robbing bees on cliffs using shaky ladders and ropes, with unfortunate hunters being stung and falling off. They date from about 7000 BC in Spain and 5000 BC in India. In some parts of the world honey collection goes on in the same haphazard way.

Beekeeping has not yet become bee farming. A smart American gentleman, the Reverend L. L. Langstroth, used his head and designed the modern beehive in 1851, writing about it two years later and revolutionising the business of caring for bees. But even given the convenience of their modern dwellings, bees know their job better than any beekeeper and are better left to get on with it. Farming other animals, the farmer is boss. The wise beekeeper knows that the bees are boss. By watching them carefully for a long time, and watching the weather and

watching the flowers, he can begin to gauge minor improvements in his techniques and timings to help his bees. Therein lies the fascination of beekeeping.

But it is still hot, heavy, uncomfortable, demanding work that doesn't pay well. Where is the beekeeper without back problems? Where is the glamour? How can a beekeeper get a summer tan through layers of spaceman-like protective gear?

Honey hunters have never had it easy. Through the centuries they have needed to be brave, strong and agile. Many ingenious ways have been devised to persuade bees to stay in one place but there was always a snag: before the Langstroth hive, the bees usually had to be destroyed in order to get at the honey.

The most common system throughout the world was to visit the bees in their own homes. Men claimed rights to certain holes in rocks and trees, raided them annually and passed them on in their wills. There are still trees in European forests that bear scars from doors cut in their trunks so that the honey gatherer could sit on a branch or a stick attached to the tree and dig out the honeycomb into his pot. Honey was always highly valued and highly priced.

The industry of the bees is even more remarkable. A bee can carry 30–40 milligrams of nectar per journey. To get a full load, a bee might visit just one bloom or a thousand depending on the type of flower. Three-quarters of nectar is evaporated in the honeymaking process, so it takes between 40,000 and 50,000 bee journeys to add one kilogram of honey to the hive supplies.

These frames get glued into the box with propolis and have to be levered out with delicacy and firmness.

A good hive produces between 75 kg and 100 kg of honey for its own use and 40 to 50 kg for the beekeeper. That means seven to ten million bee journeys a season for nectar, and half as many again for pollen per hive (figures from Frank Vernon: *Teach Yourself Beekeeping*, Hodder & Stoughton, 1977). Besides all that, they have to rear up to 90,000 young bees, making sure they reach adulthood just as the flowering of the most prolific plant in their area is at its peak. They can do with as much help and as little interference from the beekeeper as possible!

Honey, bees and particularly mead have always been held in awe by mankind. Mead and honey were food of the gods and used as sacrificial offerings from earliest times. Rameses III of Egypt is on record as offering 15 tons of honey to the Nile gods more than 3000 years ago.

People have long been curious about bees, but given the natural defences of bees, they were unwilling to stay around long enough to come to very sensible conclusions about the way the hive worked. Bees appeared to be sexless. Copulation was never observed. The queen was assumed to be a king. Aristotle, being logical, wrote that since they had stings, the worker bees could not be female, "because Nature does not give weapons for fighting to any female". Neither was he happy with the opposite view: that workers were males. He observed that "no males are in the habit of working for their offspring" (Eva Crane in *A Book of Honey*).

The only possible conclusion was that each type of bee generated more of its own kind by some sort of spiritual spontaneous combustion. That made them very holy. And since they visited heaven to collect nectar, they had the necessary purity and opportunity to be in communication with the gods. That made them wise. They knew secrets and could tell when it was going to rain. They also made a convenient storage place for human souls when the human body gave up its ghost.

The life of the hive offered huge potential for symbolism.

The bees made a noise like the humming of the heavenly spheres and yet they lived in a dark hole like the womb. They were used as omens. An eloquent speaker was rumoured to have had a swarm of bees alight on his lips when he was a babe. For very important events, people waited for lucky days when the bees swarmed. Small wonder that honey gifts and anointings accompanied all the human rites of passage in various civilisations: birth, marriage, initiation and death, and everything between and beyond. Mead made its own contribution to the celebrations.

When the Christians arrived, they were attracted by the industry and order within a beehive and the chastity of the bees. The beehive was used as a model for religious and political organisation. The Pope was seen as the king bee, lay brothers of the monasteries were the drones and the monks and workers. The bees retained their virginity, rejoiced in offspring and produced prosperity and sweetness. Of course there was a richness of parallels to be drawn—especially with the lazy drones who were chastised, chased from the hive and left to die.

Two patron saints have been offered to beekeepers. One is Saint Ambrose, whose name is fitting. He was Bishop of Milan from 374 to 397 AD and extolled the virtues of virginity in bees and humans. Wax from the virgin bees, to be burnt as candles for the virgin saints and especially the Virgin Mother, became very important in the Roman church and continued to be even into this century. Beekeeping in the middle ages in Europe was concentrated on the monasteries because of their need for wax and their expertise in mead making.

The other possibility for a patron saint, a Franciscan brother, Bartolomaeus Anglicus also wrote about the order of the hive being a model for the church, but he must have been a beekeeper himself and a keen observer. He noted that young and virgin bees worked better and made better honey than the old ones and that the old and lazy were taken out of the hive, chastised and killed. Since the bees were killed with sulphur smoke to get at their honey, he was probably comparing a young hive to an old hive, and he would have been right in saying that the young hive was the better producer.

His observations stopped just short of being very useful. Had he realised that worker bees only lived for about three weeks anyway in the summer and that it was the queen who had to be young to lay lots of eggs, then he could have revolutionised beekeeping in 1280. He might have known and decided not to mention it, since it would have meant upsetting the hierarchy of the Church. To suggest that the symbolic head of the Church was a female who mated in quick succession with up to ten males before laying 1500 eggs a day, might have been too much for the conservatism of the times. Brother Bartholomaeus himself would certainly have been chastised, cast out and possibly killed.

When a baby learns to talk, its first word in any language is often "Mama" and "Dada". We speak first about the most important thing in our lives. The same is true on a world scale. The words for honey and mead are very old words and similar in many languages. Many Indo-European languages have borrowed from Hittite which called honey "milit" and Sanskrit which used "madhu" as the root of a word for honey and mead. In Japanese, honey is "mitsu" and Chinese languages use "mi". Germanic languages are different: they use a word meaning gold or yellow, "honig".

In *The Little Book of Honey* (Judy Piatkus (Publishers) Ltd, 1984), Mavis Budd quotes an old Arab proverb which underlines the respect for honey's sweetness that we find throughout ancient literature. She writes that they say: "Some days it's honey, some days it's onions . . ." which translates as "Yuam asal, yuam basal . . ." (to the uninitiated both days sound grim).

The Bible has many references to honey. Solomon, who was the wisest man who ever lived, endorsed the use of honey, and Isaiah the prophet predicted that the Messiah would make the right choices: he would choose honey and butter. One quotation that has become a catch phrase seems to have reversed its meaning over time. In the Old Testament there are 21 references to the Promised Land as being a land "flowing with milk and honey". To me that sounds good and the phrase has been caught up as a description of prosperity. A closer look at the context gives a more realistic glimpse of the beekeeper's and cow cocky's life, and it is one that would probably have had little appeal to the tidy grape-growing Israelis.

The "land flowing with milk and honey" actually describes a barren and desolate land, out of control of man and reverting to the weeds and briars from which bees can gather nectar. Ploughed fields, trimmed hedgerows and well weeded crops have no attraction for the beekeeper or his bees, and where can cattle go when every vineyard is carefully fenced? Milk and honey flow where man is not very prosperous in the usual sense, but where he lives well and lives long.

The actual quotation goes like this:

In that day a man will keep alive a young cow and two sheep; (22) and because of the abundance of milk which they give, he will eat curds; for every one that is left in the land will eat curds and honey. (23) In that day every place where there used to be a thousand vines, worth a thousand shekels of silver, will become briers and thorns. (24) With bow and arrows men will come there, for all the land will be briers and thorns; (25) and as for all the hills which used to be hoed with a hoe, you will not come there for fear of briers and thorns; but they will become a place where cattle are let loose and where sheep tread.   (Isaiah 7: 21-25)

It was in the untamed spaces of new lands that bees would flourish. In Europe there was a taste for honey, but demand exceeded supply. The first recorded export of honeybees to America was in 1621, and by the 1800s they were common. The American Indians dreaded them as the White Man's Flies: wherever they found bees and the White Man's Foot (their name for clover) the white man was sure to be close by. Bees were exported from Europe to Australia in 1810, and there is a record of two hives

belonging to Mary Anna Bumby arriving in New Zealand from England in 1839.

Since these beginnings, the USA has become one of the biggest producers of honey (100,000 tonnes annually) with Mexico producing 45,000 tonnes and Argentina 33,000 tonnes. According to figures for 1983 quoted in *The Little Book of Honey*, the biggest producers are the USSR (180,000 tonnes) and China (120,000 tonnes). Australia has become one of the world's main exporters of honey and as much as 80 per cent goes to the United Kingdom. And New Zealanders eat, per capita, more honey than any other nation in the world.

All other factors being equal, that should mean that New Zealanders live the longest. One of honey's many fabled virtues is that it bestows long life: it is the Elixir of Youth. Apparently the beekeepers of Azerbaijan in the Caucasus live for 100 to 150 years of age, in good health and strength. When the Phoenicians arrived in ancient Britain to trade copper and tin, they were so impressed with the local honey-eating habits that they called Britain "The Isle of Honey". Plutarch, writing of the ancient Britons in the context of their honey consumption, wrote: "These Britons only begin to grow old at one hundred and twenty years of age . . ."

CHAPTER 2   WHAT'S SO SPECIAL ABOUT HONEY? HEALTH.

Bees live in ghetto conditions. There is monstrous overcrowding in a hive. Like all other animals, bees give off heat and moisture as they work. Usually there is only one small entrance to their dark, crowded home. They live in ideal conditions for bacteria to breed, and one would expect infection to sweep through their hives like bubonic plague, but bees are remarkably healthy.

There is one serious viral infection that they can pass on to their grubs by stealing contaminated honey, and very occasionally an ailing queen will produce defective grubs lacking resistance to a disease that mummifies them in their cells, but considering the millions and millions of bees that are reared successfully every year their health record is exemplary. Their only real problem is overwork and that is what most of them die from.

Bees produce honey, wax, propolis and royal jelly, all of which have antiseptic and bactericidal properties. The interior of the hive is a sterile unit. The bees are health conscious. They dispose of possible sources of infection: they drag out bees and spiders that have died and keep their floor clean of droppings. But even if the problem is too great for them, say a mouse has died in their hive, that relatively big source of infection is neutralised.

Chemists can pinpoint one action of honey that is anti-bacterial: an enzyme called glucose oxidase breaks down glucose when it is moistened, and releases oxygen. In the process it releases hydrogen peroxide which is known to kill bacteria. It is also known to be destroyed by light and heat. Some honey exposed to light and heat puzzles chemists by retaining anti-bacterial properties.

There are many mysteries still to be solved about honey. In the meantime, we have to take much on trust. Since there is no big company producing honey and employing a laboratory to substantiate claims for the wonder drug, little funding has gone into finding out exactly what honey can do and how. But there are four strong points in favour of honey as a medicine: it is cheap, plentiful, pleasant—and if it doesn't do good, at least it does no harm.

For as long as people have been eating honey, they have expected it to work miracles. Apart from giving long life, fertility and protection against devils, there is no argument that honey is a high energy source. With at least 80 per cent of its composition sugar, a tablespoonful of honey gives 60 calories (250 kilojoules of energy) and 100 grams, 300 calories (1270 kilojoules). Most of this is in the form of glucose and fructose, simple sugars which can be accepted quickly into the body. Glucose fuels the muscles with oxygen and drives out the lactic acid which makes limbs feel weary.

During the Battle of Britain in the Second World War, there were so few pilots that they had to fly day and night. They fed on honey (and probably ham and eggs as well). Honey is the one food consistently mentioned since the beginning of written records as giving that extra bit of strength to athletes, soldiers, swimmers, long distance runners and mountain climbers. (Sir Edmund Hillary was a beekeeper).

Ordinary sugar gives nearly the same amount of energy weight for weight as honey, but to break down sugar to a usable form, the body has to produce insulin. A lot of sugar stimulates high insulin production and the insulin that is left over after the sugar has been disposed of has a depressing effect so that a need for more sugar is created. That doesn't happen with honey. Even some people who suffer from diabetes can take a little honey.

Some of the benefits of honey seem contradictory. As well as giving a boost of energy, honey is soothing. It is efficient as a sedative. A spoonful of honey in a bedtime drink helps you sleep—whether the drink is milk or whisky. And honey is used as a relaxant to relieve problems of hypertension.

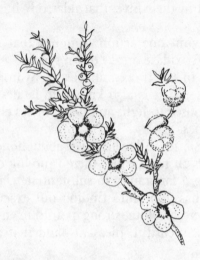

There is something about honey that agrees with the human body. (And it must agree with my dog's body: she chews dead bees, munches up scraps of wax and licks escaping honey from the concrete in the shed. She has a glossy coat.) Honey keeps things flowing. It stimulates the heart and has been used clinically to regulate the heart rhythm. Something in honey helps to maintain a balance of the red corpuscles in blood. And there is a substance named acetylcholine in it that increases bloodflow to the heart while at the same time lowering blood pressure and the rate at which the heart has to beat. For healthy arteries and circulation, it is recommended to take a daily dose of honey and water in which lemon peel has been soaked for a couple of hours. Make it a winter and summer, or spring and autumn dose, so that it is taken three months on and three months off.

The lungs and respiratory system benefit from honey. Asthma sufferers can be helped to breathe more easily by putting the stronger honeys under their nose, and honey used regularly in the diet is meant to help. For hayfever, chew cappings (the wax covers cut from the honeycomb to release the honey). Honey is also a laxative and a help in keeping the gut clean. It is a gentle medicine for chronic constipation.

In health food formulas, honey and lemon or honey and orange are often bracketed together. Honey is a particularly valuable source of vitamin C because the vitamin is not so vulnerable to light and heat when preserved in honey, but given a boost with the vitamin C from citrus fruits it is excellent for our digestive systems.

A combination of honey and vitamin C can break down poisons. When we feed ourselves harmful substances, such as alcohol, honey and lemon can repair some of the damage. The liver uses the fructose in honey to increase the rate at which it can turn alcohol into oxygen. Fructose alone can be used but honey is more effective. It has an enzyme called catalase which works with the fructose and vitamin C (and probably other ingredients which we have not yet identified) to purge out harmful substances that give our celebratory drinks their distinctive flavours.

Taking honey before a party is a useful preventative measure. Some hospitals use honey to sober patients—and honey is a blessing the "morning after". For hangovers: a tablespoon of honey stirred into the juice of a lemon with a little warm water. If the headache comes back again, take another dose.

Of course, if you eat too much honey without using the energy it gives, you will get fat. Surplus energy has to be stored as fat. But, believe it or not, honey can be useful to slimmers. I find that when I let myself get overweight, the worst part is the feeling of sluggishness that accompanies it. It is hard work to walk up a hill. Honey, because it is absorbed into the blood quickly, gives you a burst of energy and in doing so breaks down fat to release oxygen. That gives you the zest to climb another hill and break down more fat.

There is an often repeated dictum that bee stings keep off arthritis. It doesn't always work. The beekeeper who taught us beekeeping suffers from bad gout. George's wrists, abused through years of solo farming, are seized up with arthritis. Bee stings are no help at all. But honey could be.

There are those who swear by a regular usage of cider vinegar and honey to redress arthritis. (I read that and took cider vinegar and honey for years to help George's arthritis but it made no difference at all. It was easier for me to take it than persuade him to.) There has been research to show that honey, unlike sugar, leaves no deposits of uric acid to settle in the joints and irritate and stiffen them. Since Janet Pleshette in *Health on Your Plate* quotes terrible figures to forecast that in the Western world "only one person in 50 will escape arthritic or rheumatic degeneration by the age of 70", I feel it is worth trying to beat that statistic by substituting honey for sugar wherever possible.

The secret of honey seems to lie in its regular use—that is, small amounts over a long period. It is a gentle medicine well disposed towards our bodies and which leaves all our parts in better trim than when it first came into contact with them. There have been a number of well documented clinical trials where honey has been found helpful to patients recovering from strokes and operations, and beneficial to heart patients. It has been used successfully in geriatric treatment and according to a Finnish study published in 1931, giving infants a little honey in their milk does no harm and promotes bonny growth.

The best known and best documented medicinal virtues of honey are antibacterial. Swallowed or used externally, honey kills bad bugs. It would be difficult to prove that honey helps build up a resistance to infection in general, but all the evidence points that way. It is easier to demonstrate to oneself that honey is very effective in dealing with surface problems.

Swords wounds, according to ancient manuals, are best treated with honey and cobwebs. Both cobwebs and swords have gone out of fashion these days but honey for the treatment of open wounds is widespread. It is still used on battlefields as a cheap and plentiful antiseptic salve. The pleasant thing about it for the patient is that honey stops the dressing sticking to the wound. It lessens pain and reduces swelling. In places where it is difficult to bandage, honey keeps the air and harmful bacteria off an open wound, giving it a chance to heal without infection. I have found that even with ordinary kitchen and garden cuts, honey under the sticking plaster gives a quick and painless healing.

Honey is particularly useful for lip sores and it is recommended for painful sunburn, although if the sunburn is extensive, a basting with honey is not always practical (particularly if there are bees around). Steam burns respond well to honey treatment and honey helps the skin to grow again quickly after all kinds of burns. All ulcers, boils and skin eruptions are soothed and cleansed by honey. Since bacteria cannot live in its sterile environment, the infection has to die. At the same time, honey attracts moisture and keeps the skin soft so that repair work can get under way immediately.

Even teeth benefit from some of the properties of honey, though they are threatened by others: there is a substance called saccharase in honey which helps prevent dental decay. Calcium and phosphorus in the honey are essential minerals for healthy teeth, but fructose and sucrose attack the enamel, causing decay.

The good things in honey are found in other bee products: propolis, the antiseptic glue that the bees use as a gap filler and wall plaster, is excellent for teeth. But it has no sugar and is very uninteresting to chew. Propolis, ground down and made into a palatable preparation, is also good for the throat, for soothing coughs and for righting skin disorders and dressing wounds.

Now comes the complication: the honey that is the miracle cure for all bodily ailments is not just any old honey.

"Packaging" of honey is a modern problem. Standardisation for convenient marketing has meant that honey production, which is essentially a cottage industry, has had to go big. Since beekeeping is often a one man job and one man cannot safely manage more than 300 hives, honey is often sold in bulk to a central processing point. With the help of expensive fork-lift trucks, stainless steel tanks, pumps and steam, the honey is heated, filtered, blended, seeded and potted. The product is manufactured to appeal to the tastes of the majority. Beekeepers who can produce pale honey are paid a premium because the taste of the majority is for a bland, sweet, white honey, which is unfortunate. Overrefined honey is like overrefined bread and rice: much of the virtue has gone out of it.

In the days before mass processing of honey, when travellers bartered with the beekeeper in his own locality, honey fanciers noticed that lighter honeys often had more delicate floral flavours and the darker honeys more sharply defined flavours. A preference for the lighter honeys grew. Unfortunately, when honey began to be pooled for standardisation of packaging, those delicate aromas and flavours were mixed and lost. The processing could be quite violent (forcing the honey with pressure through fine filters and heating to temperatures higher than those in the hive) so that the original character was swamped and the product became little more than a spreadable sugar.

Another quality that is often lost is freshness. Because honey can keep for 2400 years, it doesn't mean that it will taste as good after that time. A perk for the beekeeper is that honey *immediately* it is taken from the hive is utterly delicious. If the bees let you get a fingerful of fresh comb to your mouth under your spaceman mask, you understand why honey stealers in the old days called it "the ambrosia of the gods". Even a few minutes later some of those flavours have gone. A few more go with extraction and a few more with storage. And it is mainly the lighter flavours that disappear.

But that is a digression. As a rough rule of thumb, so long as it is fresh—that is, so long as the colour has come from its flower source and is not the result of careless storage or contamination with a tin vessel— the darker honey is often more potently antibacterial, and has more minerals and more nutrients than the lighter honey. Lighter honeys with minimum processing are better than supermarket blends.

Recent tests at Waikato University were made on the antibacterial properties of some New Zealand honeys. Some bacteria were killed simply by the sugars and high acid content of honey (it is almost as acid as vinegar). The best results were obtained from kanuka and manuka honey, penny royal, nodding thistle, kamahi and buttercup, and the less impressive from clover, mixed pasture and various herbs.

The test gave the different honeys an area of bacteria to clear, the type of bacteria that could be found attacking a surgical wound. Manuka, kanuka and penny royal cleared an average of more than 200 square millimetres.

Clover, mixed pasture, thyme and blue borage cleared less than 50 square millimetres. (From Dr Peter C. Molan in *New Zealand Beekeeper*, 1985).

Manuka was found to retain its antibacterial activity at a twentyfold dilution and to remain effective after heating, exposure to light and storage more than a year. The team isolated the active components that they considered responsible for manuka's determindly strong showing—a group of aromatic acids related to the food preservative sodium benzoate. That means that some of the most valuable qualities of the honey for human health were linked to the particularly strong flavour and smell of manuka honey.

The tiny, delicate, white star-shaped flowers of the manuka clothe the less accessible northern hills of New Zealand in November and December. They are scrub trees growing on difficult uncultivated land. The other high achievers are weeds from neglected areas. However, clover, "mixed pasture" and herbs can only grow on well tended land. The bees can only work with the materials flowers provide, and flowers have to rely on the soil they grow in. We can harvest the rich soils of ungrazed land in our honey, where the goodness has not already been taken out in milk or crops. The other advantage of using dark honey from untamed lands is that there is less danger of taking in unsuitable elements from sprays and fertilizer.

CHAPTER 3   WHAT'S SO SPECIAL ABOUT HONEY? BEAUTY.

Sparkling beauty radiates from sparkling good health—so if you are a honey eater, your skin is already glowing, your hair lustrous and your eyes bright. Honey for external use gilds the lily.

I admit I was sceptical when I read recipes telling me to smear honey over my face and hair. The logical part of me had classified honey as sticky and messy—and definitely a food to go in the mouth and not around it.

However, I chose a summer afternoon when nobody was in the house to try to unravel my prejudices. I took two recipes from Mavis Budd's *The Little Book of Honey*: one for the face and one for the hair.

For a "cleansing and nourishing face mask" she suggested mixing in equal parts of honey, egg yolk and either sour cream or fine oatmeal. I had no sour cream or oatmeal, so I whizzed some porridge oats in the coffee grinder. That was my first mistake. The honey was granulated. Another mistake. Following instructions, I applied it "liberally". Then it had to wait 20 minutes. So I began on the hair.

Queen Anne was said to have recommended a two to one mixture of honey and olive oil. Well, I suppose what was good enough for Queen Anne . . . I tried warming the olive oil and honey to make them mix better. I had problems because globs of honey-lubricated porridge oats were slipping down my rather pointed nose, and I had to keep dashing to the window to make sure nobody was coming who could catch me at it.

"Dip the tips of the fingers into the mixture and massage the scalp for several minutes", the recipe said. But I have thick, wiry hair. The honey sat on top of the hair and the olive oil dripped back into the saucer. It would have needed a pound of honey and a litre of oil to make an impression. I felt so silly. This sticky, matted mass of hair and the globby, dribbling face, bright yellow from the egg yolk . . .

I added a little warm water to the hair mix and the hair. That helped it to go on. More honey, more oil. Finally, I was dressed like a good salad, but I still had to wait 20 minutes for the hair magic to work. I was never taught the elegant art of sitting still and doing nothing—though that would have been the wise course of action. The washing needed pegging out. There was a good breeze.

Warning: don't hang out the washing when you are wearing honey face pack and hair lotion!

It was not just that the clothes flapped into my face at the wrong moment: there was the problem of looking down for the pegs and up to the line. The oatmeal slithered off my first chin and lurched over the others and down my neck. The egg yolk crinkled and clung as I squinted against the sun. My hair tumbled out of its towel. But of course, worst of all on this fine summer afternoon—the bees. I had forgotten about them. They found me fascinating.

Despite all, it took vanity to drive me in. The sound of a car approaching drove me into the bathroom. The honey was surprisingly easy to wash off. My face felt wonderful, from inside and out. And my hair after I had washed it was soft and shiny although it is by nature coarse and bouncy. The treatment was excellent but the operation needed a little refining . . .

Honey is a little like electricity: it is useful for all sorts of things but we're not sure exactly how it works. As a cleanser, honey's antibacterial activity drives out organisms that could cause blemishes in the skin, and its hygroscopic qualities attract moisture, but how honey penetrates the skin to leave it velvety, or caresses each hair until it shines, is part of honey's own mystery.

Youth we think of as soft and juicy; age as shrivelled and dry. Honey prevents drying and has therefore been valued for its rejuvenating powers. A regular bath in honey and asses' milk was part of Cleopatra's beauty routine—although a regular bath of any sort in those days would have added considerably to her charms, and probably given her a longer life than the average if she hadn't made friends with a couple of snakes. The Queen of Sheba, too, knew the value of honey. Beauties down the ages have set and re-set the fashion for using honey to keep their hair colour, soften their skin and keep the rounded lines of youth.

In modern beauty preparations there has been a swing back to "natural" and "organic" ingredients. The top beauty houses advertise their preparations as incorporating honey, royal jelly, wax and propolis as well as other ingredients from the kitchen: avocado, nut oils, wheatgerm, cucumber, eggs and cream. The difference between what you buy and what you can make yourself is convenience (somebody has already done the mixing to the right texture and put it in a pretty pot), perfume (probably longer lasting than the herb or flower perfumes one can make at home) and price.

"Hygroscopic" means to attract moisture—but honey does more than this. It somehow works with the skin to stimulate the skin's own lubrication machinery. A simple solution of honey and water (warm water for comfort, but honey dissolves in water at any temperature) can be used as both a skin cleanser and a conditioner for the hair. Two tablespoons of honey to a litre of water dabbed onto the face with cotton wool and left for ten minutes gives a good glow, and the rest of the mixture can be used as a hair conditioner before the final rinse.

Honey-based Beauty Potions

A honey-only face mask for a quick boost is easy so long as there are no bees around: dip your fingers into warm water and then into honey and massage gently into the face and neck. It is best not to use a coarsely granulated honey like I did, but either fine-grained creamed honey or a honey warmed to its liquid mood (granules feel like grit). Warming the fingers in water discourages the honey from sticking.

Egg white (beaten) mixed with a teaspoon of honey and used regularly is meant to take away bags from under the eyes and firm up the skin.

Eva Crane gives some Russian recipes for nourishing face packs, to make up according to the ingredients to hand in the kitchen cupboard. For a single application, use a teaspoon of liquid honey as a base and mix it with an egg yolk. Add either a teaspoon of glycerine, a tablespoon of fine oatmeal or a teaspoon or sour cream. Clean the skin first, then use a hot compress for a few minutes to open the pores. Apply the face pack in a thin layer with cotton wool and leave for 20 minutes. Wash off with warm water and you will have skin like a baby, and a rosy glow.

One could just about eat the face packs and lotions suggested by some authorities (how about eggs, honey, ground almonds and lard—good for breakfast?) but Mavis Budd recommends a special beauty drink. Her mixture, a teaspoon each of honey, lemon juice and olive oil to be taken daily before breakfast, is not nearly as bad as it sounds—if you like salad dressing.

Working hands can be rescued with honey. This recipe from Mavis Budd might not reach the hands. She says it is also good for the face and neck. And throat . . . ?

125 g pure honey

125 g cucumber juice

½ cup vodka

The instructions are to pour the cucumber juice and vodka into a bottle and store it for a week in a dark place, then filter it through muslin and stir in honey. It should be left on for several hours for maximum benefit.

Honey and lemon juice can massage away hard skin on feet, knees and elbows. Rinse off with warm water.

Eva Crane gives an early Victorian recipe for chapped hands.

½ cup lard

2 egg yolks

1 tablespoon of ground almonds

1 tablespoon honey

a few drops of almond essence

Soften the lard and mix it with the other ingredients to form a stiff paste. Mavis Budd, for the same purpose, offers one egg white, a teaspoon of glycerine, a dessertspoon of honey and a little cornflower to thicken.

— —

The texture of the lotion, ointment or cream depends on what is added to the honey, but the honey is essential. With lemon juice it softens and soothes; with egg and cream it nourishes. If you want an "all purpose lotion", then put in both egg and lemon juice with the honey, scent it with rosewater and add glycerine for ease of application. Each person

can become their own beautician with a little experimentation. Herbs can be added: comfrey, aloe vera or whatever is in the garden. Lotions with cream, flour or cornmeal suit a dry skin, and with alcohol, a standard skin. Oily skins benefit from the lemon juice.

Honey is an excellent preserver. It preserves skin and hair from the ravages of sun and wind, keeps off destructive bugs and makes a barrier against the drying that comes with age. Of course, if you are seeking a more permanent solution to the problem of disappearing beauty, honey is again your faithful agent. Honey was the main ingredient that the Egyptians used in embalming their noble dead. Some achieved nearly eternal beauty and at least an approximation of immortality.

CHAPTER 4   WHAT'S SO SPECIAL ABOUT HONEY? FOOD.

"Honey is good for you," some people say. That's hard to substantiate in terms of nutrition. Whichever way you do the analysis, 75 to 80 per cent of honey is sugars. There are more than 20 different sugars found in honey, but all of them offer the body fuel for its activities, not building materials. A further 17 per cent is water. That leaves only three to eight per cent that is interesting from the point of view of nourishment.

That small percentage is crammed with good things, but to eat enough to absorb what nutritionists call "significant amounts" you would have to eat a big pot of honey every day. Unless you were very busy that would make you very fat and not at all healthy. A chemical analysis cannot tell the whole story either: there is honey's "mystery".

Those who try to fathom the "rules" of biodynamic living and farming believe that a little goes a long way. Amazingly small quantities of a simple substance at the right time and place can replace tonnes of fertiliser on pasture. Perhaps honey can work on the same principle, encouraging other substances to fulfil a nutritional or health-giving role by its presence.

The three to eight per cent is made up of pollen grains (protein), wax, plant acids, mineral salts, gums and resins. If honey is filtered too thoroughly and under pressure, the pollen grains, wax, gums and resins are filtered out. What is left contains just a little each of potassium, sodium, magnesium, calcium, copper, iron, manganese, phosphorus, chlorine, sulphur and whatever other minerals were in the soil and used by the flowers the bees visited. Vitamins A, B_1, B_2, B_6, and C are present, and a strong contingent of acids: at least 15 including pantothenic acid, acetic acid, fornic acid, nicotinic acid, folic acid and lactic acid. Seventeen free amino acids have been counted including proline, glutamic acid, lysine and acetylcholine.

The bees introduced the enzymes: invertase (breaks down sucrose to fructose and glucose); diastase (breaks down starch); glucose oxidase (breaks down glucose to hydrogen peroxide, gluconic acid and oxygen); catalase and saccharase.

The composition of any particular honey depends on where the nectar was gathered. There is really no "average" sample since honey can vary from comb to comb in a single hive, and possibly from cell to cell within that comb. Yeasts are present in honey, as well as lipids, plant growth hormones, fatty acids and the substances that give it colour and flavour: carotene and zanthophylls. In general, the same rough rule that applies to honey and health applies to honey and nutrition: the darker the honey, the richer it is as a source of minerals and "extras" useful to the body.

Royal jelly, the food manufactured by young nurse bees to feed the grubs and which they give in great quantity to the grub that will become a queen bee, is more than 400 times richer in vitamins than honey.

Gaston L. S. Pawan writing in *The New Zealand Beekeeper* Spring, 1986 gave the following comparative table showing the average vitamin content of honey and royal jelly, in micrograms per gram:

	HONEY	ROYAL JELLY
Thiamin	0.04	18.0
Riboflavin	0.26	28.0
Nicotinic acid	1.1	111.0
Pyridoxin	0.10	10.2
Pantothenic acid	0.55	320.0
Biotin	0.001	3.1
Folic acid	0.03	0.5

Having got the technical side out of the way, we can concentrate on the best thing about honey: its flavours. Miracle food or not, it would never have earned such wholehearted acclaim through the ages if it hadn't tasted delicious.

Sugar is just sweet. Its flavour depends only on its level of refinement. A sauce made with sugar is a sweet sauce. Make instead sauces with two honeys of contrasting flavours and two unique sauces have been created.

Pooh Bear said: "I like to eat my peas with honey because it makes them taste so funny" (or words to that effect). "Funny" in grown-up language means "different". Meals prepared with honey are more interesting than those that are just sweet.

Humans have been cleverly designed with a nourishment sensing device we call a palate. On the whole, what tastes good is good. But our palate is connected to the brain and the brain is boss. The brain can tell the palate: coffee and whisky might taste bitter, but they are socially important and bring rewards that you don't know about so drink them! Other strong flavours, like garlic, ginger and chilli, the palate can reject until the right time. As a child I hated them; now I am adult they taste good.

The palate is a delicate tool and can be blunted—at least temporarily. When work, money, family and seemingly unalterable circumstances force the pace, the palate can get ignored and swamped with greasy, salty, oversweet or starchy dishes that "fill the gap" and give a quick burst of energy. In the end, those habits of eating rob us of the strength and vitality we should expect from food.

Sheer convenience sells foods that fill without giving a fair share of flavour or nourishment. Even when cow-fresh butter is cheaper than margarine, if the margarine is in a handy plastic pot and easy to spread straight from the fridge, the margarine will sell. White rice sells despite its inferior flavour because it is quick to cook. White bread conquered many households because it was sliced and wrapped in plastic, while nutty fresh-baked browns made crumbs when the children cut them.

Unfortunately, things worth having often take a little effort and honey is no exception. Sugar is easier to measure; there is no need to think about its flavour; and most recipe books are geared for sugar, not honey. Also, honey costs a little more than sugar. But there are two ways around that: keep a couple of beehives (that's the best); or grow some fruit trees and encourage the family to gorge on fruit rather than cookies.

There are rules for substituting honey for sugar which are quick and simple, but honey is worth better than "hand-me-down" recipes! It is a versatile food and a good companion in kitchen adventures. Not too much can go wrong, particularly if you respect honey's special qualities. (The relationship between the cook and honey is similar to that between the beekeeper and his bees: good results come from working with the honey and giving it the best possible conditions, not from expecting it to obey orders!)

The best way to get to know honey is to taste it: taste as many different kinds as possible and as fresh as possible. The different flavours will suggest ways they can be used. Since cooking, and particularly baking, demands the same kind of accuracy as chemistry, and good cooking needs the flair of an artist, it is best to approach a new ingredient with caution. Fortunately, honey fits snugly into all our meals and snacks and is just as delicious uncooked as cooked.

Honey uncooked is good in cool summer drinks or warm winter drinks. It mixes easily with hot or cold liquids: just stir. It has always been popular as a breakfast food with porridge, cornflakes or muesli. Adventures into salad dressings and sauces have excellent chances of success if the honey is given congenial company. Good combinations for honey cooking can include orange or lemon juice, butter or cream, ginger and cinnamon, apples, bananas and dried fruit, and nuts (particularly almonds with savoury foods and walnuts with sweet).

Honey brings out the flavours in other ingredients. Used sparingly and with a few herbs, the potential is limitless for glazing vegetables, fish, poultry and meats. Honey, with perhaps a little butter and a hint of cloves, adds a special luxury to already delicious desserts such as pears or peaches, and with chopped nuts, to bananas.

In puddings, soufflés and cheesecakes, honey is easy to use and it is fine for icing, pies and sweets. Through the ages, honey has been a huge treat in fudge, nougat, torrone, caramels and halva. And honey is a natural preservative, so it can be used in bottling, canning and freezing, and to make jams, jellies, chutneys, relishes and pickles.

That's a good start. And then there is baking.

There are advantages to using honey rather than sugar in baking: apart from added flavour, baked goods keep fresh longer because honey attracts moisture, and the appearance is often improved with the richer, darker tones of cooked honey. But it is best to start off cautiously. Either use recipes already tested for use with honey, or substitute just a part of the sugar with honey in old and favourite recipes. Here are some basic rules and suggestions, but the best way to test them is to experiment.

Temperature Most baking is done with liquid honey. To make the honey liquid, heat it gently either in a microwave oven on "defrost", or in warm water (150°C)—or even by shutting it up in a car parked in the sun! Heat slowly, or the honey on the outside will burn while the inside stays solid.

For *baking*: a lower temperature is needed, about 25–30 degrees lower than for an all-sugar recipe, otherwise flavour is lost and the honey can caramelise too quickly and make the cakes too brown.

For *preserving*: a higher temperature is needed for jams, jellies and candies. There is more moisture to boil away.

Sweetness By volume (the cupful), honey is sweeter than sugar, because it is more dense. A cup of honey weighs roughly the same as a cup and a half of sugar—a cup of finely granulated sugar is about 250 grams; honey about 375 grams. In substituting, it is important to remember the difference between weight and volume. If you prefer to cook by weighing ingredients, use a quarter more honey than the recipe specifies for sugar. If you go by volume, substitute just over two-thirds of a cup of honey for each cup of sugar.

Moisture   Honey is wetter than sugar, so in making substitutions, reduce other liquids. Use a quarter of a cup less liquid for each cup of honey substituted for sugar.

Acidity   Honey is very acid. In baking, add a quarter of a teaspoon of baking soda for each cup of honey. If there is a problem with cakes not rising properly, try more baking soda. If on the other hand there is a darker layer at the bottom of the cake, too much soda has been used. Recipes using sour milk or sour cream do not need baking soda.

Freezing   Freezing intensifies the honey flavour in baked goods.

Measuring   If the spoon or cup is lightly greased, liquid honey will not stick.

Warning Number One   One tablespoon of honey has 64 calories—which can be converted into energy or FAT.

Warning Number Two   Fresh honeys are not standardised products. Never expect one honey to behave exactly like another. Be flexible. Let the honey lead. Have fun.

Rudolf Steiner said in his *Nine Lectures on Bees* (1923): "The more honey is used as food, the less it will be needed as a remedy."

I am still in awe of honey. We have kept bees on a moderate scale for four years and at the moment we have at least five tonnes of honey in our shed. Yet I use it carefully in the kitchen, remembering the work of the bees and the work of the beekeeper in making and gathering it.

We have about 150 hives. If it takes the bees of one hive 15 million bee journeys to make a box of surplus honey for us to use, then that comes to 2,250,000,000 bee journeys to get our crop and I'm not about to squander that amount of labour.

But that is not the end of the story. To look after those hives for one year and process his honey crop, the beekeeper, who usually has to put up with punishment from an abused backbone, must lift sticky heavy boxes from awkward positions using only one centimetre fingerholds, wearing hot protective gear and being bombarded by unhappy bees on at least 26 occasions. We worked out that for our hives and using a friend's warm room and extraction equipment, we lifted and carried over the year at least 130 tonnes of honey either in 45 kilogram boxes or 30 kilogram pails.

So I am a bit mean with honey. But if it happens that dampness gets into a pail or we have a disaster and a pail of honey warms to more than 40° Celsius then I pounce on that pail as my perk and soon it is gone: there are so many ways I enjoy using it in cooking.

DRINKS

In summer, a gingery, lemony fizz made from the strongly flavoured tea tree honey (manuka) is a winner. I make 10 litres at a time because it disappears so quickly but of course quantities can be reduced. And the quantity of ginger and lemon can be adjusted to suit the family's tastes.

309 Honey Fizz

3½ cups strong dark honey (manuka is best, clover makes the drink insipid)

10 litres water

3 whites of egg, beaten

2 tablespoons ginger moistened with a little water (like prepared mustard)

juice of 6 to 10 lemons (according to taste)

¼ teaspoon dry yeast

Dissolve the honey in the water and add egg whites and moistened ginger. Bring to the boil—but be alert as it reaches boiling point. The mixture will bubble up and over the pan *very* quickly if you are not ready to take off the scum. As soon as the scum is removed, the mixture can boil away merrily with no more danger of spills. Boil for about ten minutes then take off heat source and let cool.

When lukewarm, add the juice of lemons and yeast. Stir. Keep warm (below blood temperature) for a while. If the fizz is for small children, just a few minutes' wait is enough. The mixture gets more fizzy (and a tiny bit more alcoholic) the longer you leave it, depending also on the temperature.

In cool weather, the mixture can be left overnight. Strain through a cloth or fine nylon sieve. It can go straight into 2 litre plastic bottles saved from bought soft drinks, but I prefer to let it settle first in half gallon jars, then when it is poured into the plastic bottles the drink is clearer because much of the sediment is left behind. Screw on bottle caps lightly—gas needs to escape in warm weather. To be safe, store in refrigerator.

Any left over fizz will clear like wine and can be added to other home made wines to liven up a dull brew.

Honey is a natural for all sorts of drinks. A summertime trick is to dissolve honey in a little water with lemon juice and freeze it in ice-making trays ready for "instant" cold drinks. Lemon and honey in cold tea is refreshing. And honey with a squeeze of orange or lemon in any fruit milkshake turns a snack into a heavenly adventure. The only problem is keeping up with the demand.
The wine section gives recipes for honey wine, otherwise known as mead.

Athol Brose

Eva Crane quotes an 1826 recipe for a potent Scottish drink called athol brose. It's good—but definitely not as a long cool drink for the kiddies. Dissolve 500 grams of honey in about a cup of water. "Stir with a silver spoon." Slowly mix in one litre of whisky. Stir briskly until froth rises, then bottle and keep tightly corked. (The recipe does not say how long it will stay tightly corked: 5 minutes?)

Preserving

Jams, jellies and pickles can be as successful with honey as with sugar and a whole lot more flavoursome. Use lighter flavoured honeys (clover, pohutukawa, mixed pasture) with berry fruits or simple jams, and stronger flavours for chutneys and pickles.

JAM
Three cups of fruit to 2 of honey is the usual ratio. To make sure of setting, especially for jellies, use pectin according to the instructions on the packet. (Fortunately, my family is so happy to get jam they don't mind whether it is solid or runny and we leave out the pectin but substitute the juice of 2 lemons.) Boil a little longer than you would with sugar jam because there is more moisture to be evaporated. If you are converting a sugar jam recipe to a honey jam recipe, use cup for cup about half the recommended amount of sweetener. In other words, 6 cups of sugar converts to 3 cups of honey.

CHUTNEY
Honey goes so well with garlic, ginger, spices, onions, vinegar and vegetables that there is no problem substituting honey for sugar in pickles and chutney. Two of our all-year favourites are apple chutney and garlic pickle.

Apple Chutney

2 kg apples, peeled and cut up roughly
500 g peeled and sliced onions
2/3 cup water
2 cups manuka honey
2 1/3 cups vinegar
2 tablespoons salt

1 tablespoon ground ginger
2 teaspoons cinnamon
1 teaspoon cayenne pepper
2 teaspoons curry powder
250 g sultanas

Boil up onions with apples and water until soft (20 minutes). Mix in everything else, stirring until the honey is dissolved. Boil gently and stir to stop sticking for about an hour, until all soft and golden brown. Put in hot dry jars. Either seal immediately or allow to cool and cover with a layer of wax.

Pickled Garlic

(This recipe is from Erin who used to give us a jar each for our birthday present but took pity on us when we couldn't make it last the whole year and gave us the recipe.)

250 g garlic (peeled, large cloves cut)
1 cup white or cider vinegar
2 tablespoons clover honey

¼ teaspoon celery seeds
¼ teaspoon mustard seeds

Dissolve honey in vinegar. Bring to boil and take off scum. Add seeds and boil for 5 minutes. Add garlic and boil further 5 minutes. Pack into warm sterile jars. Liquid must cover cloves. Keep for six weeks if you can for flavour to develop.

We grow a lot of garlic and love it. We also give our high garlic consumption credit for keeping away colds and flu when our more fastidious neighbours are afflicted. I have read that garlic will cure colds and chills in animals but our animals have never had the opportunity to try. (The dog loves it—but then she doesn't class herself as "animal".)

An extra strong brew I read about combines honey and garlic.

Garlic and Honey

FOR COUGHS, COLDS, FLU, SORE THROATS AND COLD SORES

Peel and leave whole 25 to 50 garlic cloves (depending on size). Submerge them in 2 to 3 cups of honey in a large glass jar with a screw top. Stand the jar on a windowsill in the sun until the cloves become opaque. Half a teaspoon is enough to cure an adult of just about anything!

While we're on cures: the standard arthritis preventative and cure is one teaspoon of dark honey to one tablespoon of cider vinegar with as much water as you need. That should be taken every day for a lifetime.

A recipe I have not yet had occasion to use is for baldness, from Mrs N. Prescott's *Household Lore*: "Rub the part morning and evening with onions, till it is red, afterwards with honey—or wash it with a decoction of boxwood."

This, of course, has nothing to do with honey, but the same lady quotes a cure for the problem of snoring: "Take 6 drops of olive oil and a pinch of mustard before getting into bed." Thought you might like to know.

Onions and Honey

An onion and honey mix should not be restricted to bald heads. Baked onions in a delicious honey sauce turns the ordinary into something special.

4 large onions	*1 teaspoon salt*
½ cup cream of chicken soup concentrate	*¼ teaspoon pepper*
½ cup water	*¼ teaspoon ground ginger*

Peel the onions and cut each one in half. Mix the remaining ingredients together and pour over the onions in a baking dish. Either bake in a medium oven for an hour, or cover and microwave on "high" for 20 minutes, basting occasionally with the sauce.

All sorts of glazes for vegetables and meats, dressings, sauces, butters, marinades, dips and spreads can use honey. (For dips, spreads and butters, see Milk section. Suit the flavour of the honey to the food to be garnished.

General Marinade for Meats

1 cup oil	*1 clove crushed garlic*
½ cup honey	*1 tablespoon chilli sauce*
½ cup cider vinegar	*1 tablespoon Worcestershire sauce*
1 chopped onion	*½ teaspoon salt*

Combine, shake and use.

Mustard, prepared and mixed 50/50 with honey is a useful BBQ variation.

For a special mint sauce, the *New Zealand Beekeeper* recommends 300 g honey, 1 tablespoon cider vinegar, 125 ml water and 3 heaped tablespoons chopped mint. Combine and bring ingredients to the boil. The sauce can be used to baste lamb or as an accompaniment.

To store mint leaves indefinitely, Eva Crane advocates half filling a 65 g jar with honey, warming the honey until it is in liquid mood then filling up the jar with as much chopped mint as can be crammed in. The alternative is keeping small bags of mint in the freezer, but since small bags of things in my freezer hide themselves under everything else, I use Eva Crane's method.

Apple Mint Jelly

In *The Little Book of Honey*, Mavis Budd goes one further and combines mint, honey and apples in a successful jelly.

2 kg apples	*300 ml water*
2 handfuls fresh mint	*750 g honey*
leaves, roughly chopped	*300 ml vinegar*

Cut apples (unpeeled) and combine with mint and water. Cover and cook till apples are soft. Mash pulp and sieve, add honey and vinegar. Bring back to boil and boil fast for 5 minutes. Pour into hot sterilised jars and cover. Especially good with cold meat.

Spinach Pie

Some of the most mouthwatering food photographs I have come across are in a publication by the Australian Honey Board. An ordinary quick-to-make and cheap-to-serve spinach pie made with honey was the first thing I tried and it tasted as good as it looked. Honey used in staple starchy foods—pastry, breads, puddings and cakes—helps keep a moist texture which in turn brings out the fresh flavours of the ingredients.

Pastry: (good for any savoury pie)

1 cup wholemeal flour	*125 g cottage cheese*
1 cup plain flour	*60 g butter*
2 teaspoons baking powder	*¼ cup honey*
¼ teaspoon salt	

Mix the dry ingredients then the cottage cheese and butter and finally work in liquid honey to make a firm dough. Roll out enough to line a 25 cm pie dish, keeping a third for the pastry lid.

 *Honey*

Filling:

500 g cooked spinach, drained
¼ cup finely chopped fennel (I actually use
slightly less dill weed because there is no
fennel in the garden, and silverbeet as a
substitute for spinach)
2 gloves garlic
375 g cottage cheese

185 g grated cheese (cheddar or
homemade)
3 large eggs
1/3 cup honey
another egg and 2 tablespoons milk for
glaze

Mix it all together, pop it in the pie and cover with pastry. Glaze top and sprinkle
on 1 teaspoon fennel seeds (dill seeds for us) and make 3 slits for steam to escape.
Bake hot at 220°C for 10 minutes then reduce temperature to 180°C and bake for
a further 50 minutes. Good hot or cold and serves 8.

Honey Dumplings

(MAKES 12)

A strange honey dessert that attracted me because I could make it from
ingredients to hand had a better reception than expected. It is an old English
recipe but tastes to me Middle Eastern, reminiscent of baklava but not so difficult
to make.

2 tablespoons butter
2 cups self raising flour (or plain flour
with 1 teaspoon baking soda)
1½ teaspoons baking powder

1 cup grated cheese
1 cup water
pinch salt

Rub butter into flour and baking powder, mix in cheese (or use a food processor)
then add water to make a dough.
Make a syrup from 3 tablespoons butter, 1 cup honey and 1 cup water.
Bring to boil then drop in dumpling mixture by the tablespoon. Cover and simmer
for 20 minutes then serve hot with whipped cream and a sprinkling of chopped
nuts.

Honey Toffee Apples

Desserts and sweet treats have always been a honey stronghold. French nougat,
Spanish torrone and the Greek halva all have a honey base and are delicious, but
the recipes are in many books. I will mention just one family favourite: honey
toffee apples.

6 crisp ripe apples on sticks
2 cups manuka honey
3/4 cup evaporated milk

3 tablespoons butter
pinch salt
1 teaspoon vanilla

Mix and heat milk and honey until it reaches 125°C at which stage a little of the mixture dropped in cold water should form a firm ball. Take off the heat source and stir in butter, salt and vanilla. Have greaseproof paper or foil ready: dip apples in caramel, let them cool and store them in the fridge (but not for too long or they will melt.)

BAKING

We don't do much baking. If we make scrumptious cakes, they only get eaten and then we get fat and complain. But since we have had ample honey and embarked on the "minimum impact" lifestyle I have experimented with the simplest kinds of cake that link us with our ancestors.

Honey Cakes

Probably the very first cakes (bread or wafers) womankind made were honey cakes. In the Bible, Abraham's wife Sarah used a honey and flour recipe to make cakes for her visitors.

She made loaves from equal weights of honey and flour—which works out in volume to 3 cups of flour to one of honey. She probably melted the honey, worked it into the flour and added a pinch of salt. She would have rolled it out to about a centimetre thick and baked it in a cool oven for half an hour. (If she had had notice of her visitors' arrival, she might have left the mixture ready rolled for a couple of days protected by big leaves. Her cool oven would have been about 150°C.)

That mixture makes a pretty hard wafer but it keeps indefinitely and even improves after a few months—excellent for camping and trekking. Another variation I have tried turned out more like bread. It was quick and simple to make. The recipe is quoted by Eva Crane using 2 kg flour, but I used 500 g and made two small loaves.

500 g flour
125 g liquid honey
hot water
rosewater

15 g anise
15 g cinnamon
pinch of cloves

Mix all ingredients to a stiff paste. Make flat cakes and sprinkle with ground ginger or other spice. Cook in a low oven until golden brown and hollow-sounding when tapped.

Be warned by my mistake: I had anise only in concentrated extract to use for attracting possums, so I used that. It is *incredibly* strong. Half a droplet was much too much.

As life became more settled, more ingredients became available and stoves more sophisticated. Simple honey wafers developed into another of my standby favourites: gingerbread.

What is it about mothers? I must have tried 30 different recipes for gingerbread and never made it quite as luscious as I remember my mother's gingerbread, even using her own recipe. Actually, there are probably as many gingerbread recipes as there have been mothers, but I have discovered that the main difference between cakes and gingerbread is that the fat and sweet ingredients (honey, syrup, sugar) are beaten together before adding the dry ingredients and then everything is beaten a little more into an easily poured batter. Milk, eggs, dried fruit and spices have cheered up the original honey-wafer recipes considerably.

Since we are in the honey business, most of my experimental gingerbreads have concentrated on the use of honey to the exclusion of golden syrup. I am now admitting defeat. Honey-made gingerbreads certainly improve as they age—but made with syrup as well they improve a lot more. The gooier the cake, the higher it gets rated in our household, so syrup is definitely *in*.

Honey Gingerbread

To make a "parkin", a Yorkshire gingerbread traditionally made for November 5 (to celebrate the night a Yorkshireman tried to blow up the British Houses of Parliament about 400 years ago), rolled oats or oatmeal are substituted for half the flour. It makes a drier cake and is less popular with us, but it lasts well and is nutritious and sustaining.

½ cup (175 g) honey	1½ teaspoons ground cloves
½ cup (75 g) brown sugar	½ teaspoon salt
1 cup (250 g) melted butter	1 teaspoon baking powder
1 cup (300 g) golden syrup	½ teaspoon baking soda
2 eggs	¾ cup (125 g) dried fruit (sultanas,
150 ml milk	chopped candied peel, and crystallised
4 cups plain flour	ginger)
2 teaspoons ground ginger	

Melt (don't boil) honey, sugar, butter and syrup together. Beat the eggs and add milk. Mix together flour, ginger, cloves, salt, baking powder and baking soda. Add the egg/milk mixture to the melted fat/honey mixture, tip in the flour mixture, stir it all together and mix in dried fruit. Pour into a square tin lined with baking paper. Bake in a medium oven (180°C) for 40 minutes. Cut while hot. Although it keeps well, you might want to keep it out of sight for a longer life! Freeze it in the baking paper but already cut.

Cosy Cat Biscuits

(JANET'S RECIPE)

Actually these are made from a traditional German recipe and called Lebkuchen, but I first met them in the shape of cats at the home of so many cats (live and otherwise) that the owners and collectors of catty items had lost count somewhere up in the thousands. The virtue of these biscuits is that they can and should be made at least two weeks before they are to be eaten. They can be made in any shape and are popular in Germany for hanging on the Christmas tree. When they are first baked they are rock hard (bore a hole through the dough before baking if you want to hang the biscuits) and should be kept in an airtight jar for a couple of weeks until they are just right.

50 g butter	1 teaspoon ground cloves
1 cup honey	1 teaspoon ground nutmeg
¾ cup brown sugar	1 teaspoon ground allspice
1 tablespoon lemon juice	½ teaspoon baking soda
1 tablespoon grated lemon rind	3 cups flour (more if necessary)
2 teaspoons ground cinnamon	

Measure all ingredients except baking soda and flour into medium sized saucepan. Stir over low heat until blended and sugar is no longer grainy. Do not boil. Take off heat and cool to room temperature.
Sift baking soda into 1 cup of flour and stir into melted mixture. Gradually add more flour until dough is firm enough to roll out on a floured board. Roll out about 5 mm thick and cut into shapes. (Make holes with a matchstick).
Bake at 180°C for about 10 minutes until the edges brown slightly. Cool. Use water ice for icing.
Makes about 50 biscuits.

Wine

PREAMBLE

A winemaker is an optimist. At least for the first year. After that, one's optimism is justified, and you become an expert. Pride comes before a fall: the next batch gets labelled "Cooking" or "Wait", or the worst, "Distil"! But you are still an optimist so you become an innovator, an experimenter, an adventurer—and very popular because you have so much wine. Somebody has to taste it. Besides that, wine which was so awful last year has mysteriously improved.

We remember our wines by the parties they generated. There was the Pink Plonk. That fooled a lot of previously confirmed beer drinkers. Old Honeypuff tried to float back up the hill using Graham's beach umbrella as a parachute. Graham got frisky too.

The mulled wine for a June Christmas was more successful than it should have been: sweet warm spiced wine on a cold night and everybody drank heaps. They thought they were merry and danced all night—and only next day when they woke refreshed and ready for work did they realise we'd boiled all the alcohol away and the merriness was of their own making.

There was the Silly Games party (peach and plum) and George's Arabian Nights 50th (kiwi fruit) and the bonfire party which got rained out. That was nearly a disaster: no wine was just right, but we blended the sweet (lemon) with the dry (rhubarb) and threw in some sprigs of mint. It worked.

I think if it weren't for airlocks, everybody would make wine. They only cost a few cents each at the chemist's shop but they are a psychological barrier. Glass tubes with bulges must belong in the laboratory with clever scientists and chemicals and mathematical mysteries. Does it help to know they are plastic? They are only to stop dust and flies falling in the wine while letting out the air. They are basically using the same principle as "S" bends in loos—and "S" bends don't stop people using loos.

So do things the wrong way round like we did: buy a handful of airlocks (fermentation locks) and rubber corks to fit onto gallon jars, or if there is a lull in the supply of gallon jars, half-gallon jars. Winemaking is sociable from the very beginning: ask all your friends to save half-gallon jars for you. And never turn them down. There's no such thing as "too many".

(A note on capacities and sizes of bottles, jars, flagons, half-gallon and gallon jars, casks, crocks and carboys: they are confusing. Besides problems with conversions to metrics in an old fashioned industry slow to change its technical terms, there are difficulties with differences in American gallons and Imperial gallons. I use the term "gallon jar" to describe big glass jars that hold about 4 litres [more or less] with either one glass handle [American gallon] or two glass handles [Imperial gallon]. Some big glass "gallon" jars have wide necks and no handles at all but they're bigger than "half-gallon" jars, very few of which hold half a gallon. Usually printed somewhere in raised-up glass, they advertise a specific capacity: 2.25 litres, 2.5 litres, 1.8 litres. When I use the term "gallon" and "half-gallon" with reference to glass jars, I am describing a shape rather than a specific quantity. Wine and home-brew shops that sell the jars usually recognise those terms in the same way.)

When you have your fermentation locks, you are all set up for wine-making. The rest can be improvised.

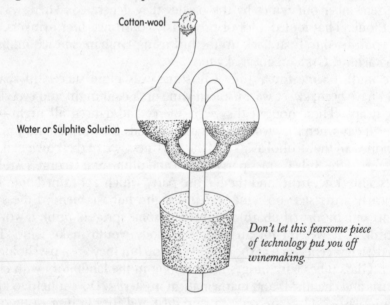

Cotton-wool

Water or Sulphite Solution

Don't let this fearsome piece of technology put you off winemaking.

Two unrelated incidents set us off on the winemaking trail. One, fair enough, was a delicious glass of orange wine. We had a huge surplus of oranges from our orchard in Kerikeri, but that alone was not enough to get us going. The ultimate stimulus was the glass jars themselves. We fell in love with a beautiful twisted green glass gallon pitcher and a magnificent five-gallon monster. This was oveseas. We had to find an excuse to bring them home, so we promised ourselves we would fill them with wine.

We have done that many times over and the glass jars are, to me, still part of the enchantment of winemaking. When the wine clears behind the glass to a pink, a golden, a full glowing amber or a fragile apple white, the translucent liquid is too pretty to drink. I get over that stage, but it's lovely while it lasts.

I think it is a mistake to get too technical about amateur winemaking. When a few basic procedures are mastered, an instinct develops enough to guide one between the boundaries of what is possible and what is unwise. There are a multitude of variables affecting wine. It is all very well to say the temperature must be within a certain range, but with no more than a normal house and its limited space, who can do that? So many little things make a difference: the chemical composition of the fruit, the quality of water, the type of yeast, balances of acids, of nutrients and of trace elements, and of course timing. It would be too frustrating to aim for perfection. A tasty drop is as much as we ask. And I would never expect to repeat a wine exactly. I leave that to real vintners.

When there were lots of gods walking about on the earth, which was just before the living memory of people several thousand years ago, wine brewed from honey (mead) was part of the staple diet. Only after humans in the warm climate around the Mediterranean organised themselves enough to grow grapes did fruit wine take over. All that is needed for wine is liquid, sugar, yeast, small quantities of yeast food, and time. Grapes

have all the yeast food that yeasts need and they also carry suitable wine yeasts on their skins. It would be difficult not to make wine with grapes gathered on a warm wet day and left a while to do their own thing.

Most other fruits and vegetables, with a little help, can produce conditions as friendly to yeasts.

Between the time when the gods did their shopping and now, millions of people must have made reasonable wines from millions of recipes. As with making cheese or bread, no special skill is needed: just timely encouragement and a sense of adventure. And patience.

Waiting is the worst part, especially at the beginning. We took immense trouble with our first wine. Four pages in our record book fuss about its progress. And all without conclusion: it never had a chance to mature because we had to "taste" it so often. More recent wines get a summary of ingredients, dates and a comment an flavour. It is easy to assess which wines were successful: they have gone. The not-so-good are still in the garage with faded labels. One day, when the supply runs low, we'll taste them all again and blend them.

If they are beyond hope, there is still their alcohol. Our local church Elder taught us to make a very simple still with a big paint tin, a pressure cooker and a plastic tube. Ten litres of sub-standard wine make two litres of alcohol and from that we can make a beautiful liqueur—but it is highly illegal so I can't tell you how.

Just in case you can find 50 per cent pure alcohol (pure alcohol diluted with water) here is a delicious orange and coffee liqueur recipe given to us by that same church Elder.

Currant Cat

(OR, TO THE PURISTS, QUARANTE QUATRE)

2 oranges	*1 litre pure alcohol*
44 coffee beans	*1 litre pure water*
44 sugar lumps	*44 days waiting time*

Cut a spiral around the skin of the oranges in order to insert the coffee beans. Combine all the ingredients in a jar with a tight-fitting lid. Stir occasionally. Use with discretion.

CHAPTER 1   CO-VINTNERS

Co-vintners add immeasurably to the pleasure of wine: the planning, the scavenging, the making, the blending and the drinking. And they make the waiting tolerable. There are fun jobs for all the family—and there are chores that are more fun when done together.

Our basic family unit these days is George and me. Others come and go. George is a "starter" and I am a "finisher". But for him, the wine would never begin. But for me, it would never grow to maturity. But for our wider family and friends, there would never be enough fruit, enough containers or enough drinkers. The loss of any would impoverish our wine experience.

Our record book tells its own story of who does what. My favourite meanders over the page like the Mouse's tail in *Alice in Wonderland*. It begins quite neatly in George's handwriting. It has the date: (my birthday) 11 December 1983. Its number: 17. And its description: Din's Birthday Babaco Wine (which incidentally turned out to be a revolting failure). The list of ingredients began to wander sideways. Two pages before is the clue to what was happening: Feijoa number 15, 27/4/82. The last entry on that page (in George's handwriting at the bottom of my page of scrawl) reads: "11/12/83. Racked and bottled. Lovely!"

To rack a wine means to siphon clear liquid off the dead yeast into a clean bottle. George didn't really feel like dealing with wine that evening, but the babacos we had been given (by Graham, the same neighbour who got frisky at our Pink Plonk party) were well past their best and one more hot day would have forced on us the unthinkable: to waste them. (No chooks in those days to clean up fruity excess.) So to make the slow job of forcing mouldy babaco gunk through a sieve more congenial, George

11/Dec # 17
Dins Birthday
<u>Babaco Wine</u>

Strained the gunk, then sieved. Added
3 Camden tablets because of "Wild Yeast."
Used starter bottle from Ginger Wine N° 11 —
made 4 gallons.

9 kg Babacos	2 tsp citric acid
2 gals water	1 tsp grape tannin
2 Camden tablets	12 lbs Raw Sugar
½ lb sultanas	

decided to rack at the same time the flavoursome feijoa (delicate pink, fresh and a delightful success).

We racked in the bathroom in those days. I was in the kitchen making myself a birthday cake. After a while, I heard George humming a little ditty to himself. Then song broke out. It got lustier and I went to investigate. For some reason, George can't seem to get the siphon going without taking a little taster . . . We had a very happy birthday party *à deux* with hot birthday cake and a drop of feijoa wine (fortunately we had put down 5 gallons) but the babaco wine never recovered. The tale of the Babaco Birthday wine still drips miserably off the bottom of the page complaining of "wild yeasts".

A lot of winemaking is bottle washing. We both do plenty of that. Thorough washing of everything to do with winemaking and rinsing containers in a sterilising solution is unglamorous but crucial. Since we rely on organisms we can't see to make our wine, we have to be aware of their equally tiny enemies, wild yeasts and bacteria. They cling to surfaces and float in the air. We can beat them by feeding up our own armies of "good" yeasts and giving them prime conditions to get established. Beware of wine recipes that leave the introduction of yeasts to chance. There are more baddies than goodies floating around.

The process of winemaking is all about helping the yeasts to grow. Each yeast is a one-cell fungus that grows on sugar. Like us, the fungus needs oxygen to breathe, a balanced diet and a temperature in the range that we too find comfortable.

Grape juice has the balanced diet yeast likes. Other fruit, vegetables and honey offer a satisfactory environment to the yeasts if a relatively small amount of malt or Marmite or Vegemite per 4-5 litres of liquid is added. If yeasts run out of food or oxygen or the liquid gets too hot or cold, they stop reproducing. Put the balance right and they begin again with new vigour.

The chemical descriptions of yeast food can be daunting but they are common substances to any chemist. For instance, citric acid is important to yeast, but lemon juice is a substitute. Packets of yeast nutrient are available at supply shops for winemakers, and at chemists, and they will contain a balance of nitrogen, phosphate and vitamins. For instance, the nutrients could be half citric acid, one third ammonium phosphate, and the rest potassium sulphide with small amounts of tartaric acid and magnesium sulphide. But non-chemists don't have to bother with that.

In fact, we get away with using very much less than our winemaking books suggest. I usually stir in a good dollop of goodies to start the yeast off on the right foot and let the yeasts find what they need after that. It is best to be more careful to begin with. If the yeast has all its food available, it might be more resistant to changes in temperature and keep on reproducing steadily. I have never seen that written anywhere, but I am using the (proven) theory that one (this one) works better on a cold day with porridge (sugar and cream) for breakfast and a whisky to go to bed.

Yeasts break down sugar to get the oxygen they need. If they can get oxygen from the air, they will be lazy about attacking the sugar. This is the reason that winemakers shut air out of bottles with fermentation locks. It is a modern refinement to induce yeasts to work more steadily and efficiently on our behalf, and to make more alcohol.

Alcohol and carbon dioxide are the waste products of the yeasts, produced in equal proportions when sugar is digested. To make a medium wine, the proportion of sugar needed to juice, or juice and water mix (the must), is 300 grams per litre. From this sugar, the yeasts will expel 150 grams as carbon dioxide and 150 grams as alcohol. This works out at about 15 per cent alcohol by weight per litre. Since alcohol is a preservative, that volume of alcohol is enough to keep the initial fruit juices from deteriorating. The precise alcohol content varies according to yeasts used, their working conditions and the recipe.

Old fashioned recipes do not suggest the use of fermentation locks. To begin a mead, many recipes tell you to use a wide shallow dish and to float a piece of toast carrying a cargo of yeast on top. To give the yeast free access to oxygen initially is a good way of encouraging vigorous reproduction, but if the supply is not reduced, the wine will end up sweet and without very high alcohol content or keeping qualities.

In the old days, winemakers had access to a variety of sizes in wooden casks. That gave them advantages and disadvantages against today's amateurs using glass jars. Wood cannot be cleaned as thoroughly as glass, so that meant that a good brew one year would probably leave a residue of palatable yeasts to start off the next year's wine. It also meant that a contaminated wine could blacklist a cask for ever. Casks are suitable because the wood insulates and keeps the temperature even, it is dark inside which yeasts enjoy, and a worthwhile quantity of wine can be made in a single container. The greater the volume of wine, the more steadily it works.

Probably wine has always been made in two stages: the dramatic beginning when yeasts celebrate their finds of sugar, warmth, moistness and good food with bubbles and hissing; then the long, steady work phase when they build up their families and clans over generations of yeasts until supplies run out and they rest, hibernate or die.

These primary and secondary fermentations are described as aerobic (with free oxygen) and anaerobic (closed vessel with fermentation lock). To change wine from one kind of fermentation to the next, and to keep it free from deposits of dead yeast (which affect the flavour), the wine has to be physically transferred from one bottle to another through plastic tubing. It takes time, but this is the human contribution to the process of winemaking. We spend hours clearing up the yeast's mess and are given in return its toxic waste-products to drink. A funny kind of arrangement, but who's knocking it?

CHAPTER 2   MAKING IT

A wine is my despairing response to a glut of fruit. One day, when I am completely organised and have nature under control, I will initiate wines: just a few litres of this and that, all perfectly cared for and served with a proper wine fancier's patter. In the meantime, we have to cope with bulk. At that point when we have gorged ourselves on plums and peaches, we've puréed them, juiced them and frozen them and still we rescue them just in time by the 20 litre bucket—then my thoughts turn to wine.

Our very first wine was from black Albany Surprise grapes. We moved from the orchard to the seaside in the winter. George took pity on a top-heavy old grapevine collapsed in the middle of the lawn. We propped it up with the whirligig washing line and that spring it gave us 45 kg of grapes. I still remember being shut in the basement with a new whimpering puppy (now my fat old Poo) and this huge vat of grapes while George went to a meeting. I had to squash every single grape by hand. I felt like Rumplestiltskin's would-be victim.

Everybody was ready with suggestions, from the "just chuck 'em in" variety to the ultra-technical. For our first few wines, we relied on C.J.J. Berry in *First Steps in Winemaking* (Amateur Winemaker Publication Ltd, 6th ed., 1979). His advice never let us down. We have evolved our own system now, but I still go back to Berry with my problems.

Plum wine is a good one to begin with. Our well-remembered Pink Plonk was plum—a glorious rich colour and it matured very quickly. It was begun from frozen plums in July and the last drop drunk in February the following year.

The freezer is an enormous help. Usually when the fruit glut is happening, everything else is happening too. I just wash the fruit, throw out anything bad, soft or wounded, bag up the rest and fill the freezer. I am forced to get the wine going at the very first opportunity because I run out of freezer space. Freezing the fruit begins the softening process. (With kiwi fruit there is an added advantage: if you take the furry fruit straight from the freezer and drop them in boiling water, their skins come off reasonably easily.)

You need a big plastic dustbin with a lid. Tip in the fresh or frozen fruit but keep a note of its weight. The simplest mnemonic for remembering proportions of fruit, sugar and water is in imperial measurements: to one gallon of water add 3 lb of fruit and 3 lb of sugar. Metrically, that is: to 4.5 litres of water, add 1.35 kg of fruit and 1.35 kg of sugar. If honey is to be substituted for sugar, increase the amount of honey to 1.7 kg. I normally mix honey and sugar, and mix types of sugar. There is no difference between white sugar and raw or brown sugar except in final flavour and colour. Raw sugar gives an amber glow which I enjoy, but for a pale apple or kiwi fruit, white sugar is the most delicate partner to the fruit.

Cover the frozen plums in the dustbin with white sugar and keep a note of how much you have used. Tip in any frozen lemon juice or orange juice or other small amounts of fruit you are bored with in the freezer. I am better at freezing things than remembering to use them—a bit of a squirrel—so robust bulk wines like plum give me an opportunity for a clear out.

If you are using fruit straight from the tree, cut out any bad or pecked or wasp-eaten bits, wash the fruit, and pour boiling water over it, remembering to make a note of all the quantities. Boiling water helps both to soften the fruit and to kill wild yeasts and bacteria. The aim at this stage is to extract as much flavour out of the fruit as possible and whichever method you find most convenient is best. Cut up the fruit now or later. Take out the stones now or when you strain the juice. If boiling water is a problem, use cold but dissolve a couple of Camden tablets (just ask the chemist) to discourage invaders until you get your yeast established. (You could put in wine yeast at this stage, but let's pretend you choose not to.)

We leave the fruit at least overnight, and often for three or more days, covered with sugar or water, but we check it often. There are two enemies: fruit flies which carry the micro-organisms that turn wine into vinegar, and moulds (wild yeasts). Keep a close-fitting lid, or cloth and weight on the container of softening fruit. The sugar should keep the frozen fruit safe from moulds while it defrosts. If the fruit is in water, stir it morning and evening.

Initially I was frightened off by the use of any kind of chemicals in winemaking and I would still prefer to do without. But they are seductive. When I tried just a little of the pectin-destroying enzyme to help break down hard plums it halved my work at the squashing and sieving stage. It also made the wine clear very quickly. Over to you on that one, but the pectin-breaking enzyme is now my friend.

I was much taken with Mr Berry's comment on making wine in bulk. He writes: "It is very little more trouble to make five gallons than to make one (and it lasts nearly twice as long)!" So I usually begin with about 10 kg of fruit flesh and end up with about 18 variously assorted "half-gallon" bottles (half-gallon capacity ranging from 1.7 litres to 2.5 litres).

Starter Bottle

I'm not very smart about thinking ahead. Decisions tend to be "now or never". Proper winemakers plan their campaign and make a "starter bottle" two days ahead of the time that they will need it. With the bulk-steeping method of covering the whole fruit with either sugar or water (or a mixture of both if you feel inclined), there is enough time to get a starter bottle going while the fruit is softening.

A starter bottle gives the wine yeasts their recruits for the war against wild yeasts. It is a nursery for incubating healthy youngsters. If you have an army of rapidly multiplying friendly yeasts to tip into the wine must (that is, the mixture of juices, sugar and water which will become the wine), the wild yeasts will be overwhelmed and surrender without doing damage.

Recipes for starter bottles are legion. They can be varied to suit what you have on hand. Basically they need sugar, water, food for the yeast and the yeast itself in a suitable temperature. Most winemaking books insist that the solution be sterile (boiled) before the yeast is added but over the years we have neglected this instruction without dire results. Since both malt extract and Marmite or Vegemite have the nutrients that yeasts like, they can make the basis for starter bottles. Use a tablespoon of malt, a tablespoon of sugar, the juice of a lemon and a cup of water. Bring them to the boil and cool before adding a teaspoon of yeast. Pour them into a bottle and plug the top with a wad of cotton wool. Or stir half a teaspoon of Marmite or Vegemite into hot water instead of the malt. Keep the bottle pleasantly warm (up to 21°C) and bubbles will rise and gradually it will get a froth up. Shake it occasionally.

That, actually, is not what we do.

Happy yeasts make alcohol, but they are not wine connoisseurs. They don't have to drink the stuff! A wine that tastes good needs a balance of acids (too much and it tastes medicinal or bitter, too little and there is no tang to it) and it needs tannin to help it clear and give it interest. You can make wine without tannin but you'd be better off drinking a glass of water.

Grapes have a good balance of acids and their skins have the necessary tannin. Vegetables and flowers have too little in the way of acids, rhubarb has too much. Since we were never sure which fruits had the right balance of acids and tannin, we developed the habit of putting everything into the starter bottle to play safe. The system has worked well for us up to now but could to with refining.

For our starter bottles, we squeeze a cup of grapefruit juice (or whatever citrus is around the house). In theory the best juice to use is the one that the wine will be made from, but two days before starting the wine we don't usually have enough of that particular fruit's juice. Since we're making about 36 litres at a time, a cup of citrus juice doesn't interfere with the flavour of the final wine. We add a cup of water (spring water— we're lucky: beware of heavily treated water) and half a cup of raw sugar. Then, to be on the safe side, we add half a teaspoon of tartaric acid and either half a teaspoon of bought grape tannin or a cup of cold strong tea. Half a teaspoon of granulated yeast with half a teaspoon of nutrient settles nicely in that mixture and gives us a good embryo work force.

Sterilising

Keeping things clean is a part of our routine—"deep clean" that is, not just surface clean.

We are taking chances by not boiling the starter bottle mixture before putting in the yeasts, but because our regular cleansing programme is thorough we know there are few places where bugs could become a threat.

For instance: as soon as a bottle of wine is finished, we rinse it. Then it is washed in a regular fashion and thoroughly rinsed to get out residue detergent. Before I put it away, I make a solution with a Camden tablet melted in boiling water. Camden tablets are sodium metabisulphite, a safe and easy-to-use chemical that provides the harder-to-use sulphur dioxide as a sterilising agent. If Camden tablets are not available, sodium or potassium metabisulphite is an alternative. Dissolve 115 grams of the metabisulphite in 1.5 litres of warm water. Sealed and kept in a cool dark place, it will last about six months until the smell weakens or it discolours. One teaspoon (5 ml) is equal to one Camden tablet.

When the water cools, I swill the bottle and put a top on it. Before I use it, the botttle is again rinsed with a Camden solution. That routine has become so much a habit that it is no longer a chore. We also use Camden tablets to sterilise the must before adding the starter bottle to it. And we were neurotic about fruit flies, any flies, any nasties. The animals are definitely never allowed anywhere near food at any of its stages.

These precautions are so natural to us and so much a part of the modern understanding of hygiene, that if I forget to say: "wash hands" or "sterilise bottle" it doesn't mean that the action can be neglected. Obviously, it is necessary to be aware of what your plastic dustbin held before you pile in the wine fruit. Bacteria from milk or meat products could ruin the wine. You'd give it a good scrub and sterilise it.

Back to your plums ... Your plums have now unfrozen. The 1.5 kg of sugar you sprinkled over your 12 kg of plum flesh has dissolved and an attractive red juice is oozing up the sides of the dustbin. You were a bit behind schedule and have only just prepared your starter bottle, but never fear, there are at least two days of work ahead for you and your softening agents. The plums have to give up all their juiciness. You have already written down in your new Wine Records book the weight of the fruit and made a calculation of the water and sugar you will need. Use up some of the water ration (not too much: remember, all the must you make now will have to go through filters and that is a slow job if there is a lot of liquid) and pour boiling water over the fruit. If the plums are well ripened and of a soft variety, their flesh should be easy to squash between your fingers after an overnight soaking. If they are of a tougher variety, use the pectin-destroying enzyme to soften them so that squashing doesn't become finger-punishing hard work. Wait until the water cools, then add one teaspoon (5 ml) of Pectolin or Pectase to 5 kg of fruit. Leave it to work for 24 hours, stirring when you pass by (at least twice daily).

It is a good precaution to stir in a Camden tablet solution while the must is at this stage. It is vulnerable to all kinds of moulds and air-carried bacteria, and the fruit probably already carried on its skin the dreaded vinegar bacteria. Small fruits such as blackberries and boysenberries are often heavily infected—they need careful picking over for overripe or mouldy segments. The recommended rate is 5 millilitres of sterilising solution (one Camden tablet) per 5 litres of must. In cooler weather and where bulk must is being carefully tended, you could probably get away with fewer tablets—but no less than two.

When the fruit is soft, get everybody you can find to wash their hands and help you squash it.

The moment I look forward to most in the winemaking process is tipping in the starter bottle. To me, that is when the watery, fruity mush becomes wine. It's not drinkable, but the potential is there. The knowledge that the magic moment is near keeps me going through the next stage: sieving and filtering.

FROM PULPY MESS TO WINE MUST
Getting the juice off the pulp takes time. It would be logical to begin experiments in winemaking with small quantities and then the straining operation would be no hassle. The job of filtering 12 kg of fruit by hand through a modest household nylon sieve tends to get put off till the last possible minute—which is not always a bad thing because the "minute" (couple of hours) is usually in the evening after some of the fruit flies have gone to bed. Some. Never all.

Fruit flies are marvellous beasties. They manufacture themselves spontaneously out of the air in a sealed and sterilised room. They are just there, where there were none before. They are enemies and cannot be allowed at any stage to come into contact with must. And they're cunning: while you are chasing one around the kitchen with murder in your heart, six more materialise.

I cover the floor with newspaper and set up two 20 litre plastic buckets (my nylon sieve can just straddle one without falling in and the other is for waste strained pulp) and a big white plastic vat with a lid—all well scrubbed and sterilised. On hand, apart from the sieve, is a coarse plastic colander with a handle, a glass measuring jug for scooping out the pulpy must, a plastic 5 litre measuring jug to measure the final quantity of must and a long plastic stirring spoon. Those are pieces of equipment that we have gradually acquired. We didn't begin with them all and substitutes are in order. One day I might find a large sieve and that will speed things along.

A wine press is an excellent help for large quantities, but messy. The simple hand method I find quicker in the long run, unless really huge quantities are involved, as for cider.

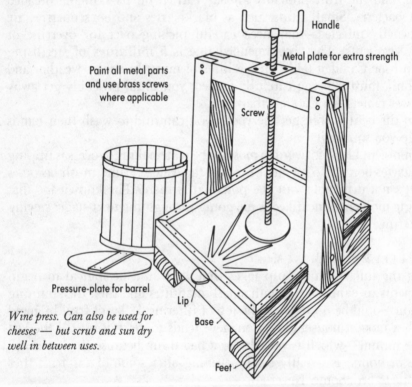

Handle

Metal plate for extra strength

Paint all metal parts and use brass screws where applicable

Screw

Pressure-plate for barrel

Lip

Wine press. Can also be used for cheeses — but scrub and sun dry well in between uses.

Base

Feet

If we are aiming for a wine of medium sweetness (usually the most popular) and we have used 12 kg of fruit (including pits), I would expect to use 10 kg of sugar or its equivalent. (Our record book is in a mixture of metric and imperial measurements which makes the mathematics tricky but the mnemonics easy: for example, for our last plum wine which was pleasantly dry, I have noted that we used 27 lb of frozen red and white plums to 9 gallons of juice and water and 9 kg of sweetener.)

More sugar can always be added later in the process of winemaking. Many books say it should be. With this particular plum wine, 1.5 kg has already been sprinkled on the plums. I would pour another 6 kg into the big white plastic vat and cover it with enough boiling water (measured) to dissolve it while I am doing the sieving. (The rest of the sugar can be added at the various rackings, or to give a boost if fermentation slows down.)

By this time, I am so well organised that there is nothing left with which I can distract myself and I have to start pouring the pulp. I hold the plastic colander above the sieve with one hand, to collect the larger globs and let the nylon mesh sift out the smaller particles. Both clog up rapidly. Set up the newspapers near the kitchen sink so that the waste bucket is beside you and the cold tap within reach. Some books advise filtering through muslin, but that would take more than my quota of patience.

While I am going through this routine, I am thinking rebellious thoughts like: "What's so glamorous about winemaking?" but actually I just enjoy making a fuss and soon it's all over. The juice is all in the buckets and the waste ready for the compost (a *small* amount to the chooks) and by then George has done the dishes and made up the fire and we can feel pleasantly virtuous over a hot drink.

The sugar has melted in the big white vat. We measure in the juicy must, put in the rest of the water, making it just warm for the yeast, adjust citric acid, yeast nutrients and tannin for 10 gallons, and the happy moment arrives: we tip in the frothy starter bottle and stir. The wine is on its way. If we weren't so tired, we could finish the process, but the myriad of junior yeasts are content to expand from their crowded nursery and make whoopee overnight, splashing about gorging themselves on sugar in the new spacious maternity unit. So long as they are tightly covered against fruit fly attack, we can leave them. If the night is not warm we leave the stove glowing.

By the morning there is a definitely "winey" smell when we lift the lid. Brown bubbles have tried to climb up the side of the white vat. There is a sizzle and hiss as we lift the lid.

Pouring the new wine into clean "gallon" jars is a pleasant task. Fill only to the shoulder of the bottle so that there is plenty of air available and space for the wine to froth. Sterilise corks and airlocks, half-fill the airlocks with Camden solution, fit them to the jars and wad the outlets with cotton wool to stop the more determined bugs from taking a dive through the water.

If the temperature is warm and you have miscalculated the space for expansion, you could soon have a vigorous mess. Our last plum was particularly lusty. It frothed up its air locks and blew out the cotton wool. If an airing cupboard is your only warm place to store the bottles (there will be about 14 cumbersome, heavy bottles by this stage, all with high airlocks), it is best *not* to move the sheets and blankets to the shelf below the wine. I was caught that way once—brown sludge over everything.

First ferment can go on for a few days or weeks. It can be far less dramatic than I have described. It can, as with our last plum, keep going crazily for well over a month, although that is unusual. Each time I racked the wine to try to quieten it down, it blew more bubbles up through its airlocks. It was doing the same six months later!

Racking

Although racking is the next official stage in the winemaking process, concentrate for a while on your scavenging team. Encourage, bribe, threaten—whatever works: you will very soon need up to 20 "half-gallon" bottles.

Wine bottles that still smell of wine are the best. Soak off the old labels, wash out thoroughly and prise off the tin necklace. I treated extra-large spirit bottles with suspicion when they were first brought to me, but used them in an emergency and have found them to be satisfactory although I wouldn't trust them to take the kind of pressure that wine can build. With some trepidation I also used vinegar bottles. Well washed they were okay too, but anything that stays cloudy after it is washed or smells oily or is in any way suspicious, I jettison.

Racking soon becomes a way of life. We began making wine in 1980. I calculate that we have made about 340 gallons (1530 litres) of wine. If each were racked an average of four times, that means we have coaxed 1360 gallons, or 6120 litres of wine along a thin plastic tube 5 mm across. We would have washed at least 3000 bottles. Believe it or not, we've drunk it all!

When the first dramatic aerobic fermentation calms, the wine is still cloudy but it is usually possible to see through the glass a line at the bottom where sediment has fallen. This is a mixture of fruit particles and dead yeast cells, called lees. If the wine is left to sit on that mixture for too long it can spoil the flavour.

Some books suggest that as many as seven rackings are necessary per wine, others say to bottle after the second. Ours gets three or four depending on how the wine behaves. If it is a really tasty wine, it gets drunk before it gets a chance to be racked the fourth time. It goes from the jar to the glass—sometimes via a decanter for elegance! If it is not good, it waits through more rackings in its jar. What is the point of bottling a wine if it is not delicious? In other words, our wines have never yet got beyond the half-gallon jar stage. They are strictly wines for sharing and drinking.

It is worth investing in a little plastic tap to fit on the end of about a metre of plastic tubing. To rack wine from lees, put the full bottle (carefully without disturbing the sediment) at a higher level than an empty container—bench to floor will do. (Winemaking shops sell gadgets about a metre high that hold jars above the workbench. They save backache and make it easier to see the line of sediment.) Put the bare end of the plastic tube into the full bottle, open the tap, bend below the full bottle and bring the wine towards you with suction. When it has travelled up the tube and has begun to descend towards you, you can aim the tap at the empty jar instead of your mouth. Of course, there are those of us who stay there just that little bit longer to test the wine . . . Usually for the first few rackings it is pretty horrible, but you can get used to anything with practice, so George tells me!

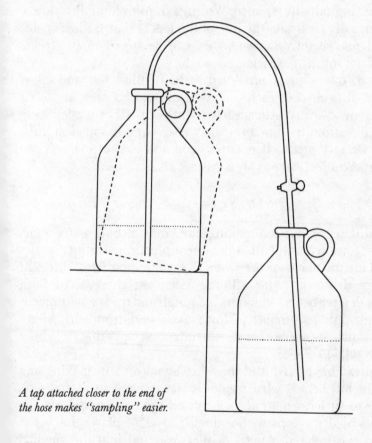

A tap attached closer to the end of the hose makes "sampling" easier.

When to rack? Berry says to wait until the wine clears after the primary fermentation. We find that impractical. We need the gallon jars for the next wine queueing up behind. Our first racking is usually three to six weeks from tipping in the starter bottle. By that time, the murk has cleared enough to give a hint of the demarcation between lees and wine.

Wine

I hate wasting anything. At this stage about a quarter of the container looks as though it is lees. I siphon down to that quarter, take out the siphon tube, then tip the lees into another bottle, very gently until only the finer, harder, white lees are left. Those have to be thrown away, but I collect the dubious murk from all the jars and keep that separately under an airlock until it has settled further and there is more wine to siphon off.

Unless you have a crazy, over-enthusiastic wine like our last plum, the wine should be ready to settle down to its slower secondary fermentation, the anaerobic one. Fill the botttles to within 2 cm of the bung, top up the Camden water in the airlocks and wait until the colour and lovely clarity of the wine is gradually revealed. Within a couple of months (slower in winter) it is usually clear and the line of the lees is sharp. Rack again. These lees need not be thrown away, they can be stored in the fridge and used as a starter for the next wine.

At this racking, our wine is promoted to half-gallon jars and taken away for storage. It is checked each time we run out of a brew and need something different to drink. After a few months, if it has a good taste but is still working strongly—has a raw fizzy taste—and has made a thick deposit of lees, we rack again. If it tastes good and has no fizziness, we rack and drink it. You just *have* to keep tasting!

Storage

There is a big difference between making our kinds of bulk party wine, and making wine for, say, competition or more sophisticated dinner parties than we have. Our treatment of the wines is cavalier and I feel diffident about associating Mr Berry's name with the system we have evolved. Both he and the wines deserve better—but ours is a rough and ready environment and survival is the only requirement. Most make it and, from what I have observed, are as much appreciated as those tender beverages that have been properly mollycoddled.

All that is a preamble to say: read the other books on winemaking and do what they say, but here is what we do! It was too expensive and took too much space to fit fermentation locks on all the half-gallon jars. To begin with, we sealed the tops with a double layer of plastic foodwrap secured with an elastic band. After a while we found that this method had two disadvantages. As the wine fermented, the carbon dioxide lifted the food wrap and stretched it so that too much air was let in. The other problem was worse: mice and wasps punctured the plastic and let in fruit flies. So we did what all the books told us not to do: we used the plastic foodwrap and then screwed the tin caps back on the half-gallon bottles,

116

leaving them just loose enough to let carbon dioxide escape. That works well for us but it is not an approved method.

Before the jars go into store, it is important to label them. We write the type of wine, the date it was born and its number. The number tallies with our record book: we could make several plum, peach or kiwi fruit wines in a season and eventually we hope to find the perfect recipe by comparing results from each batch. (Vain hope, but one has to have ambition!) It is very easy to forget over the course of months and years which wine was which, and very frustrating. Even more irritating is to have gone to the trouble of labelling and find that the ink has faded into invisibility.

The ideal storage area is dark (with a light for viewing your bottles), cool, vermin-free and easy of access. Even more ideal would be a place near a tap and bench where the wines could be racked without having to transport them down muddy paths and up stairs. A compromise is the usual answer. We have wines everywhere—some long forgotten, some regularly stumbled over. At last I have found my dream shed. All I have to do is insulate the roof with polystyrene to keep it cool, get rid of the ingrained waste-oil smell and keep out the rats and ants . . . it was the concrete floor that attracted me. Have to start somewhere.

Temperature and Time

Commercial wine producers take control of both temperature and time. They have to achieve repeatable results within a limited period in order to please their market and their shareholders. With expensive and sophisticated machinery, they make water into wine on demand. The amateur still has to rely on a miracle—a complex series of miracles. Besides all the chemical reactions happening in conjunction with the organic workings of the yeasts, varying temperatures tease and influence all the interactions.

At all stages, what happens depends on temperature. Yeasts are survivors and can withstand considerable fluctuations in temperature, but like human animals, they operate better at some temperatures than at others. Their comfortable range is about the same as ours. Above 38°C they die, and below 10°C they hibernate. They multiply fast when it is warm (21°C), work steadily when it is cooler (16°C) and plod along doggedly as the temperature gets cold, towards 10°C.

Wine needs all these stages in sequence; warm for the first ferment, cooler for the second and chilly for a slow maturing in the store room. The problem is that in very few parts of the world does the temperature stay steady. We have hot days and cool nights, cold snaps, heat waves,

Wine

unpredictable patches of wind and rain and, unless we have immense stainless steel vats with thermostats, the temperature of our wine rises and falls and the yeasts stop and start their work.

That is part of the reason why two wines made to the same recipe by the same person using fruit from the same tree on consecutive years are different. Another part of the reason is that the fruit has had different temperature during its life, more or less sun, more or less rain, a variation in available food . . . A recipe in a wine book can only offer guidelines, not a formula, which is fortunate: it gives scope to the scientist, the artist, the craftsman and me.

The obvious time to make wines is when the fruit is ripe at the end of summer. If climates were temperate and reliable, there would be hot days for the rapid ferment stage, cooler days after the first racking and long cold winter days for storage. But we like to make wine all the year around because we drink it all the year round—and we wouldn't have a hope of using up our surplus fruit if we limited our "season".

As always, we reached a compromise. During its extreme youth the wine is allowed to stay beside the kitchen stove. As a teenager it is confined to the wash house. While it reaches maturity it is banished to the garage, under the house or the shed. It is worth taking some trouble to find places where your wines can work at the proper speed for their stage of development. A continued rapid ferment in a hot environment is dramatically satsifying for the winemaker: he can see those bubbles rising and know something is happening, but the wine works itself to death and is flat and dull. Wine left semi-dormant in a place too cold takes up valuable space and containers. A cheap cupboard made from car cases and a hundred-watt electric light bulb could rescue it from a lingering death.

However carefully you tend them, some wines are rebellious. They stay cloudy or their ferments stick. Time and temperature usually cure both these problems although there are tricks to use if patience is short.

HAZES AND STUCK FERMENTS
In a lot of recipes, fruit has to be boiled to soften it. Starches and pectins are released that can take some time to sink into the lees. Other times, wines from previously satisfactory recipes play up, stick and refuse to clear.

We had a peach wine that stayed obstinately muddy from January, when the ferment began, until August. We could have waited. We could have tried the trick of moving it to either a hotter or a colder temperature. It would probably have cleared. But we were bored with it and needed the jars. There was no pressure in some of the airlocks although the mixture was sweet. (That is a tremendous advantage of fermentation locks: a

118

displacement of water shows that some carbon dioxide is being made and the wine is "working" even when no bubbles are visible.)

Our August record book entry reads: "Slow working. Muddy. Added Pectolin and yeast nutrient and re-racked. Sept. 19: Clear, sweet, acceptable. Racked into 13 ½Gs'. Blended with dry Plum No. 33. OK for Players Bonfire Halloween party."

If the haze hadn't cleared with that treatment, we could have added white of egg to help precipitate the suspended particles, or isinglass or bentonite, or we could have filtered it. More likely, since we were in no hurry, we could have hidden it away in jars until it behaved itself. It might have turned out to be a far better wine.

When fermentation stops prematurely, there are three possibilities: a drop in temperature; the yeasts have been swamped with too much sugar; or they have run out of nutrients. All those are easily remedied. A good stir is often a help or a racking to allow in a little oxygen to give the yeast a boost.

Real problems have arrived when the wine has stopped working and tastes nasty. If it tastes like vinegar, vinegar fly (*Drosophila melanogaster*) and vinegar bacillus (*Mycoderma aceti*) have done it. There is no remedy. (How could there be with names like that?) Be proud of your delicious home-made salad dressing made with secret formula wine vinegar.

If it tastes like medicine, there was too much acid in the fruit, or too little, or too much tannin. We have had that problem with lemon wine and rhubarb wine. I should have read the recipes more carefully and added calcium carbonate to counteract the acid (or tannin) in the early stages, except that other brews made to the same recipes turned out fine. The lemon we used to make the Currant Cat. The rhubarb is still in a 10 gallon drum: I have just tipped in half a bottle of Eno's fruit salts— it is an antacid and we have nothing to lose: Alka Seltzer is my next weapon.

A white powdery scum on the top of the bottle is bad news. Act quickly, or the wine will turn to carbon dioxide and then to water. Take off the film (caused by bacteria and an interaction with too much oxygen), filter the wine through filter papers or cotton wool and begin the ferment again with fresh yeast and probably more sugar.

Adjustments and refinements are possible. If you want a white wine made whiter, try adding dried-milk powder (casein) and then racking it. If the wine is flat and insipid, add strong tea or grape tannin. If your wine has darkened after contact with the air, a Camden tablet solution will stabilise it; darkening because of iron in the water can be put right with citric acid. Too dry: add sugar; too sweet: try adding lemon juice, or blend with a dry wine. If Eno's fruit salts does not solve the problems

Wine

of our rhubarb wine, I boil up honey with spices, tip in some of the lemon wine and serve it gently warmed as "mulled wine".

If you have made a wine in bulk and, when you taste it, it is just perfect, there is a way to stop fermentation right there: add one dissolved Camden tablet per 4.5 litres. So far we have never done that. We prefer to have a party and drink it.

Hydrometer

The purchase of a hydrometer indicates that you really mean business as a winemaker. Through its proper use (again, I refer you to Mr Berry), you can calculate the exact amount of sugar you should use and the alcohol content of your wine. We used a hydrometer for our first wine. Our notes are impressively technical.

Blending

Some wines are super just as they are. If we had time to be more fussy with our winemaking, more would be that way. But blending is perfectly acceptable in winemaking circles. We blend (or rather, George does) to please the palate, for social reasons and because it is fun.

The palate is a personal affair: his is more sensitive than mine and I have never disagreed with his judgement. The social reasons depend on who is drinking our mix. For youngsters and ageing aunts we usually mix on the sweet side and as colourfully as possible. For guests with discernment, we mix dry and include a few surprises. If there's a whole gang we usually mix a little bit sweeter than our own preference because it is more-ish and makes the party go.

When nothing is ready, nothing is delicious and we look at rows and rows of pretty, useless bottles, we decide on a blending session with five or six different bottles. By the time we have found the ideal blend they all taste pretty good.

Records

Keep them. It's worth it. (You might want to write a book one day!)

CHAPTER 3   HONEY WINE

Honey wine is the ultimate. Before there were men in the world to make fruit wine, the gods dined off honey mead. They called it Amrita, Ambrosia and Nectar. (Oh dear. Quite beside the point, that reminds me of my very first pantomime. The funny man said: "He took Ambrosia and

Nect'har" and everybody laughed. I asked my Mummy why and she said:
"Never mind dear, you'll understand when you're a big girl.") Even the
word for mead, from the Sanskrit "medhu" is found in so many ancient
and modern languages that it had to be among the first batch of words
anybody made up.

It's not only being old that makes mead special, but what it does for
the drinker. There are too many stories from too many civilisations about
the qualities of mead and honey for them all to be dismissed. An awful
lot of people have certainly believed that an extraordinary long life and
vigorous old age, robust health, fertility and unusual sexual potency are
the rewards of regular mead quaffing. In Bryan Acton and Peter Duncan's
useful booklet, *Making Mead*, they make delicate references to orgiastic
uses of mead through the ages and on an international scale. Mead, before
anyone understood beekeeping or the chemistry of fermentation, was a
gift from heaven and had to be shared and enjoyed with proper wholehearted
religious abandon.

For a long time, mead was reserved for religious celebrations. Although
its use was widespread, honey and mead were never in abundant supply.
Harvesting the honeycomb from wild bees was a difficult and
uncomfortable job, and fermenting the honey to make a drinkable alcoholic
beverage was a specialist skill.

Monks in medieval monasteries in Europe began to keep bees in
worthwhile numbers because wax made by the bees was considered the
most pure for church candles. (Because bees were never seen to copulate,
they were therefore all virgin and therefore suitable servants to make wax
to burn for the Virgin Mother.) Mead-making skills were refined in the
monasteries and it was only in the 1800s, when sugar became cheaper
than honey, that fruit wines and beers became the popular beverages.

Mead had its own patron saint. It probably needed one. Saint
Bartholomew used to be invoked to bless the new mead on 24 August—
a good time in the northern hemisphere, just after the honey crop was
gathered in. Before the chemical side of fermentation was sufficiently
analysed, meadmakers must have suffered the frustration of many failures.
Honey on its own is low on the nutrients that yeast needs to complete
its job. The yeasts would often have died of starvation before they had
completed the job of breaking down all the honey sugars into alcohol
and carbon dioxide. That would have meant a very sweet drink, low in
alcohol. Often, mead was mixed with spices, probably to offset the cloying
sweetness. Nowadays, by giving yeasts proper food, we can make mead
as dry as we wish.

Extracting honey from the comb is a messy business. Even with modern
centrifuge extractors, filters clog up continually with wax, pollen, bits

of bee and crystallised honey. All that has to be washed off—and it seems a terrible shame to waste it. Before extractors, honey would have been filtered through cloths rather than nylon mesh and there would have been even more waste.

Water and honey would eventually have made some kind of a mead, left in a warm place, but the monasteries had one other asset: their wooden barrels. They probably stored their honey washings in barrels already impregnated with suitable yeasts from years of meadmaking and the transition from water to wine would become an annual miracle. Sterilised plastic pails can't be relied upon to perform the same miracle.

The old-fashioned way to make mead was to saturate the "washings" from honey filters and pails and extracting equipment until it was dense enough to float an egg, with an area the size of a coin showing above water. That kind of primitive hydrometer showed the proper balance of water to sugars in which yeasts could thrive.

Honey has active antibacterial properties so even in the unhygienic environment before people realised it was a good idea to wash their hands before touching foods, honey wine would have been safe to drink. On the other hand, there are many different kinds of yeast that are attracted by a warm honey and water home to raise their young. Some make pleasant wine, some less pleasant. Some monasteries were famed for their mead and others had to find a different hobby. Good yeasts were monastery treasures and jealously guarded.

These days we have more control. Various strains of yeast have been isolated and we can choose which we will introduce into our honey must.

There are two strong schools of thought about whether or not honey should be boiled. There are those who champion "natural" mead saying that there is a virtue in leaving wax, pollen and "extras" to filter out of the wine naturally, and others who recommend boiling honey to kill "wild" yeasts and skim off the impurities. We have tried both ways and both are good.

Brother Adam of Buckhurst Abbey and Brian Dennis are acknowledged modern authorities on meadmaking. They combined to write a book, *Mead and Honey Wines*, which promotes boiling. For a small quantity of mead, boiling the honey means that results will be reliable and repeatable. Recipes vary considerably on the recommended length of time for boiling the honey. Some say just bring the honey to the boil and skim, others say to boil for an hour. There are disadvantages with both: too short a boiling means that particles of wax stay in suspension and are a nuisance in clearing the wine; and too long a boiling changes the flavour of the honey.

Ten minutes at a gentle rolling boil is a reasonable compromise. The point at which the honey comes to the boil is the danger moment. If left a second too long, brown froth mounts the sides of the pan and cascades over like a volcano erupting, and it is very hot and unpleasant to clean up. Skim off the scum when it has changed colour but before it overflows, and the boiling honey is no more trouble.

To make mead in quantity it just isn't practical to boil all the honey or even to use boiling water. We have to rely on Camden tablets to discourage unwanted yeasts. Bryan Acton and Peter Duncan describe clearly the rules of modern meadmaking. Unlike monks in the old days, we can help nature along. Using honey and water only, meads in the old days could take as long as eight years to ferment and mature. Now, with good, filtered honey and if we buy suitable yeast, add nutrients and balance tannin and acids, we can get a satisfying product in a year or two. Even so, for superior meads, a fuller flavour develops with longer maturing. (That's hearsay. We have never managed to keep any of our better tasting wines long enough.)

Things can get very technical. Acton and Duncan favour a chemical approach to meadmaking. They suggest that "advanced" winemakers would use "refined" techniques using ammonium phosphate, potassium phosphate, magnesium sulphate, Vitamin B_1, tannic acid, malic acid and citric acid. They discourage as a "beginner's" approach the use of rough equivalents: lemon, Marmite, Epsom salts, nutrient tablets and strong tea. When we finally summon up courage to fill our plastic 44 gallon drum with mead, I will be happy to brand myself a "beginner" rather than "advanced"—if I can find 88 lemons at the right moment.

Straight mead is made from honey only. Metheglyn used to be popular when yeasts were poorer and mead was more of a sweet ale than a wine. It was made by adding cloves, mace, cinnamon, ginger and the rind of orange and lemon to straight mead to give flavour and interest.

Metheglyns are still fun to make and excellent for mulled wine in the winter, but they have their problems. The spices are inclined to cloud the wine so that it takes a long time to clear, and since all honeys taste different, it is quite difficult to get the right balance between honey and spice flavours. If making a few experiments appeals to you, bring a selection of spices to the boil, simmer them for a while and when they have cooled, filter, add yeast and nutrients and make wine as for mead. I would advise small quantities to start with.

Acton and Duncan trace the origin of the word metheglyn to a Welsh word meaning medicine. Herbs were used rather than spices and the drink was consumed medicinally among the Welsh. In fact it sounds much more like medicine than a social drink when we read a recipe for an ounce (about 30 grams) each of seven different herbs including cowslip, elderflower and rosemary. You could try caraway seeds, marjoram or lemon balm, but my approach would be the safer one: make the mead first, then experiment by infusing a little of each herb afterwards.

Hippocras was another medicinal mead made with herbs, but also with grapes. It was particularly popular at Greek and Roman festivals because honey enriched with the grape juice was a better environment for the yeasts and they could produce more alcohol. Apparently our wine today made with sweeter grapes and good yeasts reaches the same strength as the hippocras: about 15 per cent alcohol. Piment was the grape and honey mix without herbs.

Soma was another mead mixed with herbs, but which herbs they were we don't know. The gods drank it and any human who managed to steal it and drink achieved (or suffered) immortality. Another food of the gods was haoma, fermented honey mixed with hallucinogens.

Cyser was a particularly popular drink when the monasteries in England had control of the liquor market. Honey and apple juice made a strong drink and apple juice was cheap compared with honey.

Then there was sack. In books we had to read at school, especially Shakespeare, they were always talking about sack. Now I know what it is. It is a sweet mead using 2.5 kg of honey to 4.5 litres of water with rue and fennel root added. I'll make some when my little rue plant expands a bit.

Melomels we make all the time. With our lifestyle, we're back to the position of the middle ages: homegrown honey is cheaper than imported sugar, so we use honey. We boil the honey in water before adding it to the fruit because we have found that the wine takes too long to clear otherwise. We get some lovely flavours if we balance the honey and the type of fruit. Manuka goes particularly well with our plum and peach. Clover brings out the flavour of kiwi fruit.

At this point I should list some recipes. I have a record book with 37 successful wines we have made, mostly in huge quantities and nearly all of them have been drunk with pleasure. But we have never repeated a single wine. We simply use whatever fruit we have and follow the general principles of winemaking. I don't consider any of our lists of ingredients and procedures to be proper recipes, even though they have worked for us. I would rather refer you to the many winemaking books so that you can experiment under more expert guidance.

But I would do so with strong encouragement, saying: don't be daunted. Winemaking is sociable and fun. With due regard to hygiene, practically every effort can be made drinkable, even if it needs some blending and imaginative presentation. And beginners can make as good a wine as the experts, with a little luck and patience. The craft of wine making is fascinating. One day I'm going to learn to do it properly.

The following summary of steps in bulk winemaking (based on bulk Pink Plum Plonk from 12 kg plums, 12 kg sugar/honey and 36 litres of water) may be useful:

- Buy fermentation locks and a packet of Camden tablets.

- Buy a winemaking book—preferably C.J.J. Berry's. There are many subtleties beyond the scope of our homely experiments.

- Ask friends to collect "half-gallon" glass jars.

- Assemble large plastic containers with lids, and "gallon" glass jars.

- Either: take plums out of freezer, note their weight and cover them with sugar (amount recorded) in a large, lidded plastic container.
  Or: pick wash and trim out imperfections of fresh ripe fruit, weigh it, and cover with sugar (amount recorded) in a large plastic container with a lid.

- Make a starter bottle and keep it in a warm place for at least 48 hours.

- When plums are partially unfrozen, cut roughly. Pour on measured quantity of boiling water and add 2 dissolved Camden tablets.

- If plums are still hard after 2 days, add pectolin and leave further 24 hours stirring twice daily. Keep covered.

- Add lemon juice, or put in cut lemons with frozen plums.

- Squash plums (the hardest part—there are fruit crushing machines with iron fingers for committed wine makers).

- Filter the pulp (the boring part—mainly because the filter blocks constantly and needs rinsing). Make yourself as comfortable as possible. Enemy: fruit flies.

- Add the rest of the sugar, diluted. If using honey, boil with water and skim off scum.

- Add the rest of the water at a temperature to bring the whole must to a comfortable "tepid"—28 to 30°C.

- Check your recipe. Exact quantities will depend on type of fruit and whether the end product is to be sweet, medium or dry wine and whether you are adding all the sugar at once or in instalments.

- Tip in starter bottle. The best part! It's almost wine now. Stir. Cover. Keep in a warm place.

- Bottle—either immediately or next day. Fill sterilised gallon jars only

Wine

to the shoulder of the bottle. Fit fermentation locks primed with Camden solution and topped with cotton wool. Leave in warm place.

- When the frenzied action of bubbly brown gunk has subsided and there is a visible residue at the bottom of the jar, rack into clean "gallon" jars, fill to near stopper and replace fermentation locks.

- When wine has cleared and fermentation is slow, rack into sterilised "half-gallon" jars. Store in a cool place. Check every few months and rack again when there is significant residue.

- Drink when it tastes good. To stop further fermentation use Camden solution.

PART FIVE

Chooks

PREAMBLE

Who needs a golden egg? A real one tastes better. Each day our crazy chooks leave me ten or so eggs while they go off to scratch bugs and fertilise the grass. After three years of egg collecting, to lift the lids of the nesting boxes and take out warm clean eggs is still a highlight of my day.

They're not always clean eggs and I sometimes have to talk severely to my chooks because there are not as many eggs as there should be—but that is my fault. Chooks can't help laying. Well bred young chickens, given regular food and pleasing surroundings, average an egg at least two days out of three through the year.

The strange thing is that so few people keep chickens. They deliver regular, top quality food conveniently packaged, give wonderful manure and keep their area free of slugs, crickets, beetles and grubs. After a couple of years of laying, they can still give a little meat for the table. What more could any reasonably stingy householder require?

Over-production in eggs is never a problem. Neighbours, friends and the local shops snap them up. The yolks are bright gold, the egg white nestles close to the yolk when the shell is broken instead of slipping away like water and, above all, the taste is worth tasting.

The practical question to ask about keeping chooks is not "shall we keep them?" but "how many?"

How Many?

We began with six. Now we have 17 and expect twelve eggs a day. Sometimes it is 13 and sometimes 8. There are a number of reasons why we don't get 17.

One reason is old Doodle-Doo-No-Cock. She has never laid. She is Madam of the run and almost Master. She has grown long red wattles and holds her tail upright, and on two occasions I have heard her achieve a real crow. But she has a gentle nature. She calms the other hens. She is always last into the food, sings gently all day, and if I am late letting them out she is the one who complains loudly to jog my memory.

(We would never agree with an old quote from Dorothy Hartley's book *Food in England*. "If your Hen chance to crow, which is an evill and unnantural [sic] infirmity in her, you shall forthwith pull her wings and give her wheat scorched and mixt with powder of Chaulke and keepe her . . . from the companie of all other Pulline." Markham.)

If any hen is in trouble, Doodle-Doo sticks with it and nurses it back to health. (Perhaps a traumatic experience of her own affected her psyche—and hormones. As a pullet she got hooked up in fishnetting and spent a cold night alone.) She would not let Hoppity out of her sight for three weeks after Spike (our young cattle dog) took a lump out of Hoppity's leg—that was before Hoppity was called Hoppity of course. And we don't really expect Hoppity to lay because it takes all her effort to enjoy life, being so lopsided.

Then there's Mama. Mama is a big Black Orpington who was given to us towards the end of her life to hatch eggs for us. We didn't expect her to lay. But we found a nest of 30 small brown eggs under a clump of grass beside the run where she was bringing up three aggressive young pullets.

That brings it down to 14 regular layers, and it is fair to expect at least one to have a good reason for taking a holiday. So I take 60 eggs to the supermarket each week and keep 12 for ourselves. The eggs I sell never get to the open shelves: the workers in the shop buy them.

The answer to "how many" usually depends on how much space is available. A chook house is the size of a small garden shed and can fit in anywhere, but chooks let loose in a garden will destroy every plant. They enjoy an orchard and help the trees by eating caterpillars and insect pests, but beware of any orchard where trees have been sprayed. Spray used five years before can find its way into the eggs.

If space is very limited, chooks can be kept successfully indoors all the time. If there is a little more room, they can either have permanent outside runs or live in movable coops that have inside/outside quarters. More room still and they could have a run divided into two: use one half until it is muddy or messy then put them in the other half and plant veges in the first.

If there is any land available fenced off from the garden, free range chooks can have a good life. I feel strongly that the most miserable animals, chooks or humans, are the bored ones. I would not consider turning my chooks into egg machines, each in its wire cage. Chooks are for pleasure as well as eggs and they can only give pleasure if they are happy.

Our chooks work for me from the time that they wake in the morning and start feeding until after lunch. By that time most of the eggs are laid. After that, their time is their own until dusk when they filter back home and choose their spot on the perch. We close their door when we take the dogs for their "goodnight" walk. The arrangement works well. The chooks have about five hours to scratch grass, fallen fruit, shells, seeds, gravel and meaty bugs, and to have their dust baths. They walk long distances, take short flights, invent dramas and choose companions for their wanderings. And they keep healthy. We are privileged to have the space for them.

In no way could our chickens be called a commercial venture, even though we sell the surplus eggs. With the best management and scrupulous attention to detail, the profit margin is very small between the cost of food and the return from eggs, though food costs can be cut by feeding home grown produce and scraps, We are content to feed passengers like Doodle-Doo-No-Cock, Hoppity and Mama, and because we give them about a bucket of mash instead of measuring exactly, we just cover costs and possibly get our eggs free. (We gave away Myrtle, so maybe that was our profit. Myrtle was a white chook who developed a nasty habit of eating brown eggs. We gave her away to an all-white chookery.)

If we throw back at ourselves the question, "Why keep chooks?", the answer has to be because we enjoy them. Like the dogs, the cat, the donkeys,

the rabbits, the pigs—even the sheep and cows. And the bees. They all take a great deal of capital outlay for fencing and housing, and there are continuing costs for maintenance and feed, and always improvements to be made to storage sheds, fencing, housing, water supply and equipment.

Even when they are established in their pens, houses, sties, hutches, kennels and hives, the animals contribute relatively little to our income. We still have to go out to work, but we need to spend two or three hours each day feeding, cleaning, chasing, milking—and processing.

There is no sound excuse for that kind of time and money investment. We are definitely badly paid servants to our animals—but very happy and well fed ones. I think it's a smashing way of living and to hell with the cash flow!

We would certainly be richer living in a flat in town and we would have all the time in the world to be sociable if we bought food from the shops. Perhaps we should be sensible and move. But I would have to take the donkeys. And the dogs of course. Couldn't leave the pigs. I'd miss my chooks . . .

Which brings me back to the question of how many chooks. The answer for us is as many as possible without overcrowding. We're about to indulge in a rooster because they're beautiful and I like their crowing and it keeps the chooks happy. (I don't know how Doodle-Doo will react.) We're on the lookout for bantams because they have bright eyes and interesting colours. Perhaps a few guinea fowl . . . and ducks. The sensible answer is: begin with six and see whether you and they get on.

Which Ones?

White chooks lay white eggs, brown chooks lay brown eggs and big black chooks lay smaller paler brown eggs. (That might be common knowledge, but it was a revelation when we began keeping chooks.) Therefore, if you want brown eggs, the problem of which chooks to choose is easily solved: Rhode Island Reds or Brown Shavers. But things are never as simple as that! We have found that our Brown Shavers have gentle natures and are willing to be befriended by humans, but the White Leghorns lay larger eggs more regularly. Against the Whites : they are scatty. The Black Orpingtons are big strong birds, meaty and good scavengers, but their eggs are smaller and they are adept at finding impossible places to lay and hide their eggs. If you want to breed for the table, try the Blacks.

We have settled for a mixture. They tend to hunt and squabble according to their colour groupings and the coop was more orderly when Doodle-Doo (brown) was boss before Black Mama began competing in a particularly raucous voice, but they all find their places on the roost and the bullying is not serious. Chooks can lay for years and years, but there is a percentage drop in egg production each year. We keep ours two years then cull. Keeping a mixture of breeds helps us to colour code the chooks for age. (I would find it hard to tell one White Leghorn from another. A friend tried spraypainting all their tails different colours, but the tail feathers fell out.)

In general, chickens are classed according to body weight. The lighter chooks lay more and larger eggs, and need less food; the heavier are better eating and usually better foragers and tougher survivors.

Having decided on which chickens to get (probably local availability will make the decision in the end) the age of the stock is the next important factor. We began with as few problems as possible by buying pullets (young females) at "point of lay". They just had time to settle into their new home and get used to different food rations before they began work producing a remarkably regular one egg a day per chook. (I get this feeling that it is my pleasure and my choice to feed them, but an undeserved joy to receive the daily gift of an egg. After all, I feed my dog every day and all she gives me is love . . .)

Cheaper chooks could be bought from commercial batteries after they have done one season of 100 per cent plus laying (sometimes the lighting and food arrangements in batteries coax three eggs from a chook in 30 hours). They would probably give another season of good laying, but they would have to be taught to adapt to their different environment. Sometimes they lose all their feathers when moved from the constant warmth of the battery and they have to learn to roost and forage. They would have a rough time if introduced into a henhouse where other hens were already established, particularly Black Orpingtons.

Day-old chicks is another option. The chicks are appealing, but they need light, warmth, special feeding and constant care for the first few weeks of their lives. The outlay in specialised equipment would counter the low price of the chicks unless a large number were to be reared.

Eggs are the other option. A broody hen and a separate coop are necesssary. A box that opens into a netted run is fairly simple to make and both the fertile eggs and the broody hen can be found among country neighbours. While she is sitting on the eggs, a broody hen eats and drinks very little.

Black Mama was excellent, though we tried to put too many eggs under her. Ten or so instead of 16 would have been less frustrating for all of us. We were constantly popping back eggs that had fallen out of the nest. Even so, she would have hatched them all if it hadn't been for the thunder. We were warned that thunder kills chicks in the egg at a certain stage— and it thundered. Only three survived.

Even with three female chicks, we wondered about the economics of

raising our own pullets against buying at point of lay. Mama was a ferocious forager and taught the chicks vigorous feeding habits early on—sending their food and sometimes the chicks in showers against the netting with her big feet while teaching them to scratch for bugs. We had to wait three weeks for the eggs to hatch (no eggs from Mama of course—her eggs from that period alone would have paid for half a point-of-lay pullet!) and for six weeks they needed to be kept in a special area where they could be protected. We chose the garden, but they became more adventurous, bigger and more destructive every day.

So that means about a week of five feeds a day on chick mash, six weeks of three meals a day, and another 12 to 14 weeks feeding mother and hungry pullets for no eggs. They wasted so much food with their scratching that they had to be fed as much as the laying hens properly equipped in the hen house. Their housing was also a bit of a problem. Black Mama was extremely protective and attacked any hen that came near her territory, so they had to be separated until the pullets were full grown. When it was time to introduce them to the other hens, the youngsters were so spoilt and bossy they disrupted routine for weeks.

Apart from the fun of raising chicks, I would go for point-of-lay pullets. Of course, chicks could be reared in a brooder, but I haven't the patience to play mother hen.

CHAPTER 1   HOUSING

We inherited a chook house, but a Scotch Pine fell on top of it and crushed it. That particular shelter was 2 metres long and 1.5 metres wide, had two nesting boxes and only one door, stoop height. We kept our first six chooks there and they had a netted run in an old orchard. When we built the new house, we improved on the size and the entrance but made a different set of mistakes.

We built the second house with timber from a demolished workshed. It is 3 metres long by 3 metres wide, with full person-standing-room and a full-sized door. The door had glass in the top panel which we replaced with netting too small for the sparrows to fly through. After our first rainstorm we put a sloping sheet of tin over the netting as the rain had driven in and made a very smelly mess of our beautiful new chook house. We also stopped all the knot holes in the walls and nail holes in the tin roof. It is very important for the chooks to stay dry—we had to evacuate our mob to a spare bedroom in the farm cottage until their own house was renovated and dried out.

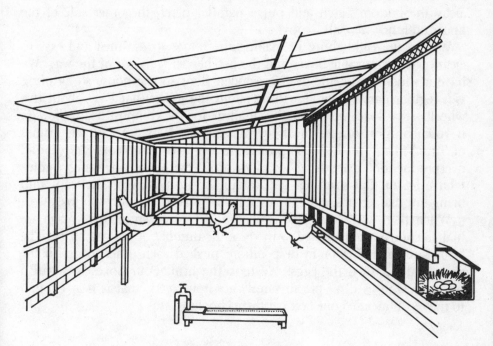

Luxury chook accommodation to house about twenty hens.

Ventilation is also important. We put a chook door in the bottom of the big door and, at the far end of the hut, cut off the top of the wall which was under a deep roof overhang and put wire mesh there for light and through ventilation.

A second major mistake was the placing of our nesting boxes. In our crushed chook house they had been off to one side. In the new one, we put them at the far end of the run, directly opposite the door. We fed the chooks just inside the door. Chooks always scratch when they feed. That meant that the direction of their scratching was towards their nesting quarters. Within a day of covering the floor with fresh fragrant hay, it was stacked in a mountain on top of their nesting boxes. When we tried a sawdust floor-covering, they filled the nesting boxes with sawdust. The boxes should either have been placed out of the direct line of fire or lifted. It was too late for us to do either, so we slotted in a movable baffle board half a metre in front of the nesting boxes. The floor covering banked against the plank instead of filling the boxes with mess.

Initially we put in two perches, one above the other. We used peach tree branches, but anything two or three inches in diameter is suitable. The chooks soon showed us that we were giving them problems. They

all wanted the top perch and there wasn't room for them all. So we took away the bottom perch and put a parallel perch the other side of the house and they were all happy.

We did the right thing in making the house streamlined and easy to clean, with removable boxes and the perches set well out of the way. We have a solid tongue-and-groove wooden floor to the house so cleaning is a regular chore. The best thing about the job is that I get about five wheelbarrow loads of top quality manure for the compost heap. (Beware if your compost heap is near the house. Chook manure attracts armies of flies.) The finished compost gives me two problems: weeds and overproduction. Everything we plant grows with overwhelming vigour. I have learnt that seedlings get lost in the lush growth that leaps into being but that shrubs, trees and established plants respond with joy.

When there were six hens, two nesting boxes were plenty. When we had 18 chooks we neglected to increase the number of nesting boxes. The birds laid on the floor in desperation, pushed each other to get in the nests and smashed the eggs. We took the hint. Four boxes was still a bit mean, but as three of our family are non-layers, that is near enough to the recommended one box per three chooks.

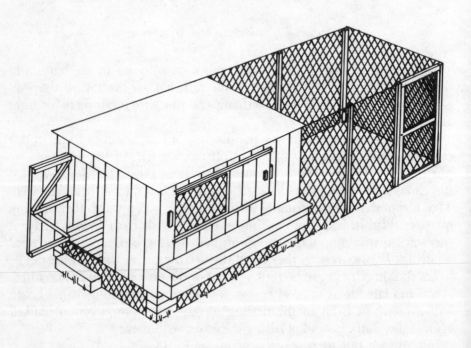

Lucky chooks to get this efficient piece of real estate. Beware of rats and ferrets — they might still dig under the wire mesh.

Another refinement that the chooks approved of is the lining for their nesting boxes. Initially we put hay in them, but it quickly became soiled and matted. Now we give them the shredded paper used as packing, collecting it from a photo shop in town. They find that soft and warm and keep it beautifully clean. The only snag is that Mama sometimes prefers to sleep in it rather than fly all the way up to the roost.

Feeders presented a new set of problems. The books said: "Feeders are easy for the handyman to make". We're not exactly handymen but buying was out of the question. Trial and error again. We used wooden offcuts and made a covered chute into a box. First problem: the mash jammed, so we made a straight-sided chute. Next problem: the chooks could get their feet in to scratch out the feed and waste it. We made the entrance too narrow and they couldn't get their heads in. Solution: we widened the entrance again and raised the feeder on a couple of bricks so that they couldn't perch, eat and scratch all at the same time.

For water we are unscientific. I steamed some vegetables in my best heavy copper bottom stainless steel saucepan, but I forgot to put in water. The copper bottom peeled half off the steel bottom—no good for cooking but a fine heavy bowl for chook water. It gets dirty but we clean it each day.

The chook house as we have it now works well for our number of free range chooks.

We seem to do things the hard way with our "try it and see" philosophy but it has two big advantages. By using materials to hand then adapting where necessary, we can filter time and money into the project instead of beginning with a hefty input of both. And better: we have to watch the animals closely and learn from them. The chooks gradually get us trained.

More efficient chook farmers have described ideal housing compromises for hens. The movable run, the slatted henhouse and the "deep litter" system are all possibilities.

Movable runs or "folds" have a house and covered-in run. These are usually elongated pyramids with perches running through the middle that double as carrying poles. They have a weatherproof house and wire mesh over the run. The idea is to move them every day to new grass so that each patch has time to recover from scratching and droppings.

The theory is fine, but anything well constructed of timber gets very heavy. For 20 chooks, the run would need to be about 5 metres by 2 metres, and even for six it couldn't be much less than 3 metres by 2 metres. It would need two people to shift it every day and then I would find it a struggle. Had we chosen that style of residence for our feathered ladies,

we would have found two other problems: we haven't much flat ground; and the chook house being small and low would be difficult to clean out.

A traditional way around the weight of the chook house is to put it on wheels and have the netting run detachable. If there is a canny carpenter in the family that is probably the best way, especially if the design can include a lift-off top for easy cleaning.

Hens can be housed permanently indoors if there are lights to encourage winter egg production. They need dry shavings, straw—or I have read of people using factory reject coffee grounds—to a depth of about half a metre. They can scratch around in that reasonably happily. These "deep litter" houses are often used in conjunction with outdoor runs, also deep litter. The problem with confined outdoor areas is that they get wet, muddy and smelly unless you are prepared to sacrifice about two bales of straw a week or the equivalent in woodshavings, leaves or grass clippings.

An easy-care system would be to have the hen house with slats on the floor, but even that would have disadvantages. Chooks are messy eaters and lose much of their mash and grain onto the floor. Burrowing vermin would soon take up residence under a slatted floor and they might hop in and steal eggs as well.

A compromise is usually the answer: your own needs and situation balanced against perfection. Perfection as far as the chooks are concerned would be a leafy forest floor to scratch and trees for roosting: but they would have to fight their own battles against rats, wild cats, hawks, stoats and in some places foxes and wild dogs.

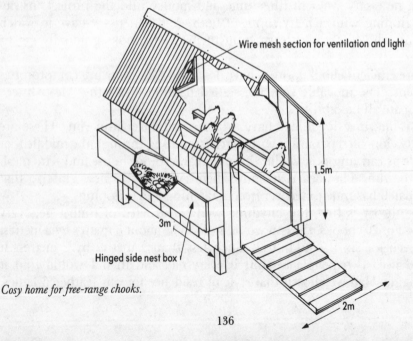

Cosy home for free-range chooks.

Lice and fleas can be a nuisance if chooks are kept indoors. If they are free to wander, they organise dust baths for themselves and keep reasonably free of irritation. (Don't worry if they look scrawny and have bald patches in the autumn: chooks moult. They go off the lay for a few weeks while they grow new feathers for the winter.) If the birds have to be restricted within a small area, they need a patch of earth for regular dust bathing, or a box of fine sand. We also squirt around the henhouse with a flea killer when we give it a thorough clean (about four times a year, spring, summer, autumn and winter. The nesting boxes get tidied up in between.) We use the same spray for the dogs, the pigs and the chook house.

Ideal measurements inside a hen house provide for 200 mm per bird on a roost, the perch being 75 mm wide and rounded on top. Some books recommend that perches should be low—about half a metre off the floor in case heavier birds cannot reach them. That might be necessary for birds with clipped wings, but our chooks, even Hoppity, manage perches 1.5 metres high. Nesting boxes, one to every three hens, should be raised off floor level (or have a baffle board to prevent mess getting into them), and be below the level of the roosts. Most hens prefer to sleep on the perches though pullets from batteries have to be taught—physically put on the perches for a few nights. When our elderly Mama began sleeping in a nesting box, we tried tipping her out each night but now we've let her win. Age deserves some consideration, even in the hen house.

CHAPTER 2   FOOD, DRINK AND EXERCISE

The cost of chooks' food has to balance the value of their eggs. Good commercial layers' mash fed early in the morning should ensure a regular supply of eggs by mid-afternoon. Keeping that in mind, the details of our chooks' menu are the usual mixture of compromise and necessity.

When I have asked other chook keepers what they feed their birds, a reply that doesn't help me in the least is "household scraps". I am a mean housekeeper—we don't have any scraps. Anything left from one meal is served at the next. The dogs squabble for bread crusts and cheese rinds; the donkeys demand imperfect fruit; the housecow steals it. The rabbits take carrot tops and outside vege leaves. Occasionally the chickens get the fat from fried sausages, but now the pigs need that.

The poor chooks are right at the end of the queue—and my compost heap comes off the worst of all—which is all wrong because the chooks give us back first rate instant food and fertiliser.

Since our chooks have the afternoon to pick at weeds and bugs in the

grass and the orchard, their need for greens is not as great as if they were cooped up. Some authorities suggest tying whole cabbages so that the birds can leap or flutter up to them—mainly to give them exercise and

Proud Mama Black Orpington teaches her chicks vigorous scratching to unearth bugs — and often sends them flying with the shower of dirt.

to counteract boredom. Boredom leads to bad habits: they can revert to pecking themselves, pulling out their feathers and fighting. Egg eating can begin from boredom and that is a very difficult problem to halt.

Hens do lay quite happily without any commercial and expensive layers' mash, but not so often. (Purists might object to the antibiotics that are included in mash and pellets for the sake of battery hens.) There are many foods they really enjoy, but what is not paid for in cash is paid for in labour. Well trained efficient foragers, for instance the Black Orpingtons, will peck at most things, cooked or raw, but other chooks are fussier and like "kitchen scrap" food cooked. Where there is a large family, a chookpot could be kept in the kitchen for potato peelings, maize husks, carrots and the tops and bottoms of things that go into winter soups, plus odd bits of meat and fish—but then it has to be boiled and cooled and that can be a smelly and lengthy procedure. An outside heat source or a stockpot system, like the old haybox, is the more efficient.

That is one extreme—lots of trouble for not many eggs. An old timer with chooks free ranging everywhere (including his house) uses the other extreme: he gives his chooks a small bowl of blood and bone and feeds them whole maize. That is probably the least trouble and the cheapest method.

What you give will depend on how much time and money is budgeted for the chooks. But some things they must have. Clean constant water is one necessity. If you could feed your chooks a regular supply of boiled eels they would probably be the best layers in the district. From eels (or fish meal and blood and bone) they can get protein for strong bodies; fats and oils for energy; vitamin B for growth and maximum production; vitamin D, calcium and phosphorus for strong egg shells and healthy bones. From grains and grass they get carbohydrates for energy; vitamin A for growth and disease resistance; vitamin K for healthy blood. If their diet is low in zinc for skin and feathers, manganese for strong shells and good hatching rate, and iodine for metabolism, these are all available in supplements.

Commercial mash has it all and if laying hens are fed exclusively on mash or pellets, they need between 100 g and 150 g per bird per day according to their body build. If the chooks are free ranging or getting supplementary kitchen scraps the amount can be cut to half or less. (If the egg laying goes down too much—feed more mash.) In the winter when our chooks have shorter hours for foraging, we feed more mash. So long as they have exercise they do not overfeed and the chooks tell us how much they want.

It is easy to overfeed chooks that are confined. We brought home three point-of-lay pullets for a neighbour when we bought our own. She loved them too tenderly. It was cool weather and she kept them inside and over-fed them. They began laying enormous eggs instantly while we had to wait three weeks for ours to begin producing the usual beginners' tiny eggs. Each day I was given a gleeful bulletin: "Another three eggs today!" I began to feel there was something wrong with our management until came the indignant bulletin: "One has died and one is sick. Its innards came out with the egg!" It was only then that we realised the young chooks were getting no exercise.

Hens don't chew—their "teeth" are in their chest. They can swallow anything, including stones, and these go into the crop which is for temporary storage. Grains, slugs and small stones are moistened and then continue through the gullet where they are mixed with acids and enzymes. Their destination is the gizzard which is a hard, muscular bag. Its contractions crush the grain and slugs against the sharp stones and grind them into a cream. From there, what happens inside a chicken is much the same as what happens inside us. But for their system, birds do need stones. Free rangers can find their own grit, but cooped chickens need a bowl of small gravel, flint or oyster shell.

If you have no means of feeding your chooks a daily eel (and only particularly privileged birds would be so lucky) then they might need an extra source of calcium and phosphorus. Soft egg shells are a real

nuisance because they can break so easily and begin cooks on the habit of egg eating. Crushed oyster or shellfish shells are a good source of calcium, or the egg shells can be baked to sterilise them, crushed in a plastic bag, and fed back in the mash. There are two schools of thought on the egg shells: one is that chooks will peck at eggs if they have them and the other is that they will peck at eggs if they don't have them. Ours pecked at eggs before they had shells and continue to peck at eggs after they had them.

Other people have told me: "Egg pecking is easy to cure. Just give them a curried egg." We did that. I filled empty egg shells with wet curry powder, stuck them back in the nest and the hens ate them. So I filled them with mustard. They ate them. I made a mixture of mustard, curry and cayenne pepper. The hens ate them, their combs went a deeper red and their feathers positively glistened—and still they ate the eggs. Only the brown ones. They still smash and eat the brown eggs—even the brown hens do it. The habit has spread and the only way I can see to stop it now is to kill the lot and begin again. (The curried egg trick can be disastrous for chooks less resilient than ours. Beware.)

I don't know why they began egg pecking. Our Brown Shavers lived at peace with the older White Leghorns and when it became time for the Whites to make way for younger birds, we brought in more White Leghorns. Very soon brown eggs were breaking. I bored a hole in the door of the henhouse and spied on them. I caught two Whites paddling in a broken egg and painted their necks with pink primer which I happened to be using at the time! I watched again and saw the culprit break an egg. That was Myrtle; I gave her away, but the eggs kept breaking. I even saw Black Mama peck an egg while she was broody. They were all at it. Now it is a race each day to see how many brown eggs I can gather before the peckers get there—not very satisfactory, but the price one pays for a sentimental attachment to one's hens.

I try to make excuses for them. Some brown eggs sometimes have paper-thin shells and their destruction could be a genuine accident, especially when for no good reason all the chooks decide to lay in the same nesting box. Also, I have noticed that there are fewer breakages when the nesting boxes have fresh hay or shredded paper. The chooks might still have a few lessons to teach me.

CHAPTER 3 HEALTH AND HAPPINESS

Happy chooks croon. They chirrup and gurgle and make gentle purring noises. I always talk to the chooks. If I creep up silently and open the door or the egg hatches, they fly all over the place and squawk. Chat to them and they chat back. The purpose of most human chatting (though I have never read this in a learned book) seems to be to soothe and reassure: "Yes, we're still friends." The chooks respond in the same way as the dogs, the donkeys, the housecow and George.

If there's something to tell, their calling becomes strident. If I am late and they want to be let out, they cackle loudly. When one lays an egg, her song is triumphant. (If she has laid outside, she is careful to run away from the nest before she begins to let us know. Even chickens are not so stupid that they would draw attention to a nest.)

If they're wet or bored or hungry or thirsty, the peaceful contented hum of chook noise disappears. Doodle-Doo paces the floor rather than perch on the roost and Black Mama becomes loud and bossy. If they are really miserable, there is only silence and sudden squawks and showers of feathers as they take scatty flight and peck bad temperedly at each other.

Hens are simple creatures. So long as they are fed, watered, sheltered and clean they stay healthy. They enjoy sunshine and variety like the rest of us but can adapt to most routines. If they are kept in relatively small numbers and replaced every two or three years so that the problems of old age don't catch up with them, there shouldn't be any health problems.

A chook that is out of sorts is easy to spot. Her comb loses its brightness and flops. Her eyes go dull and wrinkled and her skin looks flaky. She might start losing feathers. When this happened to our White Leghorns, it was entirely our own fault. We had six. Three died within days. One recovered but never laid again. Two began to lay again after three weeks.

We had done an awful thing: after making peach wine, we tipped the squeezed but fermenting peaches out for the chooks. A little at a time and they would have enjoyed them, but we tipped out the lot. The Blacks are survivors. They have strong systems and ate away gladly but did not suffer. The browns (Brown Shavers) are more timid and we had only three. They were kept away by the Whites. The Whites ate the lot. We tried putting bicarbonate of soda in their drinking water but it was too late. They scoured horribly. We felt very bad about it, but they had a marvellous party and probably left this world with few regrets.

It is usually not worth calling out the vet for chicken ailments if chooks are kept on a modest scale. The bill is bound to be higher than the value of the chickens. If a chook is crook, kill it and bury it, then clean out and disinfect the chook house.

Ailments spread through the droppings. It is important to keep a clean, dry chook house. Fortunately there is an incentive to put this chore high on the list. I don't enjoy the thought of cleaning out the hens, but once I begin I am rewarded with barrowloads of wonderful compost material

and tree mulch. It is best to choose a sunny dry day without too much wind—wind whipping chook dust into your face while you're trying to shovel it up is no fun.

As soon as I let the chooks out, I shovel rapidly so that the house will have time to dry again after a scrub with disinfectant. We spray disinfectant and insecticide into corners, and especially where the roosts are nailed to the sides, because that is where mites hide in the day, ready to run along the poles and up the legs of the sleeping chooks at night. When the place is cleaned out and smelling like a hospital, with fresh bedding in the nesting boxes and hay or untreated sawdust on the floor, the chooks

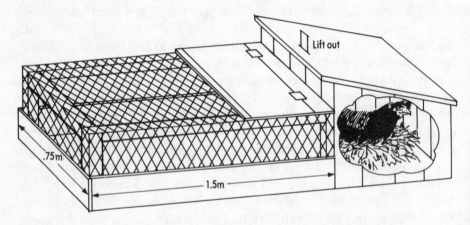

Pleasant temporary home for broody chook and newly hatched chicks.

croon their blessings and I am doubly rewarded. I have no statistics, but I am sure more eggs are laid and fewer broken whenever we have a good clean out.

White Leghorns bought as point-of-lay pullets and bred specially for egg laying, seldom go broody. Our Brown Shavers, also a strain specially bred for egg laying, sometimes go part-broody, but I wouldn't trust them with eggs. The Black Orpingtons, home-reared from eggs, are heavy, motherly birds and quite often go broody. Left to themselves, they might stay broody for a month—which means no eggs and one of the nesting boxes constantly occupied. We left Black Mama broody the last time: she let the other chooks in to lay under her wings and then kept the eggs safe from peckers. She earned her keep as a security guard.

Our never-fail method of bringing chooks off the brood is to put them in a rabbit cage. The cages have wire mesh floors well off the ground. Apparently this works because the temperature of the hen's underbelly is lowered to below hatching temperature. Three days with food and water available is always enough to get the chooks standing up and ready to go home to their friends in the flock. They lay again in about a week. Some people dip their chooks in cold water or hang cages in trees, but I am glad we have the rabbit cages.

If you wanted to breed from your own chooks, you would have to learn to pick out the good specimens to be mothers. I enjoy the succinct description of indicators of good breeding in *Fream's Elements of Agriculture* edited by D. H. Robinson (Thirteenth Edition 1956, John Murray, London):

> Indications of quality are difficult to define yet in every animal there are indications of "breeding" or of "coarseness". In poultry this lack of quality is nearly always associated with heavy beetling eyebrows, a large coarse head, a fat beefy comb, harsh-textured skin and round shanks. The indications of a good bird are a head with bold prominent eyes, a soft-textured comb, and wattles and flat-sided shanks. Only birds answering to this description should remain for any length of time in the laying house.

Professor Robinson recommends frequent handling of hens to check that they are in good condition and in lay. Each hen should have egg-laying records and he suggests the use of multi-coloured rings to distinguish one from another and to indicate the month they came in to lay, the month they went off and how many times they went broody. We are not so efficient. I am grateful to see twelve unbroken eggs and to hear a happy noise. If there are "passengers" in the flock, then they probably make a different kind of contribution. For instance, we should have disposed of Hoppity when Spike broke her ankle, but she brought out such devoted care in Doodle-Doo that we couldn't bear to. Now she has developed a hop and skip that makes her the fastest chook in the flock. She is so pleased with herself, she has come back into lay—although it has taken nine months. She began by laying half-sized eggs like a pullet, but they arrived every day and gradually came up to full size.

To tell whether a bird is in lay takes a little practice. Bright red comb and wattles indicate good health. The distance between the pelvic bones and the breast bone is the indicator of laying capacity. Below the tail, the two pelvic bones, side by side, project backwards from the skeleton. Beyond them is the breast bone. If there is room for four fingers between the pelvic bones and breast bone and between the two pelvic bones, the hen is probably in lay. If she is not, the distance will be halved.

Laying in the second season of a bird's life is generally about 60 per cent of its first year.

Professor Robinson makes the comment: "It cannot be too strongly emphasised that the normal condition of poultry is to be healthy and that disease and ailments are abnormal." For the record, he lists some of the more common complaints but stresses that good feeding and clean housing should avoid all problems.

A type of bacillary diarrhoea can be inherited and can affect young chicks. Coccidiosis is causes by an intestinal parasite and is passed on very easily in a dirty house. Young hens that haven't learnt to roost can catch cold. Worms are another problem in dirty houses. There are external parasites: mites can suck the chooks' blood at night and hide in the day; lice are normal but are kept in control with dust baths or can be discouraged with insect powder. Fowl Pest is a bad disease which should be reported immediately to appropriate authorities. The birds get drowsy, their feathers ruffle up and they lose their appetites. They breathe rapidly, make strangled noises and can get partially paralysed. Egg production falls and the chooks die.

Predators are the only problem we have encountered.* Our chooks are shut in every night. Mice cohabit with them but nothing bigger can get into the closed chook house. Keeping only adult chickens, we are not worried by hawks. Spike, our farm dog, posed the only threat. We made the chook entrance so small that we thought he couldn't get in but we didn't realise how small he could make himself or how fast he could move. He is still fascinated by the chooks, but never trusted near the chook house on his own. Vicki, springer spaniel, was sufficiently awed by a neighbour's chooks, ducks, geese and turkeys at an early age to find them totally uninteresting.

*Not quite the only problem—see footnote on page 148.

CHAPTER 4   HARVEST AND CULL

There are two harvests: eggs and meat. Eggs are pure delight: no killing, scalding, plucking, singeing, pulling or jointing. The only possible embarrassment with eggs is oversupply—but that doesn't last long. A market is created wherever a neighbour samples a fresh egg from loved hens.

Particularly for free-range eggs, the market is unlimited. We have been conditioned to accept external uniformity as a standard of acceptability in bought eggs, but when taste is allowed to make the decision to buy, home eggs win. In winter I find it awkward going to town: I have to disappoint so many of the people I meet because the chooks do not lay as many eggs in the winter as in the summer (shorter daylight hours and moulting time drop the numbers). Converts to "real" eggs dread going back to the tasteless yolks and watery whites of the mass produced and long-time-stored eggs sold in bulk.

Per egg unit, farm eggs are more expensive to produce. Sometimes they are more expensive to buy than the cost-efficient units of a commercial eggery. I am content to take an average kind of price from our local supermarket, knowing that I can supply on a basis of "whenever" and "however many". My labour I count as my pleasure and our reward is unlimited access to the eggs—and the fun of picking them out of the nests every day.

There are ways to store eggs, but even in winter the chooks give up a few eggs and it would take more discipline than we have to use the stored eggs rather than fresh ones. I froze some about three years ago and they are still at the bottom of the freezer. When I find them again, the piggies will enjoy them. Eggs can't be frozen in their shells, but they're fine either separated, whites from yolks, or as single eggs, yolks broken and stirred into the whites. I have read that eggs can be frozen into ice cube trays, but our eggs are too big to fit. Perhaps there are trays that make bigger ice cubes.

Carla Emery in her *Old Fashioned Recipe Book* (Bantam Books, 1971) has worked out how much thawed egg equals one egg: 1½ tablespoons of thawed egg yolk equals one fresh egg yolk; 2 tablespoons of thawed egg white equals one fresh egg white; and 3 tablespoons of thawed whole egg equals one fresh egg. Two ounces (57 g) is a "standard" sized cooking egg, according to that Kiwi cook's bible, *Edmonds Cookery Book*.

Eggs can be preserved in their shells. The general idea is to stop air getting to them. I remember that as a child during the war my mother had an earthenware crock of duck eggs in waterglass (sodium silicate). It is best not to wash eggs that are to be preserved. There is a protective film over the pores through which the egg "breathes" and the more thoroughly the shell is sealed, the better the eggs will last.

Fresh eggs, between a day and four days old, are best and for some reason infertile eggs last longer than eggs from hens run with a rooster. Waterglass, or sodium silicate, can be bought and is used in a proportion of one part waterglass to nine of water. Boil the water and cool it. Add the waterglass and pour it into an earthenware, glass, enamel or plastic container. Cover to slow evaporation, but keep the fluid topped up. Eggs and more waterglass can be added as necessary. The fluid starts off clear but gradually goes milky and jelly-like.

Other methods of sealing eggs against bacteria and evaporation use a bought plastic-based solution applied with a paint brush, or lard or mineral

oil or gum arabic or butter. Buttered, larded and oiled eggs can be packed in drums of sawdust or oatmeal. They last better packed small end down, though with our eggs it is often hard to tell which end is which. Brining we have never tried, but the recipe is: 13.5 litres of water to 570 ml of quicklime and one cup of salt. Always store the eggs in a cool place but don't let them freeze.

Hard boiled eggs can be pickled (without their shells). That gives them a life of about two months. Bring spiced vinegar to the boil, cool it, then put in the hard boiled eggs. Seal, wait a couple of weeks, then try them.

When an egg is fresh it has very little air inside and it will not float. As it gets older, air enters and the egg begins to dry out. In water an elderly egg will dance on its pointed end (the bigger end has the air cushion). If it is really bad, it will float. Be careful when you throw it away: rotten eggs can explode and make a most embarrassing pong.

The meat harvest is a little more trouble. First there is the horrid job of killing chooks that you have fed and chatted to and fussed over for a couple of years. They have given so many beautiful eggs, asked so little and now ... After you have hardened your heart, taken a deep breath and caught one, hold it upside down by the feet and chop its head off. The quicker the better. Some people have the knack of pulling and twisting the neck. We wait a few seconds for the bird to stop flapping, then rest the head on the grass or a block of wood and chop fairly near the head in order to miss the crop.

For this operation, we make sure the dogs are locked up, and choose an outside place where a mess doesn't matter. The headless birds flap around distressingly after they should be dead and "bleed" themselves.

Ignore them and finish the killing. You'll feel like a murderer anyway, so you might as well carry on with the job: while the bodies are still warm and before the feather follicles have had time to close and harden, begin plucking. For the inexperienced (me) it is a long and frustrating job and makes my fingers ache. The feathers need a firm, controlled tweak to make them come out without tearing the skin. If there's a wind blowing, they get up your nose and in your hair but you can't do anything about it because your fingers are all bloody and feathery ... Books say: "lay out a newspaper to collect the feathers", but the wind usually has other ideas. Books also instruct that soft feathers on breast and sides should be plucked first, then the wings, back and pin feathers. A foot is the easiest part to hang on to: I just pluck down from the leg, wherever is convenient. Some feather follicles stay in the flesh and may need tweezers. One problem is speed: with a lot of chooks to pluck, you need to keep up the pace so that the others don't cool down. Fortunately, their feathers are good insulation.

Scalding makes the job easier if you are organised. Then you really can pluck onto newspapers and tidy up as you go, because the feathers are wet. The idea is to have water boiling in a large container while you do the killing, then dip the chooks for no more than half a minute. Longer and the skin will come off with the feathers. Some people douse in cold water first so that the bird gets a thorough wetting. Start on the wing and tail feathers, then leg and body feathers and finally pin feathers. That's the ideal.

When we had Maori neighbours who were professional *hangi* organisers (a *hangi* uses a hole in the ground covered with hot stones as an oven), they rigged up a mechanical plucker for the large numbers of chooks they needed to pluck. There were rubber "fingers" on wheels which could be operated from the back of a tractor. Plucking was a very sociable occasion.

When the feathers are out, the body has to be singed to rid it of long hairs and down. A flame from rolled up brown paper or newspaper does the job.

If the hens being culled are quite old, it might not be worth keeping the whole carcass. Old roosters could also be too skinny. You could just cut off the legs and bury the rest. In fact, you could save the whole plucking routine by skinning the legs, feathers and all, and refrigerating them straight away.

The quick way is tempting, but we usually decide to give the chooks the whole works. A wartime upbringing and the knowledge that our chuck-away habits are making a hole in the sky and cluttering up the planet forces us to see any kind of waste as unseemly. The oldest chooks make excellent broth or stock, and Scottish tradition maintains that cock-a-leekie soup is sweetest with the most tried and tough old rooster.

So the next stage is also unavoidable: drawing or disembowelling the birds. The head is already off. Take off the feet at the knee joint. (To go the full distance in anti-waste, scald the feet to take off the skin and claws and stew what remains slowly, beginning in cold salted water. Good soup stock.) Cut off the preening gland—an oil bag at the tail end.

Feel through the neck opening for the places where the innards attach to the skeleton and loosen them. Pull them out. Beware of the bile sack attached to the liver. It has a green liquid which is excellent for getting fat off the hands but horribly bitter if it touches the meat.

Among the mass of intestines and jumble that come out of the chook, will be the "giblets". They are valuable. Heart, liver and gizzard are worth recovering. The gizzard has to be peeled. Slit it around and empty it out and take the muscle from the yellowish skin.

Cut around the back vent and discard. Loosen the lungs from the body wall of the chest cavity and the kidneys from the back cavity. It is unlikely

they will come out cleanly. Finally, make a nick in the neck to pull out the wind pipe and crop. Pull firmly but gently, making sure the crop is clear because it tears easily and makes a mess.

Obviously any way you can get the innards out is a good way, providing nothing critical is punctured. Practice gives each of us our own method.

The flesh needs to rest in a cool place for 24 hours, probably the fridge, before it is frozen but giblets can be frozen straight away. I prefer to boil up scrawny bits of bird straight away and freeze the stock. Then I want nothing to do with cooking or eating chicken for at least three days.

Summary

- Chose light chooks for eggs and heavy chooks for meat.

- Begin with a few and house according to your space: in a deep litter run for a small garden or, ideally, free range.

- Housing is for protection and shelter. Special needs: ventilation and a place for eggs.

- Chooks need food and water daily.

- Clean, happy chooks are healthy chooks.

- Replace layers after two years.

- One free-range chook gives about 50 kg of compost material a year (feathers are excellent for producing nitrogen). Considering that one light chook needs about 36.5 kg of layers' mash for a year (at 100 g per day), lays about 200 eggs (at 50 g each, about 10 kg) and she finally gives her own flesh—she's a fair bargain.

Footnote: a sad one

With animals, there are always dramas. Nothing stays the same for long. All our chooks are dead.

The story began when a friend rang to say that there was a spare rooster in town and would we have him? The children had brought him home from school when he was young, but now he crowed all day and had begun to frighten the little ones.

The very day I took the call and said "Yes, please", Doodle-Doo began to look off colour. I had been worried about her reaction if we brought a male into the family, but I hadn't expected her to be psychic. Within three days her comb had turned from red to purple and she could hardly move. I bopped her on the head with a big stone and gave her a quick funeral. She was a kind chook and I was sad to see her go.

We handed over two pots of honey and Spiderman arrived, neatly trussed. A handsome rooster, brilliant red comb and wattles, white with brown markings, four times as heavy as the hens and with a most distinctive waddling strut. We undid the ropes on his feet (strong spurs beginning to bud out) and opened the hatch for the hens to come out and meet him.

No hens emerged. Usually they scrabbled to be first out of the door. Then Black Mama emerged. The others sidled out in her shadow while she took up a position challenging Spiderman. We watched spellbound. Black Mama drew herself up like Queen Victoria. Spiderman looked rather silly and began to trail one wing uncertainly along the ground. That had no effect. Black Mama flew at him.

They fought, both leaping off the ground and attacking with imaginary spurs. We were very proud of Mama. The dignity of the hen house was gloriously defended. Then the donkey chased all the watching hens through the hedge and they had to regroup.

They worked out their pecking order and the hens submitted stoically as Spiderman picked and chose among them and did his work. He was blatantly racist, favouring blacks and browns and ignoring the whites. The chook house was a contented place: the hens made their crooning happy noises and eggs, after a few days, appeared regularly. Even the egg-pecking problem seemed to disappear, although there were a few accidental breakages because one of the blacks laid eggs with a thin very rough shell.

Spiderman was a bit of a pain. He crowed all day and all night. He also attacked me twice, the second time drawing blood. But the hens were happy and I found his strut so amusing to watch that I was willing to give him a third chance.

Then about a month after he arrived—during a particularly long, wet, warm winter—the tips of his beautiful red comb began to go a dull purple. And one of the Whites looked the same. We gave them a day. The white's comb flopped and went purple, the other whites looked blotchy.

So we killed them all. We emptied the hen house, scrubbed it out with disinfectant and opened it to the wind and sun. In a month or two we will stock up again.

I felt miserable and guilty about our failure to keep our chooks healthy. But I met in town the friend from whom we bought the farm. He said that every few years they had done the same. Bugs had built up in a wet year, or disease had been introduced by mice and sparrows sharing the life of the hens. That made me feel a little better. Life, death, new life. That's the rhythm with we animals.

Chooks

CHAPTER 5   CHICKEN FEED

I have used the terms "chook", hen and chicken as if they all meant the same thing. "Domestic fowl" or "poultry" is the way the dictionary describes the animals that I want to talk about. Pullets are young hens, capons are castrated males and cocks or roosters the males. All those terms apart from chooks (which doesn't appear at all in my dictionaries) can be applied to other birds as well. I hope my meaning is clear.

Another set of terms that I have found confusing is those that apply to the dead chook: boilers, broilers, roasters and fryers and spring chicken. The type of chicken meat that is born, reared and sold in a plastic bag is another kind altogether, but for farm-grown chooks their lifestyle determines the treatment of their carcass.

Our White Leghorns and Brown Shavers, after two years of laying, are definitely boilers. There is very little meat anywhere except on their legs and breast, and if they were roasted they would be tough. Pressure cooked, shredded and served in a sauce the meat is tasty; chopped up fine and cooked slowly, made into soup or casseroled for a long time it makes a good meal. Probably the best way to deal with culled chooks is to boil them slowly with a few vegetables for several hours until the flesh falls off the bones, then the flesh and stock can be used separately.

It is easier to hatch chicks in the spring but they are ready to moult and go off the lay in winter. Some egg producers (forget commercial batteries, they have their own systems) rear chicks in the autumn in order to get more winter eggs. "Spring chickens" are the culled males, sorted out when the hens begin to lay. The young tender cockerels are definitely roasters. Other roasters may be young hens that were slow to lay or produced small eggs.

Slightly older hens that have done some laying but are lazy with a strong tendency to go broody might get culled out and be sold as broilers in the summer. It is an American term and broilers are often prepared by cutting the carcass in halves.

Fryers are definitely young birds and usually they are jointed when they are prepared for sale or for the freezer. You could roast a fryer but not necessarily fry a roaster. Fryers are specially bred to be the meatiest bird, given a rich diet of grain and killed before they have ever been surprised by the miracle of an egg.

If you have raised your own chicks from eggs it is likely you will have a mixture of pullets and young cockerels. The males are your home-reared Sunday roast and will taste quite different from plastic chicken. Dorothy Hartley in *Food in England* gives some useful reminders about stuffing a bird.

150

The purpose of stuffing, before the days of plastic chicken meat, was not simply to give flavour. It was to prevent the hollow carcass from drying out. In the old days, cooks put strips of fat pork or beefsteak or lard inside the chicken that was to be roasted so that the fat could be absorbed from the inside and the savoury steam would permeate the meat. Sometimes they just basted the inside with oil or butter if it was a small bird and would take a short time to cook.

Larger older birds (they can be made quite tender with slow roasting for several hours) should have suet mixed in with their stuffing, but should also be basted inside before they are stuffed. The basting will help the cooking until the suet begins to melt and carry on the work. (Suet needs to cook for at least 40 minutes.)

Regular recipes for doing things with eggs and chicken meat are legion in microwave, standard and gourmet cookery books. The following ideas are for home-reared fowl whose tenderness you are unwilling to guarantee.

For instance: a recipe for Fowl Jelly found in an old cookery book without a cover. It begins: "Take ten pounds of the leg of beef, two cow-heels, a knuckle of veal, a couple of old fowl and the trimmings of any thing at hand, with bones, etc, broken in pieces . . ." But I can see why that one is not included in modern cookery books.

Boiled Fowl (Sudden Death)

This one also belongs to the good old days:

"Place a large pan of cold water on the fire, go out and catch a young fowl, chop its head off, and let it bleed until the water boils. Draw it, and plunge it in the water, when the feathers and skin will come off altogether easily . . ."

If you are still feeling like a chicken meal after all that, split it in half, salt and pepper it, toast it over a hot fire turning frequently and in 20 minutes it is good to eat. Okay for back-to-basics camping if you're *really* hungry but not quite in the style of modern barbecue parties!

Chicken Broth

Old fashioned chicken broth tastes of nothing except the vegetables when made with supermarket chooks, but try it with home-fed chickens for a different experience. The basic broth can be turned into a meal by serving it with noodles or plopping in some dumplings.

Chooks

Stew a hen or two, allowing 1 teaspoon salt per kilogram of chicken. Put in a cut-up carrot, an onion, a stick of celery, a clove or two and a few peppercorns. Bring it slowly to the boil and simmer until the meat falls off—between two and four hours. Let it cool. Take out the bones and any uninviting bits. Perhaps add a teaspoon of turmeric for a richer colour. Then bring it to the boil again ready to drop in the dumplings.

Dumpling mixture

2 cups wholewheat flour   *½ cup milk*
pinch of salt   *2 eggs, beaten*
3 tablespoons baking powder

Mix all the ingredients together. Either drop tablespoonfuls of the mixture into the soup and continue to simmer it for a further half hour, or bake the dumplings in a hot oven (220°C) until crispy.

Old Fowl Pot Roast

The secret of getting the flavour but not the chewiness from an old bird is always to cook it very slowly for a long time. The recipes don't make exotic reading, but they can be adapted to use whatever ingredients you have available and they have that quality of an "honest homecooked meal" to give family and friends the feeling of having dined well. The major advantage is that they can be prepared well in advance and left to cook gently all day while you join in whatever fun everybody else is having. Why should the cook miss out?

Lay slices of bacon on the bottom of a greased casserole. Salt and pepper chicken joints and lay them on the bacon. (Boil up giblets and back for stock). Cut up root vegetables (carrots, parsnips, turnips) and pack them around the joints with small potatoes and peas and beans, a sprinkling of herbs, and mushrooms if you have them. Kumaras, pumpkin, choko—anything can go in. Fill up the casserole with tasty stock, add a touch of garlic and then batten down. The tighter the lid the better. If you have some leftover pastry, seal the lid with it. And bake very slowly until you're absolutely ravenous—up to 4 hours. Bon appetit!

Pot Luck Chicken Pie

Carla Emery's correspondent, Ivy Isaacson, found a way of making two chooks serve 20 people in the kind of dish that could be taken to a pot luck meal.

Stew up two birds with carrot, celery and chopped up onion until the meat falls from the bones. Pick the meat from the bones and keep the broth separate. Mash up the vegetables with the broth and use enough to moisten a small loaf torn in pieces, and four cups of corn bread. Add another cup of chopped onion and one of chopped celery and tip the mixture into a buttered pan about 30 × 40 cm. Cover the mixture with a layer of chicken meat and and then make a white sauce with ¼ cup melted butter, ¾ cup flour and 2 cups of milk. Add 6 beaten eggs and pour the sauce over the chicken meat. Sprinkle the whole pie with buttered breadcrumbs and bake for about an hour at 175°C until golden.

Cock-a-leekie

More useful is the recipe for traditional Scottish *Cock-a-leekie*. Simple, tasty and nutritious.

The oldest and toughest bird will do, hen or rooster. Pluck, draw and clean but don't truss the bird. Lay it on the bottom of a strong casserole pot, well greased. Cut leeks in reasonably thin 5 mm slices on the diagonal and pack in round the bird. Add salt and pepper and a couple of handfuls of barley. Cover the whole lot with water—up to six litres. Then simmer gently, letting as little steam as possible escape for hours and hours, until the bird is a rag and the leek is pulp. Flick out the bones and serve with home-made wholemeal bread and farm butter for the ultimate cold winter night's Cup o' Soup.

PART SIX

Buns

PREAMBLE

I dream for my rabbits. One day I will make them a huge outside run with a little wooden house in the middle and hills and stumps for them to play around. Luscious weeds, herbs and vegetables will pop up overnight. One day, I really will. That's if Basil and Bonnie can wait. They are already seven years old, which is getting on for rabbits. They ask so little from us and give us so much that they are inclined to slide to the bottom of the list of "things to be done".

They live now in two perfectly respectable townhouses in the garden and their windows look into our windows. Originally each of their houses was three flats housing three rabbits but I took down the partitions.

Basil is black, a Chinchilla-New Zealand White cross, and Bonnie is pure white, pure New Zealand White. When they were younger they worked hard. Basil had five does in his harem and did his work willingly and efficiently. Between us we kept a shop supplied with tender, lean, nutritious rabbit meat.

Basil and Bonnie, very special buns.

155

Buns

In their retirement, Basil and Bonnie live in bachelor quarters side by side. In together, neither would have any peace: Basil would demand his conjugal rights more than was good for him, and if *that* didn't kill him, Bonnie probably would. Females will fight fiercely to protect their territories—and Bonnie is at least twice Basil's weight.

Basil is sociable. He gets on well with the dog—dog doesn't get on so well with him. Vicki, who is meant to be a hunting dog, gets terribly embarrassed when Basil hops over and kisses her nose. Basil can come into the house. He uses a box in the corner for his toileting—he was never taught but he never misses. His own cage is immaculate.

Bonnie is not so fussy. She's a good Mum but slovenly, and she is not sociable. Basil expects to be fed small amounts, tender shoots and good variety. Bonnie chews her way through mountains of bulk anything. Basil is a prodigious drinker—two water bottles emptied every day. Bonnie's bottle lasts a week.

So how could we possibly eat rabbits?

We don't eat Basil and Bonnie: they are "family". On the other hand, we watched proudly while two of their children were sliced up in a television cookery demonstration. It seems mean and terrible to rear rabbits for meat— even though their meat is exceptionally good to eat, with low fat, high protein, fine texture and pleasant mild taste.

And of course it *is* mean and terrible.

Those soft cuddly rabbits grow up trusting us to feed and keep them in every comfort. As it gets near slaughter time, I feel like the old witch in Hansel and Gretel fattening up the children for her stew pot. At the grim moment when I take them gently from their cage, stroking them behind the ears and telling them they won't feel a thing, I feel rotten. And George won't often admit it but he feels no better about taking them by the back legs and hitting them on the head with a hammer.

We *could* go and buy a pound of mince from the butcher and not feel a thing. But what if the butcher didn't care when he killed the animals for us to eat? That would be worse somehow. Our young rabbits are mourned. Their life is good and their death quick. When they come out of the freezer and are baked with all our home-grown vegetables that have suffered a similar fate, we feast without regrets.

How Many?

A home-reared rabbit killed at 10 to 12 weeks weighs when dressed (undressed actually) between 1.3 and 1.5 kg. One buck and two does would consider it no hardship to initiate and rear 50 young in a year. Even a big family should find one rabbit meal a week to be plenty. Home-reared rabbit meat can substitute for chicken in any recipe.

The smallest garden has room for rabbits. They are clean and quiet and if properly housed there is no smell. They are cheap to feed, take little of your time and never complain. Their droppings are first-rate fertiliser which can be spread on the garden without composting, or it can be left in a pile to become a self-maintaining worm factory.

Rabbit hutches are relatively simple to make. They should be well off the ground with the floor about waist height so that they are out of reach of dogs and cats. They have wire mesh floors so that droppings fall through and can be shovelled up comfortably. The rabbits need shelter from wind and rain, and shade from constant sun although they do like to be able to sunbathe. (One year Bonnie overdid the sunbathing and her white fur went yellow-brown.) Ferrets, weasels and stoats attack rabbits. Basil and Bonnie have both come off best in fights with night visitors (before we blocked holes in their cages with netting) but babies are vulnerable.

In calculating available space and if it is intended to keep up maximum production, either for a hungry family or for sale of surplus, it is wise to figure two cages per doe—one for her and the other for her babies after they are weaned at six to eight weeks. They get very big very quickly and up to fourteen young rabbits can give Mum a tiring time if left with her too long, especially if she is pregnant with the next family.

We were always short of cages. If we wanted to let the young grow bigger than ten weeks, we needed to separate the does and bucks. In a confined space they get stroppy and fight, and the bucks spray the does, discolouring their fur. Often, too, they begin to victimise the smaller rabbits and vandalise their cages. Watching them was a lesson in the consequences of city overcrowding.

Which Ones?

Unless you are a great deal more organised and determined than we were, you'll take whichever rabbits are available. Fortunately, the odds are that New Zealand Whites will be advertised "free to a good home" in your local newspaper, and they are the best meat rabbits. When we were in production, we were always delighted to spare a youngster from the hammer. It was free on the one condition that there was a suitable cage ready to receive it.

Meat rabbits are classed according to size. Small breeds weigh about one kilogram when fully grown and the heavy breeds, the Giants, weight more than six kilograms but take a long time to reach maturity.

Bonnie and Basil are both "medium", although Basil weighs about 2 kg and Bonnie must be at least 5 kg. Bonnie's offspring have averaged a dressed weight of 1.45 kg. Her daughter Lucki produced heavier young. Jodi, a Chinchilla cross like Basil, turned out progeny with a dressed weight of 1.3 kg and Peanuts (we never inquired too closely into her parentage but she was a lovely brown colour) was somewhere in between.

(Peanuts had a sad story. She was a beautiful, gentle rabbit but there must have been a touch of the wild creature in her background. She and her brother were cast-offs from children who had grown bored with their pets. Her brother was wild and destructive and went into the pot early on. Peanuts lost her spirit after a while in the cage and began to eat. She ate and ate and refused to take exercise when we let her out. She raised several successful litters but continued to grow. Her last litter of twelve big healthy babies we had to bury with her. Her hips had given way under her own weight and she couldn't feed the infants.)

There are 60-odd breeds of rabbit. Many are fancy with floppy ears, mixed colours and tufts of fur in strange places, or they are shaggy or prized for their wool, like Angora. But for meat, stick to Californian Whites, New Zealand Whites or Palomino breeds, with perhaps a lighter buck for a variety of colours in the young.

If you want to preserve the skin for the fur, then the Whites are no good. The fur falls out. You will have to decide on a compromise. The Whites are fast growing, being ready for killing in eight to ten weeks. The breeds with good fur are slower growing and usually more expensive stock to buy. The also have to be allowed to reach maturity through several moults if the skin is to be in peak condition.

CHAPTER 1 HOUSING

Our very first hutches we adapted from instructions given in an American VITA (Volunteers in Technical Assistance) book *Raising Rabbits* by H. D. Attfield (VITA Publication, 1977) and were designed to be made cheaply in third world countries. We bought nothing except the square mesh for the flooring. The rest we picked up off the beach or scavenged.

The self-cleaning mesh floors are the key to happy rabbit management (one centimetre squares, or one by two oblongs are ideal). Three rabbits can be housed between divisions in one three-metre-long hutch.

For pleasure and exercise and a bit of variety in their lives, I would strongly recommend some kind of fun for warm days in the garden. An enclosed pen on the lawn needs netting underneath it because rabbits dig. A rough patch well fenced with some shade or a box for shelter will keep your rabbits' ears perked forward and their bodies healthy. Good for mistress

too. Those are precious moments when I can sit on the grass with my friendly rabbits and hear the sounds that they hear and take notice of the little weeds and bugs.

Whatever materials you can find for building the hutches—car cases, fibrolite, demolition timber, tin, tea tree or bamboo—there are a few basic requirements:

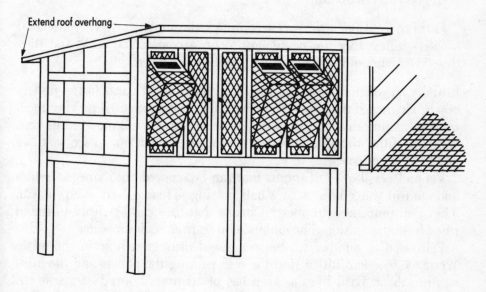

As well as giving protection from dogs, cats and ferrets, raised hutches allow good ventilation and make it easy to shovel out the excellent rabbit manure that drops below.

For *protection* of your rabbits from beasts with teeth and claws, the cages should be off the ground. If there are human young within range, a system of double door catches guards against the kind of disaster where an innocent wants to give a leaf to the baby bunnies and suddenly there are a dozen miniature rabbits running in every direction.

Shelter from wind, sun and rain are important. Basil caught pneumonia from long wet grass one time. Bonnie got sunburnt. There should be a draught-free corner in their cages, from whichever direction the wind is attacking. The roof should be sound and although they enjoy some sunshine, if rabbits get too hot, they die.

Light and *air* are important to these field creatures even if they have been bred in cages. A sloping roof with an overhang lets in the light and the rain runs off.

A warning: rabbits gnaw. Arsenic in treated timber is not good for them.

Cages will vary according to weather conditions. Where there are cold winters, cages will need to be more solid and possibly have the shelter of a lean-to or shed. Even in our mild climate, Bonnie and Basil appreciate a wooden box to sit in, on or behind. Where it is hot and damp, rabbits need good air circulation.

Furniture and *amenities* vary according to the idiosyncrasies of individual rabbits—unless they are being farmed on a commercial scale and then the convenience of the operator has to take precedence.

Initially we offered Basil his food and water in elegant, heavy pottery bowls. He treated them as exercise equipment and practised picking them up and landing them upside down. True to character, Bonnie sat in hers. When we filled them with pellets they scraped them out to see what we had hidden underneath.

Vet and pet shops sell spouts that can be screwed onto vinegar bottles and control water flow with a ball bearing. These solved one problem. They clip onto the wire mesh doors so that they can be slipped off and filled from the outside. The rabbits soon learn to suck the water.

Pellets go in another tin hopper poked through a hole in the mesh. We made wooden lids to stop the rain ruining the pellets and the birds stealing them. Basil likes to keep hay at all times hooked in a wire net attached to the wall of his cage. Bonnie keeps nothing. The same amount of hay that lasts Basil a week disappears in ten minutes from Bonnie's cage so that there is no need for a net. Books on rabbit keeping suggest making a mesh manger for green food to hang outside the door so that food can be pulled to the inside. It's a good idea. But in practice, Basil and Bonnie have plenty of space and never trample the food in their "kitchen" area or confuse it with their "loo" area.

Some books suggest that a scratching block as part of the hutch furniture will keep the rabbits' toenails short but that didn't work with our lot. Occasional nail clipping is more effective. But all the rabbits appreciated a chewing block. They like prunings from the fruit trees and fresh logs (especially willow). If these are not available they will chew their cages or nesting boxes. Peanut's brother chewed right through the wire mesh of his cage door.

Other furniture is optional. If rabbits are more for fun than for commerce and there is space in their cages, they enjoy odd shaped logs and a variety of boxes. Bonnie rearranges her furniture frequently and gets noisily irritated with me if I put it back the way I want it. Basil likes his left exactly as it always has been.

Curtains can be a comfort. Whichever way you have cunningly faced the cages to escape the wind and the rain, the weather has a way of beating you. On those vile days when the wind drives buckets of sharp miserable icicles straight to the back of cages and into feedbowls, a weighted sacking curtain anchored to the roof with a couple of bricks is a help. For the more organised, a sack or plastic can be stapled above the door and thrown back over the roof when not needed.

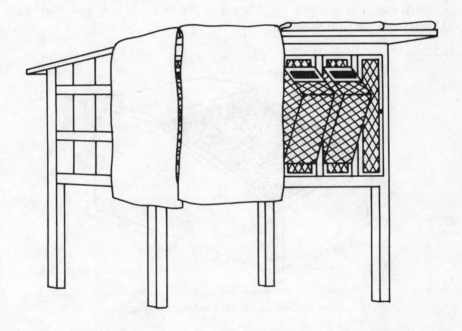

Mating boxes are put in a few days before the doe is due to kindle (have the buns). If you put it in too soon, she might use it as a lavatory. Even nesting boxes make allowances for local weather conditions. They are simple boxes like seed boxes but with high sides tapering to a lower front section. For colder climates or winter babies, the floor of the box needs to be wooden but that is too hot in summer and a mesh floor padded with hay gives better ventilation. In winter, a half lid over the high back portion makes it cosier for the baby rabbits (who arrive furless and blind) and gives the doe somewhere warm to sit away from the demands of her young.

Put hay or shredded paper packaging in the nesting box and make it cosy, but the doe will rearrange everything you organise. When the time is near, she plucks out soft underbelly fur and makes a nest wherever she thinks fit—usually somewhere quite inappropriate. With tact and gentle persuasion you can wear her down until the nest is in the nesting box. All is well until you wake up on the coldest morning of the winter and find she has left the babies blue and miserable lying on the wire mesh. Unless quite obviously dead, gather them up and plop them into the nest. They are amazingly resilient. The doe will cover the baby rabbits completely in a cloud of white fluff. Check occasionally that one hasn't crawled out and wedged itself between the nesting box and cage wall. Mums can't (or won't) count.

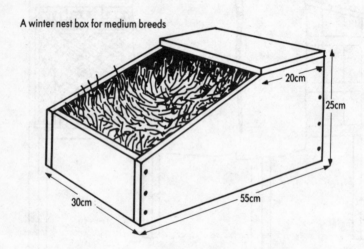

A winter nest box for medium breeds

20cm

25cm

30cm

55cm

Room for Mum Bun to take a rest on the top platform.

BUILDING THE CAGES

Attfield in *Raising Rabbits* gives detailed plans and instructions for building cheap cages—even suggesting a roof from flattened tin cans. Our hutches built to his specifications have stood the test of seven years' exposure to weather, sea salt, rabbits and a major change of location. We had to saw off the legs to get them on the truck for their move, but they are still sound. And very heavy. We used a sheet of second-hand corrugated iron for roofing. It doesn't look bad when it is painted.

During construction, be alert to any sharp edges of netting, tin or nails that could hurt the rabbits. The other danger points are places where manure could pile up. Beware of ledges and anywhere difficult to clean as stale droppings are the most common source of rabbit disease.

CHAPTER 2 FOOD, HEALTH AND EXERCISE

Food

Pellets containing all things necessary to a rabbit's diet are available at pet shops, vet shops and many supermarkets. In small packets they are expensive but one of the above outlets can usually obtain them for you in bulk. They provide a convenient way of feeding rabbits, particularly if a neighbour is feeding the rabbits for you while you are away or you are busy.

We keep pellets as a standby, but I'm mean with them. Rabbits are so easy to feed. If they have a mixture of foods when they are young, they will eat practically everything in the garden—or house. They love bread and biscuits and cake and apples and pears and peaches. Carrots and radishes they will eat, but they prefer just .the tops. Cabbage and all herbs are good, including clover, sorrel, dandelions, soft thistles, plantains, chickweed, nasturtium, marigold and grass. Be careful with lettuce: too much and they can scour, especially young ones. Leaves off trees go down well: willow, leaves from fruit trees, bamboo. Even rhubarb leaves they can eat without harm. Hard, dark leaves are suspect and avoid Deadly Nightshade, potato and tomato leaves. If you have corn, peanuts, sunflower seeds or other grains to spare they make good food.

Hay can be left hooked onto the side of the cage to be nibbled at all times for roughage. Other foodstuffs need to be limited, except to pregnant does or growing young rabbits. They can have as much as they can eat.

If you want to fatten young rabbits for the kill, feed them mostly pellets with enough greenstuff for variety. Nursing or pregnant does need up to a cup of pellets or mash a day, but bucks and resting does need only half a cup.

There are comprehensive charts showing the ideal ratio of food to weight for certain types of rabbit in Harlan Attfield's rabbit book, but I have found it best to go by what the rabbits tell me. I cut down the pellets as hard as I can and feed a variety of weeds and oddments when I pass their cages. If they get hungry in the evening they stand at their cage doors and rattle them. If they've had enough they sit and doze. If you love your rabbits, you are more likely to have problems with overweight than underweight.

Water

Rabbits need water at all times. If drinking spouts are not available, clip a bottle on the inside of the cage, upside down with its neck in a bowl filled with water. As the rabbit drinks the water, the bottle will refill the bowl.

That system is not suitable for destructive or overactive rabbits.

One time I went through a healthy phase and tried giving all the animals cider vinegar because it cures everything. Husband refused it. Dogs ignored it. Rabbits had no choice. It was meant to make the young ones grow bigger and stronger. When it came to slaughter time, the haves and the have nots were much of a muchness. But of course they were healthy rabbits anyway. It might have been different if they had been under stress.

Rabbits like milk, but to give it to them means putting it into their water bottles and then having to clean them out. Mine don't get it very often!

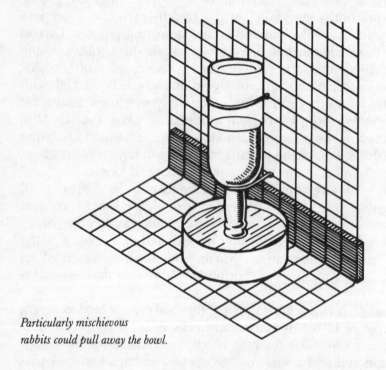

Particularly mischievous rabbits could pull away the bowl.

Hygiene and Health

So long as cages are clean and ventilated and there is a warm place in them, there should be no health problems.

Young rabbits are the most vulnerable. Scrub out cages and nesting boxes with disinfectant between each litter and dry in the sun. Make sure no scraps of food are left on the cage floor to mix with droppings and make yukky compost heaps.

Health indicators in rabbits are the same as for other land mammals. Buns should be active and interested in what is going on (except at siesta time) and have clear, bright eyes. Their fur quickly goes dull and lumpy-looking if anything is wrong and their ears flop. Runny eyes or nose are a bad sign, and ears should be clean and dry inside. Watch out for sore feet.

There *are* nasty things that can happen. There is an intestinal parasite that can infect very young rabbits with coccidiosis, especially in damp places. Clean hutches are the best prevention. We've never had it. (Nor have our rabbits.) Ear mange is caused by another small parasite that digs under the skin but can be swabbed away with a solution your vet will tell you about. Same for skin mange.

Sore feet can come from too much thumping on a rough floor. The books say to bathe the back feet and apply ointment—but those back legs are powerful kickers and rabbits can wriggle like mad when you're trying to help them. Best to keep them content with plenty of space and they won't bang their legs so much. Outside exercise gives them a chance to get rid of pent-up energy.

In the wild, rabbits can find warm burrows or sheltered dips in the ground away from wind and rain. Shut up in hutches, they can get chilled and are vulnerable to colds and pneumonia. The best antidote is plenty of exercise and green vegetables. If a rabbit is downcast, try keeping it on a diet of green stuff for a while. If after a couple of days it is still miserable, hunched up, sneezing, wiping its nose and eyes, and not eating, the vet can give it an injection to bring it right. You have to love your rabbits extravagantly to call the vet: Bonnie grew a tumour on her back leg. The operation to cut it off and sew up the leg cost the equivalent of six new young does!

Exercise and Happiness

Having an exercise area for rabbits is an indulgence. None of the serious rabbit books mention it as necessary. But then, medical books often forget to point out that female humans do better if given a meal out occasionally!

Basil just loves the big life outside his cage. His ears are still cheekily forward-tilting a week after helping me plant comfrey behind the compost heap. To show his pleasure at being out after a long boring winter he ran in circles round me, grunting. His pleasure might have had something to do with Bonnie. She always shows a maidenly resistance to being taken out of her cage because it usually means *one thing*! But she actually frolicked a while with Basil before she found a disused pig pen, took up residence and spent the rest of the afternoon gnawing its well weathered side struts.

It was my fault that Basil caught pneumonia. His regular outside run was in long wet grass and the day was cold—I forgot him. It is a better rule just to take advantage of warm days.

Rabbits are companionable and appreciate it if you can spare a while with them. They need to be in a fenced place. Across an open paddock I could probably outrun Basil, since he has spent all his life in a cage and wouldn't know where to run, but I could lose him in the bush. Once he and Bonnie have sniffed out the boundary fence they work out their own territories and settle down.

A warning: don't exercise a buck and a doe together unless you want them mated (Basil doesn't even ask first). And a reassurance: if you have a fenced vegie garden, that's a suitable place for them to exercise. Our rabbits expect food to be picked for them and take little interest in growing leaves. Basil nibbles a bit and digs a few holes but does no damage that the garden cares about.

CHAPTER 3 HANDLING, BREEDING AND KEEPING RECORDS

Rabbits have their own dignity. They don't like to be rushed at or crowded or smothered. Some, like Basil, are naturally curious. He will come to the front of his cage to examine a visitor and stand happily while his fur is ruffled the wrong way. (He's more like a dog than a cat in the way he prefers to be caressed. He gets bored with having his fur stroked in one direction: he prefers his rump scratched or a rub behind his ears.) Bonnie on the other hand scoots to the back of her cage when she sees visitors. Both of them hate the initial pick-up, however quickly and painlessly I try to do it.

I usually remember to wear a long-sleeved shirt because rabbits have claws. The smaller they are, the sharper the claws. Their instinct is to struggle and they kick with those back legs. My arms have often been covered with tramline patterns of scratches, but I prefer that to the ways I have seen some rabbit handlers toss rabbits around by their ears or legs. *Don't* pick them up by the ears—that hurts them. And their front legs are very weak, not even jointed into their shoulders like ours are but held just by flesh and muscle.

Adult rabbits should be taken firmly by the loose skin behind their ears, with the other hand supporting their rump. Scoop up the rabbit so that you take all the weight with the supporting arm and tuck the rabbit into your waist with its head under your arm. Lighter rabbits you can hold as if they were standing upright—still by the scruff of the neck but with their legs turned away from you and a supporting hand under the rump. It is not a good idea to carry them any distance this way. The pressure is still on their neck. They are bound to struggle and get bruised and sore behind the ears.

Once Basil and Bonnie have been lifted from their cages, they settle down happily to the carrying part, although the dog is inclined to put on her "great hunter" expression and follow closely, upsetting them a bit. Actually, she is just jealous that they are getting the cuddles.

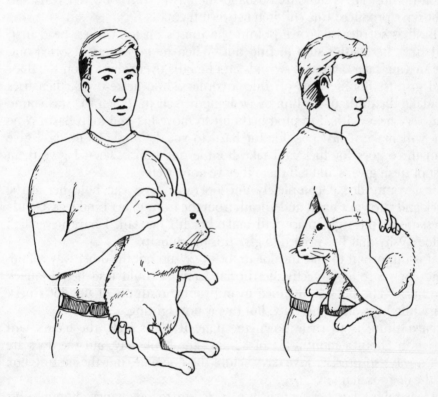

Rabbits usually struggle when they're picked up and their claws are sharp.

Breeding

Medium weight rabbits can breed at six to nine months, but a doe needs to be strong and mature enough to nurse the babies. If does are to have a long and healthy breeding life, it is better to wait until they are a year old before the first mating. Make sure your doe and buck are not closely related otherwise inherited weaknesses can become exaggerated.

MATING

My preparation for the rabbits to mate is to clear Basil's cage of all his toys, furniture and box. I choose a warm dry day before the evening feed and make sure the dog is out of the way. Rabbits can be put off by spectators, human and other. Bonnie knows what's coming and tries to hide. I take her from her cage, pop her in with Basil and stand back.

Bonnie's display of reluctance is actually all show. She and Basil are good friends. He is the only husband she has known for seven years and they have produced fine children between them.

Basil is so pleased to see Bonnie, he jumps on top of her: head first, tail first, he doesn't stop to find out. When he gets himself sorted out, the mating takes about 1½ seconds and he falls over sideways on the floor and grunts. Bonnie runs off into a corner while he recovers, then tries to make life difficult for him by wedging herself in. When she was young and very heavy, I had to prod her a bit to move her and help Basil. Now she will make it *just* possible for Basil to get the angle he needs. I give him three goes for luck and take Bonnie out again. Then I give them lost of fresh greens and tell them they've done well.

If a young doe is completely uncooperative, you can hold her at the neck and slip your hand underneath from the front to her hind legs. Gentle pressure in the right place will make her lift her tail. I have never had a doe so shy that I've needed to give this much help.

It is important to take the doe to the buck and not the other way round. The doe's strong protective territorial feelings could lead her to attack the buck. The buck is inclined to pull out mouthfuls of the doe's neck fur while he is doing his duty, but this is not fighting.

Next thing is to write down the date. If all is well, the babies will arrive in about a month—31 or 32 days the books say, but the does are not always so precise. Five days before the due date, put the nesting box in the doe's hutch.

Each rabbit has her own way of reacting to pregnancy. Bonnie puts on a performance at each stage. First she eats madly, even more feverishly than usual. Then she gets hyperactive and gnaws and thumps all night. She plays at making trial nests with her hay, circling her cage with huge mouthfuls trying to stuff it into corners. Then she goes dull and eats hardly anything. Then she pretends she's not going to have babies after all. Then she has them—and looks after them beautifully.

Usually she chooses night-time to kindle. Often one or two babies miss the nest and have to be rescued in the morning. Apart from checking to see if they are all alive, it is not necessary to disturb the fluff ball. The baby rabbits in fact are not worth looking at for a couple of weeks— they're pink and bald and look like short-tailed rats. Only when they grow fur and open their eyes and poke their noses from the nest at ten to twelve days do they become irresistibly adorable.

No they don't! Remember: from that time forward they are simply *food.* Unless you can persuade a neighbour's child to wheedle her father into making a suitable cage to rescue one or two of them, they are all destined for the chop and pot. Congratulate their mother by all means, but don't give names or undue attention to the young. They will soon grow into horrid, greedy, argumentative teenagers anyway.

SEXING

Sometimes you need to know the sex of a young rabbit. Behaviour will give clues, but the surest way is to take a look. Catch the rabbit by the scruff of the neck, tip it up on your lap and press back the soft folds between its back legs. Males have a circle and females a slit.

WEANING

If it is important to grow the heaviest young rabbits possible as quickly as possible, leave the babies with their mother for eight weeks. We found that, especially if it was a big litter, the pressure on the doe at about six weeks was as much as we wanted her to take. When the buns were weaned at that age they took no noticeable knock (they begin to eat solids as soon as their eyes open).

One of Jodi's litters we had to subject to an emergency weaning at four weeks because she was becoming unbalanced. The young suffered very little set-back and in fact killed out at 1.4 kg each, which was better than her previous four litters. Jodi gradually became more crazy, leaving the following litter to die and eating the next. We buried her under a pohutukawa tree.

BREEDING RECORDS

Records are a pain. I hate writing down what I have just done, but memory plays tricks. Sometimes a pattern shows up in records that will alert you to a problem that can be put right in a doe or a buck. Or an experiment can turn out to have good results, such as when we had to wean Jodi's litter early: I would have forgotten the dates and weights if they hadn't been written down.

If you have more than a couple of does, detailed records are very important. A doe that consistently produces small litters or lightweight offspring can be costing you money if you are feeding a lot of pellet food.

Buns

(Feeding green food and scraps achieves the same results as feeding pellets, but fattening takes longer.) If all the does seem to be slowing down, the buck could be the problem. The figures show exactly what is happening.

Harlan Attfield suggests a simple Doe Record Card which we found to be adequate, and quotes at length from Mrs Anne Faunce in the January 1974 *Countryside and Small Stock Journal* showing the need for fuller records for commercial breeding.

Here is all we needed on our cards:

DOE CHART

NAME:
BREED:
BOUGHT:

Date of breeding	Buck	Date due to kindle	Date kindled	No. alive	No. dead	Date of weaning	Date of killing	Dressed weight
				—				

NOTES _____

If rabbit breeding takes your fancy, there are other details you will need to know, such as the litter weights at various dates to find our how well the doe nurses. The ability to produce good milk is passed from mother to son to his daughters, so the figures affect the choice of buck. Accurate weighing can become important since a newly weaned litter can gain half a kilogram a day.

There has to be some culling and replacement in a big herd and only good records can fight biased judgement in favour of a specially appealing rabbit. There is only a small profit margin in rearing rabbits for meat and that disappears if sentiment is allowed to creep in. We made that discovery after two years—and stopped trying to raise rabbits for profit.

CHAPTER 4   HARVEST

In an honest and beautiful book that has been a huge help to me I came across this section on killing which made me feel better. Carla Emery writes in her *Old Fashioned Recipe Book* 1977:

Of killing: . . . I don't think much of people who say they like to eat meat, but they want somebody else to do the killing of the animal and go "ick" at the sight of its bleeding body. That is simple irreverence and wanting something for nothing . . . I'm sad, humble and grateful for each animal that perishes for the sake of nourishing my family. If the good Lord has a place in His heaven for the souls of chickens, cows, and pigs, I hope He has taken and will take every one of them.

Rabbits too.

So: choose a time of day when the flies aren't too bad, and a sheltered place with a sturdy tree. Fetch your first victim. Hold it by the back legs upside down until it quietens and then smack it hard behind the head with a hammer or something hard. One good smack should break its neck. Either nail one back foot to the tree nailing between two bones, or hook both back legs onto a rope suspended from a branch of a tree. Cut off the head and let it fall into a bucket placed underneath—most of the blood will come out. Nerves make the carcass "kick" a while.

Begin *skinning* by cutting the skin around the back feet and taking off the front paws completely. With a very sharp knife, but carefully so that the meat is not damaged, slit the skin from the inside of one back leg, starting at the hock joint, down through the pelvic median point and up the inside of the other leg. Peel the skin off both hind legs and cut the tail off. Steadily pull the skin downwards and off like shedding a tight sweater.

If you want to tan the hide, leave it fur downwards out of reach of dogs and cats to dry for a few hours, then fold it, fur outwards, put it in a plastic bag and freeze it until you have enough pelts to make a tanning operation worth while.

Clean the rabbit by slitting from between the back legs, down through a faint guideline on the belly. Take care not to puncture the gut inside. Remove the liver and heart. Examine the liver—if it has white-filled spots on it, the rabbit has been attacked by coccidiosis. Do not eat the meat.

Cut the gallbladder, with its green bile, from the liver, but keep healthy heart and liver for a specially tasty pâté. Let the rest of the guts fall into the pail with the head. Ease the lungs off the carcass with your fingers.

The kidneys in their beds of fat can stay there until it is time for jointing in the kitchen.

Tidy up the carcass, hose it down, clean the knives and start on the next one. Leave the carcass a day in the fridge to set, then either joint and snap freeze or leave whole and freeze.

Jointing is easy if you have sharp knives. Take off the back feet by cutting the tendons, then the front legs which are not attached to the skeleton except by muscle. The back legs break out easily at the hip joints if you cut the meat carefully through the groin.

The long body makes four good eating pieces. Cut through the breast bone longways and down close beside the backbone—the tiny bones are a nuisance until you get used to the operation. Then divide each half by cutting through the "flaps", under the lower ribs and crunch across the backbone.

Stop Press

Willie, Basil's first son and son of the ill-fated Jodi who went mad, has come home to live. His "little girl" mistress out-grew him. Willie is soft grey, heavy and a confirmed bachelor. Like Basil, he drinks a lot of water and he is fussy about his food. He will eat only the brand of pellets he is accustomed to, and likes them mixed with sunflower seeds and maize. Bonnie and Basil won't eat the pellets he likes and Bonnie leaves the sunflower seeds ... It's a good thing they are ancient and honoured members of the family because there are some excellent recipes using fussy old rabbits!

Summary

- Rabbits kept outside in sound cages are clean and friendly pets.
- Their offspring are a source of plentiful, nutritious meat.
- There is a small profit margin for careful, small-scale rabbit keeping.
- Cages are cheap and easy to make. Wire mesh for the floors has to be bought.
- Rabbit droppings are first-rate fertiliser and can be used without composting.
- When foraging round the garden, roadsides and other people's gardens for rabbit food, I have become aware of many grasses, weeds, herbs, flowers and leaves I had not noticed before. Some taste good in "human" salads. An unexpected perk from rabbit keeping.

Eating

Home grown buns, particularly if they have eaten pellets for the last few weeks of their life, taste quite different from wild ones. Ignore instructions in recipes such as "soak in vinegar for two days"—unless you want pickled rabbit which sounds quite revolting. Nor do they need washing in salt.

Pâté

We usually kill about 12 rabbits at one go. That means plenty of hearts and livers for a nutritious and delicious pâté.

Basics

rabbit livers and hearts	*onion*
bacon rashers	*cream (for a soft pâté)*

Optional

Add anything you enjoy in the way of salt, ground pepper, herbs (rosemary is good), chillies, garlic (sauté with the onions or add as powder), paprika, capers, gherkins, olives, and/or a couple of chopped, hard-boiled eggs.

Chop up the livers, hearts, bacon and onion and sauté together in butter for a short time, then mince finely. Add whatever extras take your fancy and blend in cream.

Fill a big dish or lots of little dishes, stand in cold water, cover with buttered paper and cook for about half an hour in a medium oven (180°C). When cooked, cover with a layer of melted butter. It freezes well in the pots if you can make it last that long.

Nell's Teriyaki

Nell was a devoted and intelligent Border Collie cattle dog. When she left the farm, she kept the orange trees in line in our citrus orchard. Aged 16 she began to slow down, although she could still beat the Trekka on short runs at 30 mph. When it came time to die, she went off dog food and took a fancy to sausages. For the last four days of her life, she would eat nothing but Rabbit Teriyaki. I wonder what she'll be in her next life?

It is a cook-in-the-bag dish, easy to prepare beforehand. A warning about rabbit fat: there is often quite a lot of fat around the kidneys. I find it has an unpleasant taste and avoid it, but the dogs like it.

The recipe makes plenty of sauce: it turns into a lovely jelly when cold and is popular in sandwiches or is good to use in a fried rice type of dish with any left over cooked rabbit meat.

Sauce:

3 tablespoons soy sauce	*chopped root or powdered ginger*
3 tablespoons sherry	*chopped garlic*
2 tablespoons olive oil	*salt to taste*
2 tablespoons honey or brown sugar (honey slips off the spoon easily if you pour the olive oil first)	

Mix all ingredients together and pour the sauce into a roasting bag. Add the rabbit joints, straight from the freezer or unfrozen. Swish the sauce around to coat the pieces and marinate without air in the bag for an hour or until thawed. Before putting in the oven, refasten the bag, leaving a finger-sized hole for steam to escape. Spread out the pieces to one layer deep and bake in a shallow dish for one hour in a medium oven (180° C). Don't burn your hands slitting open the bag. Good with baked spuds in their jackets with cream on them, and green beans.

Rabbit Fried Rice

This uses left-over Teriyaki or other cold rabbit meat, and is at least as good as the Teriyaki itself, but not such a formal meal. I cook too much so as to make sure there are left-overs. The recipe is the basic Thai fried rice dish that can be adapted infinitely. I keep Chinese smoked pork sausages in the freezer to slice finely (still frozen) and add that "different" flavour. A little sausage goes a long way and sets off the rabbit flavour perfectly. Quantities and ingredients can be varied to suit the family—a few cooked peas or any cooked vegetables can be added but they shouldn't swamp the meat.

2 tablespoons oil or ¾ cup dripping	*4 cups cold cooked rice*
1 tablespoon crushed garlic	*soy sauce to taste*
1 cup (boneless) cooked rabbit (plus any jellied Teriyaki sauce)	*1 chopped chilli or chilli sauce (optional)*
	1 can shrimps or crab meat (optional)
1 Chinese sausage, finely sliced	*1 cup cooked peas (optional)*
2 eggs, lightly beaten	

Heat the oil, fry garlic and add meat. Warm through. Pour the eggs in quickly and stir before they set. Add the soy sauce, then shrimps, peas and rice. Stir well and leave just long enough to heat through. Turn onto a serving dish, sprinkle with fresh ground black pepper and serve hot. (If you ordered *Khau Phat*—fried rice— on a Thai train, the rice would be pink with tomato sauce and there would be two long green spring onions and a fried egg on top—but no rabbit.)

Things that go especially well with rabbit are: bacon, apples, mushrooms, rosemary, prunes, almonds, onions and garlic, and parsley, but not necessarily all at once. Kiwi fruit or pineapple juice would help to tenderise an older rabbit. Or wine. If you do happen to need to cook an old rabbit, cover it with cold water and bring to the boil. Throw away the water and start again. Or soak it in salted or vinegared water, then stew it with celery, carrots and parsnips and serve with dumplings. Another way to disguise the strong taste of a wild rabbit is to cook it slowly in milk and cream. In general, cook rabbit a little longer than chicken.

Practically anything can be done with rabbit meat. There are rabbit broths, brawns, ragouts, blanquettes, pilaus, cups, mumbles, moulds, jellies, pies and fricassees, or you can roast rabbit, jug it, casserole it or stew it, braise it, fry it, barbecue it or serve it "en papillote".

Rabbits were more familiar in farm kitchens before the turn of the century than they are now. Kaara, the farming friend who gave me the courage to start making butter and cheese, lent me her mother's recipe books, some of which had been handed down by *her* mother. Front and back pages had disappeared from the books and sections of older books marked the pages of special recipes in the more "modern" ones. In all the books, pages were thumbed, brown and nibbled, but I have presumed that those giving the price of rabbit as 8d per lb were more modern than those quoting 7d. Even the "modern" books have pictures of little girls dressed in pinafores over layered skirts gathered in a bundle behind—and Mama wears a high, tight neck to her dress with ruffles over the bosom, long sleeves and long skirt.

Those books were a blessing when, because of "financial pressure" (we are still telling ourselves it is a temporary phase!), our only meat for a year was provided by Basil and his consorts. In the biggest book, *Cassell's Cookery*, there are 90 rabbit recipes. After reading through so many recipes, it made sense to close the books and use the basic principles to create unique masterpieces. Our present favourites have evolved from the days when the choice was rabbit—or rabbit.

The rewards for dipping into the old books were splendid insights into attitudes of a hundred years ago (it's hard to tell exactly when, but defintely Victorian). For instance, *Cassell's Cookery* says to tell whether a rabbit is young and suitable for the table, try to break the jaw between thumb and finger (if it resists, it is too old). When skinned and emptied, it advises removing the rabbit's eyes. Another more thoughtful recipe for boiled rabbit suggests cutting off the head altogether. The author is a sensitive fellow:

We hardly remember that the thing ever lived if we do not see the head, while it may excite ugly ideas to see it cut up in an attitude imitative of life; besides for the preservation of the head the poor animal sometimes suffers a slower death.

A cookbook editor, now anonymous, writing in London, had no premonition of the problems that farmers in Australia and New Zealand would have with rabbits. In a note under "Rabbit Pie" he or she writes:

Fecundity of Rabbits: The fruitfulness of this animal has been the subject of wonder to all naturalists. It breeds seven times in the year, and generally begets seven or eight young ones at a time. If we suppose this to happen regularly for a period of four years, the progeny that would spring from a single pair would amount to more than a million. As the rabbit, however, has many enemies, it can never be permitted to increase in numbers to such an extent as to prove injurious to mankind; for it not only furnishes man with an article of food, but is, by carnivorous animals of every description, mercilessly sacrificed. Notwithstanding this, however, in the time of the Roman power, they once infested the Balearic islands to such an extent, that the inhabitants were obliged to implore the assistance of a military force from Augustus to exterminate them.

The same editor advises between "Fried Rabbit" and "Rabbit à la Minute" that there are four varieties of rabbit. These are warreners, parkers, hedgehogs and sweethearts.

The warrener, as his name implies, is a member of a subterranean community, and is less effeminate than his kindred who dwell *upon* the earth and have "the world at their will", and his fur is the most esteemed. After him comes the parker, whose favourite resort is a gentleman's pleasure ground, where he usually breeds in great numbers, and from which he frequently drives away the hares. The hedgehog is a sort of vagabond rabbit that, tinker-like, roams about the country, and would have a much better coat on his back if he were more settled in his habits, and remained more at home. The sweetheart is a tame rabbit, with its fur so sleek, soft and silky that it is also used to some extent in the important branch of hat making.

(I wonder if that could account for the Mad Hatter and the March Hare getting together in *Alice in Wonderland*?)

Nothing to do with rabbits, but in the foreword of another of Kaara's old books is instruction on preparing green vegetables.

Another important point in cooking the majority of vegetables is to have plenty of water . . . it is well known how extremely disagreeable green-water is to smell; consequently, should say a cabbage be placed in a small quantity of water, this disagreeable smell becomes more concentrated . . . never on any account let it be poured down the sink, as the smell that will consequently arise will probably have the very uncomfortable result of rendering the whole house disagreeable for some time after.

How ideas towards cooking have changed, and, thank goodness, towards plumbing systems! While I digress, one more quote I find irresistible— from *The Book of Household Management* on "The Mistress".

As with the Commander of an Army, or the leader of an enterprise, so it is with the mistress of a house. Her spirit will be seen through the whole establishment; and just in proportion as she performs her duties intelligently and thoroughly, so will her domestics follow in her path.

The writer comforts the new mistress:

To be a good housewife does not necessarily imply an abandonment of proper pleasures or amusing recreation, although he (it *has* to be a he) goes on to insist on early rising and frugality as essential virtues. Then there is "The choice of Acquaintances" . . . very important to the happiness of a mistress and her family. A gossiping acquaintance, who indulges in scandal and the ridicule of her neighbours, should be avoided as a pestilence.

The mistress is advised to go out into society but to beware of "ladies who uniformly smile". Unfortunately the following pages are lost.

To return to rabbits. Milk and cream complement rabbit in a special way and they have the virtue of being ingredients readily available to us. Milk is useful too in taming the stronger flavour of wild rabbits. Basil and Bonnie attract friends from the wild. Gradually these friends get bigger and cheekier and bring their cousins and aunts into the garden to visit. They make a good meal of our vegetables and scratch craters in the lawn and finally our patience pops and out comes the shot gun.*

*A footnote to that: *please* be careful if you keep rabbits, *never* to let them get loose. The wild rabbit problem is big enough already.

Buns

Rabbit Custard Tarts

A good thing about this recipe is that it can be made in stages at convenient times. The rabbit can be left to simmer quietly while you do something else, and then cool down and wait for you. Anyone with a free moment can pull it to pieces (keep the stock for soup and sauces).

The quiche pastry (again from Kaara) can be kept in the fridge or frozen and the custard takes no time to make. Make in individual small foil pie dishes for a refreshing picnic or summer meal. The sweet and savoury mixture is unusual. Quantities and time depend on how much rabbit you start with and how many pies you make of what size.

rabbit meat	apples, sliced
pickling spices (whole peppercorns, dried chillies, cloves)	chutney, or ground mace and nutmeg

Pastry

1½ cups plain flour	130 g butter, soft and cut in chunks for the
¼ teaspoon salt	processor

Custard

3 eggs, beaten	salt and pepper to taste
1 cup cream	lemon thyme or parsley
1 cup milk	

To make the pastry, put the flour salt and butter into a food processor, or mix by hand until the mixture is the consistency of breadcrumbs (silly way of describing it really when breadcrumbs can be any size, but the phrase has become a cooking term). Mix in the eggs until the pastry holds together.

Rolled out between two pieces of go-between freezer paper, the pastry makes no mess and is easy to transport to the pie dishes.

Stew rabbit or rabbits (whole or pieces) with pickling spices. Put the rabbit or rabbits (whole or pieces) into boiling water with the pickling spices and let it simmer until tender (about 2 hours, depending on the size). Allow to cool in the juice, then remove all meat from bones.

Line foil dishes (or one big quiche dish) with pastry. Make a layer of apple slices and spread them with chutney or sprinkle with mace and nutmeg. Add rabbit meat.

Mix all the custard ingredients together and pour on top of the rabbit. Leave open or cover with a pastry lid and bake in a moderate oven (180°C) on a low shelf for about 30 minutes, or 45 minutes for a big pie.

Serve with a salad and sweet chutney.

Harvest Rabbit

This is basically a casserole, again combining sweet and savoury flavours. You can use whole small rabbits, but rabbit joints are more manageable. The only young rabbits I keep whole are the larger ones that I want to roast.

rabbit pieces	*any selection of herbs from the garden*
oil or dripping	*bacon rashers*
onions, sliced	*stock (chicken stock if you have no rabbit*
seasoned flour	*stock in the freezer. A light, white, fruit*
prunes, soaked and stoned	*wine is excellent if you make your own.)*

Fry rabbit pieces until light brown.
Cover the bottom of a casserole with slices of onion. Coat rabbit pieces with well seasoned flour and arrange each of them on two opened out prunes on top of the onions. Tuck a bunch of herbs under each and cover with a rasher of bacon. (Rabbit is a dry meat and bacon a useful complement in many recipes.) Just cover with stock and cook slowly for two hours.
Serve with fried forcemeat balls.

Fried Forcemeat Balls

These look fun if they are bright green so be generous with the herbs.
Mix chopped bacon (or suet) with herbs (chives, parsley, marjoram—whatever you have) salt and pepper and breadcrumbs. Bind together with egg. Fry them so that they are crisp and tinged with autumn brown.

Roast Rabbit

Plain roast rabbit is lovely if the rabbit is young and fresh but it is even better with an imaginative stuffing.

1 rabbit, whole
bacon rashers

Stuffing

1½ cups soft nutty breadcrumbs	*1 onion, finely chopped*
1 cup chopped apples	*3 rashers of bacon, chopped*
1 cup sultanas	*salt and pepper to taste*
½ cup chopped peanuts or sunflower seeds (roasted)	*1 egg*

Mix all together, adding a little warm water if more moisture is needed to bind.

Line the inside of the rabbit with rashers of bacon and lay the stuffing inside. Sew or pin up and truss the rabbit's limbs close to the body so that they don't dry out with cooking. Keep a sheet of aluminium foil over the rabbit for the first hour, checking at half hour intervals, basting if necessary. For the second hour, take off the foil and replace it with bacon rashers. Bake in a slow steady oven for about 2 hours.

Serve with hot baked onions in a white sauce, creamy mashed potatoes and a leafy green salad from the garden including if possible some "hot" vegetable such as radish or mustard spinach.

The main complaint I have had about rabbit is that it is full of little bones. I agree. The backbone and ribs are fiddly. If you are doing a major rabbit kill, it is a good idea to freeflow-freeze and bag the rabbit leg and back portions separately from the rib cage portions. The rib sections can all be stewed, the meat taken off and the stock frozen for soups, sauces and casseroles.

A no-fuss recipe for braised rabbit, intended for use by my mother-in-law's Indian cook, is in Mrs G. L. Routleff's *Economical Cookery Book for India* (Thacker Spink & Co., 1961). She also lists ten "Golden Rules" for the kitchen in her introduction, including these:

- haste without hurry saves worry, fuss and flurry
- a time for everything, and everything in time
- an hour lost in the morning has to be run after all the day.

She explains the difference between boiling and stewing meat. To boil meats properly, they should be put into boiling water, then the heat turned down to simmer. That way, the meat makes a skin for itself and keeps the juices inside while they cook.

Stewing is the opposite. If the water is never allowed to boil but just simmers, a rich gravy is made with the juices that escape from the meat—suitable for stews and casseroles. Never, she says, put meat into cold water and bring it to the boil.

Braised Rabbit

oil or butter for frying	1 teaspoon chopped parsley
2 carrots, chopped	1 rabbit, jointed
2 onions, chopped	2½ cups stock
1 turnip, chopped (optional—a parsnip would do)	2 rashers of bacon, chopped
	pepper, salt and mace to taste

Fry the vegetables, lay the rabbit pieces on them and cover with stock and the bacon. Season, cover and simmer for about two hours.

Rabbit Pie

In many old recipes, cider is used to tenderise older rabbits. I have substituted kiwi fruit slices with success in the traditional rabbit pie.

For this recipe, older or wild rabbits can be used. Soak wild rabbits in milk for a couple of hours before frying.
Use just the joints with bigger bones, and stew the rib sections for gravy or for stock for the pie.

bacon, in rashers and chopped	peas, or other green vegetables
bay leaf	salt and pepper
rabbit pieces	chilli sauce (optional)
oil for frying	kiwi fruit, sliced, and/or apples, sliced
parsley, chopped	stock from stewed rib pieces
onion, sliced	potatoes, thickly sliced
carrots, sliced	butter
parsnips, sliced	pastry for pie lid
mushrooms	

Line the bottom of a deep pie dish with bacon rashers and a bay leaf. Lightly fry the rabbit pieces to seal the juices and pack them into the dish with chopped bacon. Cover them with chopped parsley then slices of onion and the vegetables. Season with salt and pepper and, according to the family's taste, a little chilli sauce. The pie needs to be spicy. Use kiwi fruit slices and/or apple slices to cover the vegetables. Fill the dish with stock and finish off with thickly sliced potatoes, topped with butter and parsley. Cover with a lid of pastry (the pastry can be omitted but it looks more festive).
Put the pie in a hot oven (if it has a pastry lid, at about 225°C) and then let the oven cool to about 150°C for the rabbit to simmer until tender—about 2 hours. If the rabbit is old and you want to add a pastry lid, plan to cook longer, but for half the planned time without the lid. Alternatively, put foil over the top so that the pastry does not overbrown.

Rabbit Baked With Rice

Our generous chooks give us plenty of eggs. This recipe takes six egg yolks. I make it after making 309 Honey Fizz (page 89) or an exotic dessert which uses the whites of eggs leaving the yolks to look miserably at me from their glass containers each time I open the fridge door. This recipe is also generous with

home-made butter. The chutney we make, the pigs we are rearing: next effort—
grow the rice!

rabbit joints	*4 cups stock*
pepper	*mace*
bacon	*50 g butter*
oil, dripping or butter for frying	*6 egg yolks*
1 cup rice	*chutney*

Rub rabbit pieces with pepper and fry gently with bacon in oil, dripping or butter
until browned and half cooked. Wash rice and boil it in stock flavoured with mace
until tender and the liquid is absorbed. Let rice cool then stir in 50 g butter and
the yolks of 4 eggs (the whites too if you don't want to separate them). Butter a
casserole and lay in it the rabbit pieces and bacon. Spoon chutney on the pieces
and cover with rice. Put two more beaten egg yolks on top of the rice and bake in
a brisk oven for about 45 minutes.
(This dish can seem too bland. I usually include a chopped capsicum or chopped
red chilli and vary the colour of the rice with a teaspoon of turmeric or a dollop of
tomato sauce.)

Rabbit Tartar

This dish can be served either hot or cold, with tartar sauce.

Marinade:

honey	*chives*
olive oil	*parsley*
lemon juice	*pepper and salt*
crushed garlic	*chopped mushrooms if available*

My bias is towards hot, not very sweet foods so I leave the quantities variable for
those who prefer less garlic, less chilli, less pepper than I do.
Warm the honey with the oil and mix in other ingredients.
Marinate rabbit pieces (preferably not the ribs or backbone) then roll them in
breadcrumbs and grill them, basting with the marinade.

Tartar sauce:

To 1½ cups of mayonnaise, add 1 teaspoon chopped capers (or nasturtium seeds),
1 clove of garlic (crushed), 1 teaspoon chopped gherkins, a pinch of sugar, 3
teaspoons fresh chopped herbs (parsley, chervil and tarragon if you have them—it
is a French recipe and the French love tarragon), and a chopped hard-boiled egg.
Mix it and keep it cool.

Rabbit Patties

This is useful "instant" picnic or lunch food to have in the freezer. The only chore is taking the meat off the bones and mincing it. You can adapt the recipe to use cooked rabbit meat.

1 kg uncooked rabbit meat, minced

2 onions, minced

2 level teaspoons salt (some people like more with rabbit)

1 teaspoon black pepper

1 cup breadcrumbs

½ teaspoon paprika

½ teaspoon dried ground sage, or more fresh herbs

2 eggs, beaten

milk or cream if more moisture needed

Mix all ingredients well and make into small cakes.
Either fry and freeze between layers of freezer paper, or freeze uncooked, then fry without defrosting. Serve with apple sauce.

Rabbit Curry

The older cookery books give instructions for a type of "Western" curry—more like a stew with a small amount of curry powder added to the gravy. We prefer a more basic curry made with coconut milk. Because the rabbit is a dry meat, it can stand the last minute addition of a little cream for extra luxury.

2 tablespoons curry powder (or a mixture of coriander, clove, mace, mustard, cumin, turmeric, ginger, garam masala and chilli in whatever proportions your family prefers. I tend towards the sweeter spices with rabbit—clove, mace and ginger.)

1 jointed rabbit (or, better still, the equivalent without the small bones)

2 tablespoons clarified butter or mixture of oil and butter, for frying

2 onions, chopped

2 cloves garlic, crushed

1 cup boiling water

2 cups coconut milk

1 teaspoon salt

½ cup cream (optional)

Rub some of the curry powder into rabbit pieces. In a large pan, fry until soft onion and garlic, then add the rest of the curry powder mixture and fry on a low heat for 3 minutes stirring to stop sticking. Add boiling water and let it simmer gently until it smells good (a few minutes). Put in rabbit pieces and simmer with lid on for 1 hour. Add coconut milk and salt and cook with lid off for further hour. If preferred, add cream to curry just before serving. Serve with chutney, kiwi fruit slices or a piquant mixture of a tart apple, diced, mixed with chopped red chilli, lemon juice and salt. And of course, boiled rice.

Vintner's Rabbit

Finally, a Hudson and Halls recipe. It was actually demonstrated with our own rabbits on television! David Hudson and Peter Halls lived near a small seaside fish 'n chip shop we ran for a while and they "discovered" our rabbits. They demonstrated a version of Vintner's Rabbit which we enjoy on sentimental or festive occasions.

250 g bacon, finely chopped	*1 cup red wine*
1.5 g rabbit pieces (the equivalent of one rabbit—even if it is all legs)	*1 cup stock (chicken will do)*
2 tablespoons plain flour	*2 tablespoons cognac*
½ teaspoon ground black pepper	*2 teaspoons red currant jelly (or quince cheese)*
½ teaspoon salt	*1 bay leaf*
2 onions, finely chopped	*dried rosemary and dried thyme—a pinch*
2 cloves garlic	*juice of half a lemon*

Cook bacon in casserole, then use fat (you might need extra) to brown rabbit joints that have been dusted with flour, pepper and salt. Take out the joints as they are cooked and put them aside with the bacon. Fry onion and garlic in the bacon fat (plus oil if necessary). When they are soft, add wine and chicken stock and bring to boil, stirring in any flour sticking to the pan. Stir in cognac, jelly and herbs and return the rabbit pieces and bacon.

Cover and simmer for 1½ hours or until rabbit is tender. Take out bay leaf, add lemon juice and correct seasoning.

It is a rich dish. Serve with plain steamed vegetables and baked potatoes in their jackets.

A p p e n d i x

REGULATIONS

Beware of local regulations when it comes to beekeeping, poultry raising and rabbits. On a small scale (that is, non-commercial) there are few State or country-wide rules—except that one should not be a nuisance to one's neighbours.

One rule is very clear: "the onus is on the individual to make the necessary enquiries and to then comply with requirements" (stated in a letter from the Australian Department of Primary Industries and Energy and echoed in letters from departments and bureaus throughout Australia and New Zealand).

Health authorities naturally take a keen interest in animal operations on any scale. Even housecows should be presented for tuberculosis and brucellosis testing. A slack beekeeper who allows foul brood to go unchecked can wreck the livelihood of his neighbours and endanger national honey and bee exports. In Australia and New Zealand it is generally necessary to register with the State department of Agriculture or Primary Industries if you plan to keep bees. In New Zealand beekeeping is covered by the *Apiaries Act* 1969 which demands all hives be registered and identified with a number. The Act also covers disease control, use of pesticides and drugs, and importation of honey, bee appliances or bees.

In both Australia and New Zealand there are strict rules about which breed of rabbits can be kept in domestic situations. In most States of Australia if you wish to keep more than one rabbit you must apply for a permit from the Minister of Agriculture/Primary Industries. In New Zealand feral rabbits come under the *Agricultural Pests Destruction Act.* Exempt are nine breeds and crosses of those breeds: Californian White, Netherlands Dwarf, Dutch Dwarf, Tanxand Silver Fox, New Zealand White, Angora, Flemish Giant, Rex and Chinchilla. All rabbits must be securely housed and restricted to prevent escape and should not be allowed to graze pasture.

You must consult your local council if you wish to keep a few chooks—each council has its own requirements. In some urban areas, roosters can be kept so long as their voice boxes have been removed.

If you plan to run a small business from your produce, check the guides and Codes of your local council. In both Australia and New Zealand there are laws which govern packaging, labelling and standard weights and measures. It is also necessary to consult your local council if you want to slaughter animals. In New South Wales the Meat Industry Authority will carry out an inspection of your premises; in other States and in New Zealand contact your local Department of Health.

There are no handy volumes of reference for all these rules, but a letter or phone call to your local council will keep you out of trouble and your neighbours safe.

CHEESEMAKING

Equivalent measurements for temperature in *fahrenheit* and *celsius* (centigrade)—for cheesemaking:

FAHRENHEIT	CELSIUS	
32	0	Freezing
50	10	
55	12.8	
60	15.5	
65	18	
66	19	
68	20	
71	21	
75	24	
80	26.7	
85	29	
86	30	)
88	31	) add rennet
		) Maximum temperature
90	32.2	) for Gouda.
92	33	)

FAHRENHEIT	CELSIUS	
94	34	
95	35	
98	36.7	
100	38	Maximum temperature for Cheddar.
104	42.2	
113	45	
122	50	Maximum temperature for Cottage Cheese.
140	60	
158	70	) Pasteurise at 72°C—hold
167	75	) temperature 15 seconds and reduce to 32°C.
185	85	
194	90	
203	95	
212	100	Water boils

B i b l i o g r a p h y

Acton, B. and P. Duncan, *Making Mead*, An Amateur Winemaker Publication, Andover, Hants, 1978.

Alberta Beekeepers Association, *A Honey of a Cookbook*, Canada 1963.

Attfield, H. D., *Raising Rabbits*, A VITA Publication, Maryland U.S.A., 1977.

Barca, M. *Making Your Own Cheese and Other Dairy Products*, Nelson Homestead Series, Australia, 1978.

Beedell, S., *A Complete Guide to Wine Making and Home Brewing*, Sphere, London, 1969.

Berry, C. J. J., *First Steps in Winemaking*, Amateur Winemaker Publication Ltd, Andover, Hants, 6th Ed., 1979.

Black, M. *Home-Made Butter, Cheese and Yoghurt*, E.P. Publishing, Yorkshire, 1977.

Buchman, D., *Herbal Medicine*, Rider and Co, Hutchinson, 1985.

Budd, M., *The Little Honey Book*, Judy Piatkus (Publishers) Ltd, London, 1984.

Butler, C. G., *The World of the Honey Bee*, Collins, London, 1974.

Chapman-Taylor, R., *Beekeeping for Fun*, Ray Chapman Taylor and Ivo Davey, Auckland, 1981.

Crane, E., *A Book of Honey*, Oxford University Press, U.K., 1980.

Dadant and Sons, *The Honey Kitchen*, A Dadant Publication, Hamilton Illinois, 3rd Ed., 1986.

Dennis, B and Brother Adam of Buckhurst Abbey, *Mead and Honey Wines*.

Edmonds, *Cookery Book*, T. J. Edmonds Ltd, New Zealand, 1976.

Ellis, A., *Farmhouse Kitchen*, Hutchinson Publishing Group, London, 1977.

Emery, C., *Old Fashioned Recipe Book, An Encyclopaedia of Country Living*, Bantam Books, US and Canada, 1971.

Forster, S., *The Australian Honey Cookbook*, Australian Honey Board, Sydney, 1983.

Glynn, C., *Cheese and Cheesemaking*, MacDonald Guidelines, London, 1977.

Gordon, S., *Australian and New Zealand Complete Self Sufficienty Handbook*, Doubleday, Sydney and Auckland, 1981.

Glenfield College Home and School Association Auckland, *Maori Cookbook*, 1980.

Graham, M. and J., *The Cow Economy*, Coburn Farm Press, Maine, 1976.

Hartley, D., *Food in England*, MacDonald, London, 1954.

Hooper, T., *Guide to Bees and Honey*, Blandford Press Ltd, Dorset, 1979.

Kosikowski, F., *Cheese and Fermented Milk Foods*, published by the author, 2nd Ed., Cornell, 1977.

McKechie, D. J., *Home Winemakers' Recipes*, John McIndoe Ltd, Dunedin, 1979.

Matheson, A., *Practical Beekeeping in New Zealand*, Government Printer, Wellington, New Zealand, 1984.

Molan, Dr P., *New Zealand Beekeeper*, Summer 1985, National Beekeepers' Association of New Zealand.

New Zealand Department of Agriculture, *Beekeeping in New Zealand*, Bulletin No. 267, 1946.

Nilsson, A., *The Art of Home Cheesemaking*, Woodbridge Press Publishing Company, California, 1979.

Pain, A. D., *Making Wine at Home*, Whitcombe and Tombs Ltd, New Zealand, 1972.

Pawan, G. L. S., *New Zealand Beekeeper*, Spring 1986, National Beekeepers' Association of New Zealand.

Pearks, G., *Complete Home Winemaking*, Magnum Books, Methuen Paperbacks Ltd, 1978.

Pinder, P., *Soft Cheese*, Search Press, London, 1978.

Pleshette, J., *Health on Your Plate*, Hamlyn, U.K., 1983.

Prescott, N., *Early Settlers Household Lore*, Raphael Arts Pty Ltd, S. A., 1977.

Roads, M., *A Guide to Organic Living in Australia*, Mary Fisher Bookshop, Launceston, 1977.

Robinson, D. H. (Ed), *Fream's Elements of Agriculture*, John Murray, London, 13th Ed., 1956.

Seymour, J., *Self Sufficiency*, Faber and Faber, London, 1976.

Smith, K. and I., *The Earth Garden Book—Self Sufficiency in Australia*, Nelson, Melbourne, 1977.

Street, L. and Singer, A., *The Backyard Fair book*, Prism Press, Dorchester, 1975.

Tompkins, E. and Griffith, R. M., *Practical Beekeeping*, Garden Way Publishing, Vermont, 1980.

Van Look, D., *The Family Cow*, Garden Way Publishing, Vermont, 1976.

Vernon, F., *Teach Yourself Beekeeping*, Hodder and Stoughton, England, 1977.

Winter, T. S., *Apiary and Honeyhouse Management*, Department of Agriculture, Wellington, New Zealand, 1946.

I n d e x

Gouda, 27, 31-33
granulation, 67, 68
grapes, 73, 101, 102, 105, 107, 109, 124
grit, 139
guard bees, 43, 47

H
half-depth super/box, *see* supers
hangovers, 77
Hansen's, 27, 28
haoma, 124
Hard cheese, 31
harvest, 60, 61, 144, 146
hatching, 47
heart, 76, 77
health, 4, 6, 7, 9, 66, 74, 76-78, 80, 84, 108,
    121, 129, 139-141, 143, 144, 148, 149,
    158, 164, 165, 167
hen house, *see* chook house
Hippocras, 124
hive, 40-51, 52-60, 66, 69, 71, 72, 74, 79, 85,
    86, 130
hive tool, 50, 52, 53, 57, 59
honey, 11, 12, 35, 36, 38, 40, 43-48, 53-63,
    65-98, 107, 120-124, 149
  moods of, 67
  spreading, 65, 67, 68, 69
honey wine, *see* mead
house bee, 46, 47, 54, 55
housing, 43, 130, 132, 155
hutches, 130, 142, 157-160, 162, 164, 165, 168,
    172
hydrometer, 120, 122
hydroscopic, 81, 82
hygiene, 3, 26, 27, 110, 124, 141, 164
hypertension, 75

I
iceblock, 14
insulin, 75
Italian bees, 42

J
jam, 87, 90
jellies, 87, 90
joining hives, 60
jointing rabbits, 172
junket, 18-20

K
killing, 141, 144, 146, 149, 156, 163, 164, 169,
    171, 180
kindling, 161, 168
kiwi, fruit, 107, 127, 175

L
labelling, 25, 32, 34, 38, 99, 102, 117
Langstroth, 43, 45, 69, 70
larvae, 46, 47
laws, 41, 54, 57
laying, 143, 148
lees, 114-116, 118
leg rope, 5

M
manuka, 60, 63, 67, 68, 79, 80, 89, 124, 159
manure, 128, 134, 141, 148, 157, 162, 164, 172
market, 144
mastitis, 7
mating, 43, 72, 166, 168
mating boxes, *see* nesting boxes
matting, 22, 33
mead, 62, 67, 71, 72, 90, 101, 106, 120-124
medicine, 66, 75, 78, 119, 123, 124
melomel, 124
metheglyn, 123
milk, 1-38, 73, 80, 82, 110, 164, 170, 175, 177
milking, 2, 4-7, 9, 130
milking curd, 33
milky puds, 3, 11
moisture, 67, 74, 78, 81, 87, 88, 90, 106
money, 1, 3, 17, 130, 135, 139
mother culture, 27, 28
mould
  living, 24-26, 34, 37, 108, 111
  rigid, 22-24, 26, 32-34, 37, 38
moulting, 137
must, 105, 109-113, 122

N
nectar, 40, 41, 43, 46-48, 55, 56, 60, 65-67, 70,
    71, 73, 85, 120
nesting boxes, 127, 132-135, 137, 140-142,
    148, 160-162, 168
New Zealand White, 155, 157, 158
nuc box, 54
nucleus, 45, 54

Index
of Recipes

F

Face masks, 80, 82
Fried forcemeat balls, 179

G

Garlic and ginger spread, 36
Garlic and honey, 91
Garlic pickle, 91
Gouda cheese, 31

H

Hair conditioner, 81
Hand lotion, 83
Hangover drink, 77
Harvest rabbit, 179
Health drink, 76
Honey and lemon drinks, 90
Honey cakes, 95
Honey dumplings, 94
Honey gingerbread, 96
Honey toffee apples, 94

J

Jam with honey, 90

M

Marinade for meat, 92
Mint and honey, 93
Mushroom soup, 10

N

Nell's teriyaki, 173

O

Old fowl pot roast, 152
Onions and honey, 92
Orange and lemon spread, 35
Our rice puds, 11

P

Paté, 173
Pot luck chicken pie, 152
Pumpkin soup, 10

Q

Quiche, 11

R

Rabbit
  Baked with rice, 182
  Braised, 181
  Curry, 183
  Custard tarts, 178
  fried rice, 174
  Harvest, 179
  Nell's teriyaki, 173
  Paté, 173
  Patties, 183
  Pie, 181
  Roast, 179
  Tartar, 182
  Vintners, 184

S

Skin cleanser, 82
Spinach pie, 93
Soups
  Chilled pink mint, 10
  Mushroom, 10
  Pumpkin, 10
  Winter green vegetable, 9
Spreads
  Cream cheese, 35
  Chutney, 36
  Garlic and ginger, 36
  Orange and lemon, 36

T

309 freezer cheese, 20–24
309 Honey fizz, 89

V

Vintner's rabbit, 184

W

Winter green vegetable soup, 9